PRIME MINISTERS AT THE AUSTRALIAN NATIONAL UNIVERSITY
An Archival Guide

PRIME MINISTERS AT THE AUSTRALIAN NATIONAL UNIVERSITY
An Archival Guide

Michael Piggott & Maggie Shapley

Published by ANU eView
The Australian National University
Canberra ACT 0200, Australia
Email: anuepress@anu.edu.au
This title is also available online at: http://eview.anu.edu.au/

National Library of Australia Cataloguing-in-Publication entry

Author:	Piggott, Michael, 1948-
Title:	Prime ministers at the Australian National University : an archival guide / Michael Piggott & Maggie Shapley.
ISBN:	9780980728446 (pbk.) 9780980728453 (pdf)
Subjects:	Australian National University. Noel Butlin Archives Centre.
	Prime ministers--Australia--Archives.
	Australia--Politics and government--Archival resources.
Other Authors/Contributors:	
	Shapley, Maggie.
Dewey Number:	994.04092

All rights reserved. No part of this publication may be reproduced, stored in a retrieval system or transmitted in any form or by any means, electronic, mechanical, photocopying or otherwise, without the prior permission of the publisher.

Book design and layout by Teresa Prowse, www.madebyfruitcup.com

This edition © 2011 ANU eView

Research for this publication was supported by the Australian Government under an Australian Prime Ministers Centre Fellowship, an initiative of the Museum of Australian Democracy

Contents

Preface	vii
Acknowledgements	ix
1. Prime Ministers and the ANU	**1**
Earliest links	2
The war and its aftermath	4
Students, staff, and other connections	8
The collection connection – official documents	12
The collection connection – Butlin	13
2. Prime Ministers in the archival landscape	**17**
Papers of or about prime ministers	17
Prime ministers without papers	19
What's relevant?	20
Personal papers of prime ministers	21
Archives about prime ministers	22
Prime ministerial libraries	23
The prime ministers' portal	24
The Australian Prime Ministers Centre	26
The ANU collection	26
3. Prime Ministers in the ANU Archives	**31**
1. Three Labor dismissals	31
2. Hughes and conscription	37
3. Bruce the Businessman	41
4. 'Pig Iron' Bob	45
5. L F Fitzhardinge and W M Hughes	48
6. The IPA and three Liberal PMs	52
7. Bob Hawke and University House	56
8. Whitlam and Wave Hill	62
9. Heinz Arndt and Malcolm Fraser	68
10. The public face	71

4. The Archives 81

EDMUND BARTON, 1901–1903 81
STANLEY MELBOURNE BRUCE, 1923–1929 84
BEN CHIFLEY, 1945–1949 92
JOSEPH COOK, 1913–1914 102
JOHN CURTIN, 1941–1945 103
ALFRED DEAKIN, 1903–1904, 1905–1908, 1909–1910 107
ARTHUR FADDEN, 1941 110
ANDREW FISHER, 1908–1909, 1910–1913, 1914–1915 111
FRANK FORDE, 1945 113
MALCOLM FRASER, 1975–1983 115
JULIA GILLARD, 2010– 119
JOHN GORTON, 1968–1971 121
BOB HAWKE, 1983–1991 123
HAROLD HOLT, 1966–1967 135
JOHN HOWARD, 1996–2007 139
BILLY HUGHES, 1915–1923 141
PAUL KEATING, 1991–1996 155
JOE LYONS, 1932–1939 157
JOHN McEWEN, 1967–1968 160
BILLY McMAHON, 1971–1972 162
ROBERT MENZIES, 1939–1941, 1949–1966 164
EARLE PAGE, 1939 176
GEORGE REID, 1904–1905 178
KEVIN RUDD, 2007–2010 179
JAMES SCULLIN, 1929–1932 181
JOHN CHRISTIAN WATSON, 1904 184
GOUGH WHITLAM, 1972–1975 189

Index 199

Preface

This guide arose from the happy conjunction of two different interests. The first was a fellowship awarded in 2008 by the Australian Prime Ministers Centre. The fellowship's aim was to identify prime minister-related records in the ANU Archives. The recipient had just retired from ten years managing the University of Melbourne Archives. Its holdings, together with the collections of the ANU's Noel Butlin Archives Centre, account for the majority of Australia's extant business and trade union collections, and it can also boast of large holdings of social history archival heritage. He also knew something of the unexpected relationships a University's official archival records can document. Sir Robert Menzies, for example, had been a student at the University of Melbourne, and its Chancellor between 1967 and 1972.

A second stimulus was a continuing concern of the ANU Archives to publicise its collections. Archivists know that, to quote a famous Deputy Keeper of the UK Public Record Office, archives were drawn up 'for purposes almost infinitely varying' and 'are potentially useful to students for the information they can give on a range of subjects totally different but equally wide'. But the ANU wanted to stress to – among many others – students, scholars, librarians and the media that the nature and content of the archives should not be taken for granted. The National Library of Australia, the National Archives of Australia and university-based prime ministerial libraries do not hold everything about Australia's prime ministers. Nevertheless, that the university's official archives and the business and labour collections of the Noel Butlin Archives Centre include anything on prime ministers is a surprise to most, including on occasion their biographers. As we show in Chapter 1, there is a remarkably strong connection between prime ministers and the ANU, and because of that and other factors, also between prime ministers and the ANU Archives' collections.

Our guide does not follow the standard model of an archival finding aid. However it does sit within the pattern of published guides about sources relating to prime ministers produced by the National Archives. The first appeared in 2002, and was titled *Our First Six: Guide to Archives of Australia's Prime Ministers* by Susan Marsden and Roslyn Russell. It described collections in the National Archives and elsewhere relating to Barton, Deakin, Watson, Reid, Fisher and Cook. Since then others to appear have focused on individual prime ministers – Bruce, Lyons, Curtin and Holt.

The guide's aim is to present, through a large sampling, a picture of the nature and wealth of relevant material held by the ANU Archives. We knew we could never achieve exhaustive coverage, even if a limit on the level of descriptive detail had been set. For a start, the collection is being added to weekly, and at twenty kilometres it is too vast for us to be sure we would locate every document on our topic. In any case, the duration of the Prime Ministers Centre fellowship set a practical boundary on the guide's scope.

Apart from offering descriptions of records, we also want to encourage the collection's use. Therefore we have included in the guide not only photographs and reproductions of documents, but also examples of the archives in action, using them to present small prime ministerial moments from the past. Our inspiration here is Dr Klaus Neumann's guide *In the Interest of National Security: Civilian Internment in Australian during World War II* (National Archives, 2006). His guide consigns the actual description of archival sources to a detailed appendix. At its core are 'the internment histories of seven men and three women, whose records are held in the collection of the National Archives' (p. 3).

We trust our guide approximates its success, passion and interest, and brings new researchers to the ANU Archives.

Michael Piggott, Australian Prime Ministers Centre Fellow 2008–2009
Maggie Shapley, University Archivist, ANU Archives

Acknowledgements

Our first acknowledgement is to those who entrust their records to the ANU Archives and allow their use for research: Australian companies, businesses, trade unions, industry councils, organisations and individuals whose records are in the Noel Butlin Archives Centre, as well as Australian National University staff, departments and organisations whose records are part of the university's archives. In particular, Professor John Richards, Master of University House, and Professor Melanie Nolan, General Editor of the Australian Dictionary of Biography, facilitated the recent transfer of records which are now accessible through this guide.

The Archives is grateful for the support of the retiring Vice-Chancellor Professor Ian Chubb, the Friends of the Noel Butlin Archives Centre, and the Australian Prime Ministers' Centre at the Museum of Australian Democracy at Old Parliament House.

The authors particularly thank the staff and volunteers of the ANU Archives who have alerted us to new finds and enthusiastically searched out prime ministerial material for inclusion in the guide.

We thank Michael Richards, David Stephens and Denis Connor for checking the text, ANU photographers Neal McCracken, Stuart Hay and Darren Boyd for providing images, and indexer Barry Howarth.

CHAPTER 1
Prime Ministers and the ANU

The Fisher Government – the first national Labor government to win a parliamentary majority anywhere in the world – decided that Canberra would be our national capital. Four decades later, the Curtin and Chifley Labor Governments decided that our national capital needed a national university.

Kevin Rudd, Annual Burgmann College Lecture, Australian National University, 27 August 2009.[1]

The prime ministerial presence dominates Canberra. In the nation's psyche, the name of the prime minister and of the national capital share metonymic status as 'The Government'. Canberra is where 'the PM' lives and attends parliament, and from where he or she is typically represented in the media. This is where prime ministers are sworn in, receive foreign leaders, hold summits and make their most important announcements. This is where the Prime Minister's XI plays and prime ministers' prizes are presented.

Parliament House was not always here of course, and even since their advent, prime ministers have not occupied the Lodge consistently. In 2011 however, the link between prime minister and Canberra is indelibly fixed, while reminders of predecessors are provided by suburbs, statues, buildings, schools and so on. One prime minister, Stanley Melbourne Bruce (later Viscount Bruce of Melbourne), had even willed that he be cremated and his ashes sent to Australia to be scattered over the national capital. Canberra itself, 'the city he had helped create', said the National Archives, 'remains a monument to this Prime Minister'.[2] Arguably this could also have been said of the prime minister who shared some uncanny similarities with Bruce, Robert Menzies (later Sir Robert).

Logically, such alignment between the highest office in the land and a city the late Professor Paul Reid described as 'Australia's greatest cultural artefact'[3] is not surprising. But the current and historical association between our prime ministers and one particular Canberra institution, the Australian National University, is truly extraordinary. It seemed appropriate that when we began preparing this guide, Kevin Rudd described the ANU in a speech in late May 2009 as having a 'unique place in the national educational firmament'. His opening words were revealing:

> It's great to be back home here at the ANU – the place that, after I arrived as a student in 1976, in many ways helped shape my future, as it has done for generations of students since. The ANU gave the opportunity of a world class tertiary degree to this country boy from Queensland. The ANU equipped me with the skills to speak Mandarin and begin thinking about Australia's future place in the 21st century, the Asia-Pacific century. And somewhat more importantly, the ANU gave me Therese – whom I met over a bowl of cornflakes at Burgmann College in Orientation Week.[4]

The fact that Rudd was opening a new building for a School of Medical Research named in honour of another prime minister, John Curtin, indeed suggests strong links. In 1980 Sir Frederick White had gone so far as to call the ANU 'this academically outstanding child of the Federal Government'.[5] To appreciate just how strong and how personal the links were, we need to begin at the beginning.

Earliest links

Oscillating between a few degrees of separation, the PM–ANU association starts early. Implicit in Australia's Constitution was the requirement for a seat of government, section 125 specifying its location and control. A number of our earliest prime ministers, particularly Edmund Barton (later Sir Edmund), Alfred Deakin and George Reid (later Sir George), were key shapers of constitutional arrangements, and even before Federation, Reid (as Premier of New South Wales) ensured premiers' conference agreement that the new capital and thus the university would be inside his state.

The first government (1901–1903), led by Barton, began visiting possible sites, introduced the first Seat of Government Bill and established a Royal Commission to do further research. 'The City', the latter reported, 'is to be the seat of power, the nerve of the Commonwealth, and, in the future, the focus of its intellectual activities'.[6] The aforementioned bill was reintroduced by the short-lived government of John Christian Watson in 1904. The following year, Deakin worked with his NSW counterpart to narrow the possible sites, with thirty-six members and senators visiting the Canberra district in August 1906. Deakin's government reintroduced the Seat of Government Bill in 1908 which saw the final broad location (Canberra–Yass–Lake George triangle) resolved by October that year.

Under the new government of Andrew Fisher, the bill became law in December 1908 and the precise location was decided. Fisher was leading his second government by the time complementary legislation had been passed after the Commonwealth negotiated to have NSW cede the required land. By 1 January 1911 the Federal

Capital Territory was a reality, and a little over two years later, officially named. At the ceremony on 12 March 1913, the prime minister said 'I hope this city will be the seat of learning, as well as of politics'.[7] As one of Canberra's official historians put it: 'The idea of a national university had loomed vaguely in the shadows ever since the city was conceived'.[8]

Under Fisher, guidelines were issued for the new capital's design competition, and the paintings, maps and models provided to entrants informed them 100 acres would be allocated for a university.[9] Fisher's minister for home affairs King O'Malley expressed the hope the university would be one 'which will serve the masses as faithfully as the present universities serve the classes'.[10] The talented Griffins obliged, but the site, near Acton, remained vacant for decades while Canberra painfully and slowly took shape.

Walter Burley Griffin's 1912 map of Canberra locates the University at its present site (ANUA 138/1)

Although the 1920s were dominated by the transfer of government to Canberra and the opening of Parliament House, the decade also saw a number of proposals advanced for a university of some kind. Precisely what kind (research, postgraduate schools, teaching the locals, conducting national examinations) and indeed how many (sharing the roles) were questions on which leading academics and thinkers were happy to offer views. Equally they were asked of government committees commissioned by the Bruce government. Among the key opinion makers was Sir David Rivett, head of the Council of Scientific and Industrial Research (and incidentally the son-in-law of Alfred Deakin).

With the end of the Bruce prime ministership imminent and Wall Street's collapse just weeks away, an ordinance creating Canberra University College (CUC) was proclaimed. Affiliated with the University of Melbourne, its first two decades were 'less than glorious' wrote the ANU's official historians.[11] The College ultimately joined with the ANU. It undoubtedly falls within our theme, and it too had some remarkable prime ministerial connections. Opinion on the amalgamation issue was divided, but the possibility had been provided for in section nine of the ANU's original legislation.

The war and its aftermath

The government of John Curtin anticipated post-war needs as early as 1941. His vision was for a 'new social order', but the practical thinking came from within departments of Labour and National Service and War Organisation of Industry, and in 1942, from Post-War Reconstruction. During the period 1943–1944 interdepartmental then Cabinet committees examined national educational and research needs. Curtin's ministers and their management and policy officials coordinated policy development, but Curtin personally had enthusiastically supported ideas from military quarters for a national medical research institute, suggesting it be based in Canberra. In January 1945 he chaired the Cabinet meeting accepting the idea of the ANU.[12]

Ben Chifley ensured the passage of the Act establishing the ANU after Curtin's death, and it received assent in August 1946. There was no doubt of his support, despite a renowned dislike of budgetary excess; as treasurer and minister for post-war reconstruction he had been supportive (albeit after some prompting by his director-general H C Coombs). It was also Chifley who ruled that Curtin's name might be best perpetuated, for reasons noted above, by adding it to the new School of Medical Research, rather than, as some wanted, to the university itself. Fittingly then, in 1949 Chifley laid its foundation stone.

Ben Chifley lays the foundation stone for the John Curtin School of Medical Research in October 1949 (ANUA 15/27/1)

Robert Menzies, who defeated Chifley to become prime minister following the 1949 federal election, was both interested in and strongly supportive of the ANU. Three years earlier as opposition leader he had supported the legislation establishing the ANU, though objecting to some details. His second period as prime minister (1949–1966) coincided with the critical early development of the university. The university quickly came to realise it had his support even if it was neither always benign nor completely uncritical. And on occasion his support was needed – to secure additional funds for instance, and to defend the university against charges about left-wing professors (including a parliamentary attack from a young backbencher called Billy McMahon, later Sir William). Occasionally, as in the selection of Sir Leslie Melville as Vice-Chancellor in 1953 and the amalgamation with the CUC in 1960, Menzies intervened directly. Of course the association was also structural; the Prime Minister's Department was the source of the ANU's annual grant and Allen (later Sir Allen) Brown, the departmental head, was its representative on several interim and formal university committees.

Robert Menzies and Vice-Chancellor H C Coombs at the laying of the foundation stone for what would become the R G Menzies Building, with Pattie Menzies and Gough and Margaret Whitlam further back in the crowd (ANUA 15/111/2)

The regard and respect was mutual. In 1961, the ANU asked Menzies to lay the foundation stone of the building that was to become the R G Menzies Building and which Queen Elizabeth II opened in 1963, housing the Library's postgraduate library collections. When he retired in 1966 the University awarded him an honorary doctorate (his twentieth), and University House made him an honorary fellow. In the latter he had always shown warm interest. He spoke at its opening in 1954, attended his daughter's wedding reception there, and even donated to it an ancient Greek terracotta figure.

For much of both Menzies' incumbency and this critical period in the ANU's growth, its Chancellor was the former prime minister S M (by then Viscount) Bruce. Based in London, for the decade after his appointment in 1951 he played very much a part-time role. It suited everyone for him to be a 'hands-off' ceremonial figure and to chair Council only when in the country. By then quite elderly, Bruce fitted the role and was a useful representative in a part of the world providing many of the ANU's foundation deans and directors. Appointed initially for three years, he was genuinely concerned the ANU quickly find a local replacement while agreeing to extensions when the search stalled. He had a genuine regard for Canberra and its university and, as his will testified, backed this up with funds.

Stanley Melbourne (Lord) Bruce, the ANU's first Chancellor (right), with Sir Earle Page, then Chancellor of the University of New England in 1958 (ANUA 15/55/14)

Students, staff, and other connections

The ANU's partial forebear, the Canberra University College, certainly shared the trait of attracting prime ministerial associations. Some are interesting, if a little tenuous, such as the renown of two College staff, Laurie Fitzhardinge and Professor L F (Fin) Crisp, for fine though very different biographies of prime ministers (Billy Hughes and Ben Chifley). Crisp had served Chifley in the 1940s as, in his words, 'a former civil servant and an active Labour Party member',[13] and was also the ANU's John Curtin Lecturer in 1974. As it happens, one of his students from the 1951–1952 intake of diplomatic cadets was Peter Henderson, then beginning to court Heather Menzies, the prime minister's daughter.

The College's proudest boast is a trifecta of Whitlams, the only prime ministerial family who lived in Canberra outside politics, though John Gorton (later Sir John) is a partial exception. Gough's father, the Commonwealth Crown Solicitor Fred (H F E) Whitlam, was a College lecturer in commercial law and also served as a member of its Council (1939–1941). In the 1950s, he was also a member of the ANU's committee of legal advisers. Fred's famous son Gough appeared on the College's books as a scholarship holder though he never actually enrolled,[14] using it to study law at the University of Sydney. Gough's sister Freda Whitlam also spent several fairly undistinguished years there as a College student.[15] Paralleling Gough in gaining a CUC scholarship was James S Menzies, son of one of the prime minister's older brothers, James L Menzies. He also attended Sydney, studying medicine.

Australia has approximately forty universities. None relate to the biographies of Australia's twenty-seven prime ministers and their families to the same degree as does the ANU. This remarkable conjunction is epitomised by the 26th prime minister Kevin Rudd: he is an ANU graduate, gaining a Bachelor of Arts (Asian Studies) degree with First Class Honours in 1981, but so also is his wife Thérèse Rein – and a third of his Cabinet colleagues. Other ANU students have included Bob Hawke (PhD scholarship student, 1956–1958) and John Gorton's wife Bettina (graduating with Honours in Asian Studies 1967).

Kevin Rudd at the opening of the new J G Crawford Building in May 2010 announces the establishment of the Australian National Institute of Public Policy at the ANU (photographer: Darren Boyd)

In the year Mrs Gorton graduated she began working as a part-time research assistant on a major project compiling an English–Malay dictionary. At the time, her husband was minister for education and science, with responsibilities including the ANU, but there had been earlier links still: in 1951–1952 Senator Gorton had been a parliamentary representative on the ANU Council. Bob Hawke's student associations also extend further: while a graduate student he lectured part-time at the CUC in Introduction to Legal Method (1957–1958) and was also an elected student representative of the University Council until forced to step down in February 1957. As will be recounted later, while a student Hawke was involved in an incident very late one Sunday night at University House which led to disciplinary action and the Council resignation. He was clearly forgiven, later becoming an invited member of Council (1979–1980), and while prime minister opened ANU's new telescope at Siding Spring Observatory (1984) and the J G Crawford Building (1986).

Dr John Ritchie, General Editor of the *Australian Dictionary of Biography*, with Bob Hawke at the launch of volume 12 in 1990 (ANUA 225/526/2)

When Bob Hawke left parliament in 1992, he joined the ANU as an Adjunct Professor, and he has often returned, for instance, to attend installations, launch books and once even to open a twentieth anniversary conference on his government's record. The first ex-prime minister to gain an ANU 'golden parachute' however was Gough Whitlam, who left parliament to become Visiting Fellow in the Department of Political and Social Change, 1978–1980. He then stayed to become the ANU's first National Fellow in 1981, based in the Research School of Pacific Studies.[16]

Even during his brief frenetic years in power 1972–1975, there was contact: Whitlam gave the sixth John Curtin lecture and opened the Tandem Accelerator at the Research School of Physical Sciences, underlining continuing Labor prime ministerial association with science research: Chifley had laid the foundation stone for the School in 1949. Like Menzies before him, there was also strong affection for University House where, following Whitlam's dismissal as prime minister in 1975, he and Margaret lived for six months. In 1982 he was made an Honorary Fellow of the House, with whose Master Dr Ralph Elliott he had worked researching Italian influences in Chaucer.

Gough Whitlam with nuclear physicist Professor Sir Ernest Titterton, Director of the Research School of Physical Sciences in 1973 (ANUA 225/1315/2)

Well into Whitlam's and Hawke's retirements, the pattern continued. Prime ministers such as Malcolm Fraser launched education policies on campus, and others opened buildings. John Howard's presence at the opening of the Sir Roland Wilson Building in 1999 represented yet further connections. This was the same Wilson who, with Allen Brown, represented the government on Council in the early 1950s; who with Menzies tried (unsuccessfully) to entice Sir John Cockcroft to be Sir Douglas Copland's replacement as Vice-Chancellor, and who subsequently told Chancellor Bruce of Menzies' insistence that it had to be Melville. Officials of another kind, prime ministerial advisers such as Stephen FitzGerald and Ross Garnaut, might also be noted, moving back and forth between government and academe. But there is more.

The collection connection – official documents

Given the requirements of administration, it was inevitable that something of the aforementioned history and relationships would be reflected in the official archival records managed by the ANU Archives. At the heart of this multiple documentary 'brush-with-fame' are the minutes and agenda of Council and its committees, and the equivalent of the CUC Council. The Council records document discussions and decisions regarding, for example, policy issues, high-level appointments, serious current issues, Royal visits and budgets. Complementing them is a large and long-lived series of files of the ANU's central administration and the 'personal' collections of official papers of Vice-Chancellors, Chancellors and others of similar level and responsibility.

Forming the base of this implied pyramid is sixty years' sifted accumulation of name-identified files: records of staff and other 'employees' ranging from administrators and academics to Chancellors, and a selection of student files, as well as the graduate roll and related mandatory data which enables the issue of academic transcripts. Here too documents matching our interest can be found, completed by a final category of record series best labelled as 'various'. They include for instance the large photographic archive of the University's media office, and the research files accrued by official history projects which published accounts of the University (Foster and Varghese, 1996) and University House (Waterhouse, 2004).

While the above records are a natural by-product of practically any university, the ANU's original raison d'être was research. Aside from the inevitable presence of prime ministerial connections revealed in some academics' papers (for instance, L F Fitzhardinge and Professor Colin Campbell), the vast archives of the Australian Dictionary of Biography self-select. The ADB's publishing record since its first volume appeared in 1966 has rightly attracted praise as a national treasure, and it undoubtedly lends weight to the ANU's prime ministerial description as 'a unique place in the national educational firmament'.

Noel Butlin, Reader in the Department of Economics, became Professor of Economic History in the Research School of Social Sciences in 1962 (ANUA 225/168/1)

The collection connection – Butlin

The year 1954 is a significant point in the young ANU's development. Its first PhD degree was awarded, and its first specially designed major building, University House, was opened. One of its guests that year, the visiting Fulbright scholar and Director of Archival Management at the US National Archives T R Schellenberg, foreshadowed a new deal for archives in Australia, and appropriately it was the first full year of operation of what was to become the Noel Butlin Archives Centre (NBAC). Professor Noel Butlin had saved the archives of the Australian Agricultural Company from incineration, and through his initiative and energy, ensured they and many other business archives came to the ANU. The result today is Australia's first and largest collection of business and trade union historical source material, fittingly named in Butlin's memory following his death in 1992.

The NBAC collections support prime ministerial studies in two main ways. Their primary value derives from the Centre's holding of records created by trade unions, businesses and related organisations which include direct references to prime ministers, including the years before and after they held office. In some cases this means a collection includes documents by one of our twenty-seven (such as a 1903 letter from Alfred Deakin to the Ballarat Trades and Labour Council) or documents referring to them (such as CSR Limited seeking contributions to the Hughes Testimonial). In the more numerous and important cases however, because they were part of an organisation – typically a union member, official or representative – they were captured in records such as minutes of meetings and reports of day-to-day activities. The complete biographies of Fisher and Hughes (Waterside Workers), Curtin (Timber Workers), Chifley (Locomotive Enginemen) and Hawke (the ACTU) cannot be written without them. There are also important minute books showing first hand Watson's work as Chairman of Directors of Labor Papers Ltd and Bruce's chairing of the Melbourne Board of Paterson, Laing and Bruce.

In addition to direct contemporary evidence, the NBAC collections document context of action, including sources on some of the most important themes in prime ministerial lives. Thus a number of the unions' and unionists' collections (for instance, of Michael Easson) help document what Race Mathews called 'Victoria's War Against Whitlam',[17] namely Whitlam's efforts to reform the internal processes and governance of the ALP. Referencing the Holt, Gorton and McMahon governments, are union socialist and disarmament campaigns against Australia's involvement in the Vietnam War. Two earlier campaigns are also in evidence, both involving Menzies: the so-called 'pig iron' affair of 1938 and the 'Oust Menzies' campaign in 1953. Then there is the collection compiled on the 1998 maritime dispute, one of the most divisive issues of Howard's eleven years as prime minister. Identified in the public's eye with dogs and balaclavas and described by Paul Kelly as 'an elemental struggle',[18] the dispute is documented by several Butlin collections such as that of the ACTU.

A further kind of context to prime ministerial action is provided by union newspapers and newsletters, company journals, and journals of organisations such as the Institute of Public Affairs which are included in the archives. The Noel Butlin Archives Centre also holds substantial collections of rare and ephemeral publications, such as pamphlets, booklets, and flyers distributed to support political campaigns, for or against conscription, war, communism, green bans and nuclear disarmament, among others. These printed sources are also a source of contemporary photographs and of cartoons and caricatures of prime ministers.

Finally, the ANU campus provides enduring evidence of the prime ministerial presence: the foundation stones and opening plaques that record a prime ministerial role, and the buildings that memorialise the connections: the student residence Bruce Hall, the John Curtin School of Medical Research, the J B Chifley Building, housing the humanities library, and the R G Menzies Building, housing the Asia–Pacific library and the reading room for the ANU Archives.

Endnotes

1. Kevin Rudd, Burgmann College lecture, 27 August 2009: http://news.anu.edu.au/?p=1639.
2. *Prime Ministers of Australia* website, National Archives of Australia, primeministers.naa.gov.au.
3. Paul Reid, *Canberra following Griffin: A Design History of Australia's National Capital*, National Archives of Australia, 2002, p. 2.
4. Kevin Rudd, Speech at opening of new JCSMR building, 27 May 2009: http://news.anu.edu.au/?p=1259.
5. Sir Frederick White, 'Biographical Memoirs: Robert Gordon Menzies 1894–1978', *Historical Records of Australian Science*, vol. 5, no. 1, 1980: www.science.org.au/academy/fellows/memoirs/menzies.htm.
6. J G Crawford, *The Australian National University: Its Concept and Role*, Convocation address, University of Melbourne, 29 March 1968, p. 4 (Australian National University Archives: Crawford papers, ANUA 17/ 9).
7. Crawford, p. 4 (ANUA 17/9).
8. Jim Gibbney, *Canberra 1913–1953*, AGPS Press, 1988, p. 258.
9. Reid, pp. 18, 51.
10. A R Hoyle, *King O'Malley 'The American Bounder'*, Macmillan, 1981, p. 116.
11. S G Foster and Margaret M Varghese, *The Making of the Australian National University 1946–1996*, Allen and Unwin, 1996, p. 144.
12. Gibbney, p. 259.
13. L F Crisp, *Ben Chifley: A Biography*, Longmans, 1961, preface.
14. Foster and Varghese, p. 144.
15. Australian National University Archives: Canberra University College, ANUA 133/3, Minutes of Council meetings, 17 February 1941.
16. For an endearing and insightful recollection of this appointment by his allocated secretary, see Claire Smith, 'EGW and me', in Brij V Lal and Allison Ley (eds), *The Coombs: A House of Memories*, ANU, 2006, pp. 189–91.
17. The phrase was employed by Race Mathews for the title of the chapter he contributed to *The Whitlam Phenomenon: Fabian Papers*, McPhee Gribble/Penguin Books, 1986, pp. 109–29.
18. Paul Kelly, *The March of Patriots: The Struggle for Modern Australia*, Melbourne University Press, 2009, p. 380.

CHAPTER 2
Prime Ministers in the archival landscape

To appreciate the significance of what the ANU Archives has on prime ministers, it is useful to consider the pattern of prime ministerial documentation nationally. To do that, a distinction must first to be made about an easily misunderstood feature of archives.

Papers of or about prime ministers

The 'of/about' distinction concerns direct and indirect associations. To refer to a collection of personal papers *of* a prime minister typically means that person (with the assistance of staff) accumulated and retained records, which might be diaries, letters received, copies of letters sent, drafts of speeches, important single documents like birth and marriage certificates, business papers such as tax returns, a passport, mementos from early schooling, scrapbooks of newspaper cuttings, and perhaps some albums of photos. There may even be objects inextricably linked to the documents, such as a clipping of baby hair enclosed with a letter.

To date, scholars have especially prized diaries, notebooks, intimate correspondence and today's more ubiquitous virtual equivalents when they contained extensive details of the 'inner life' and the thinking behind action. Of the Deakin papers for example, Graeme Powell wrote that they formed 'the finest collection of Prime Ministerial papers in Australia' in that they 'fully document ... [his] entire public and private life'.[1] The historical, political and psychological research they have supported since John La Nauze wrote his two-volume biography in 1965 is continuing testimony of their value.[2] This gold is all the purer free of restrictions on use, and over the years a number of the prime ministerial biographies were produced with unfettered and, for the duration, exclusive access.

Note that in saying such documentation is *of* a prime minister, archivists avoid describing it as *by* that person. Such a preposition normally implies authorship, whereas the process of filing and preserving documents is broader. The term 'by' is reserved for statements such as:

> There are some letters handwritten *by* Alfred Deakin in 1903–1904 in the archives *of* the Ballarat Trades and Labour Council preserved at the Noel Butlin Archives Centre, ANU (NBAC E97/7).

The hypothetical prime minister's papers described above are a typical composite case. In real life, many factors influence the span, physical order, condition, longevity, content, motivation behind and ultimate location of this kind of documentation. Collections *of* a prime minister's papers can be fought over, split, copied, broken up for sale, and deliberately destroyed – Billy Hughes for instance being known to burn letters 'as soon as read'.[3] Sometimes their fate is considered while still being added to; sometimes the inheriting family will have to be courted with infinite patience, as we learn when collecting institutions such as the National Library share their acquisition stories.[4]

Returning to our distinction and our example, there are also collections which include material or information *about* a prime minister. They are the 'see also' collections which complement the primary focus; the collections about which the world of online commerce would note: 'Customers who viewed this also viewed …' or similar advice. Collections *about* prime ministers would be the papers of people and records of organisations they had a relationship with. For example they could be represented in the collections of their parents (because they maintained an album of press notices) and in the collections of people written to (who kept a file of their letters). Again, they could be represented in the administrative records of organisations such as employers, trade unions and various sporting and social clubs. Their words may be reported in the media, minutes of meetings, and by diarists and bloggers. They may even be caught, so to speak, in documentation where there is no obvious direct relationship: for instance inadvertently included in a photograph taken at a social function or recorded by CCTV footage in the foyer of the building where the function was held. They would be referred to in secondary sources such as newspapers and other printed material.

The of/about distinction has an important implication. Although it may not always be obvious to inexperienced scholars and journalists, often the most rewarding source of a prime minister's views and thoughts is not in their own collection but in collections preserved elsewhere by their correspondents. This is especially the case when no copies of the letters sent were retained by the writer. The most famous (or notorious) Australian instance involved the Nobel-prizewinning novelist Patrick White, who even appealed to his correspondents to destroy or return his letters, but they were also approached by the National Library seeking those same letters.

This archival version of Sir Christopher Wren's epitaph ('Lector, si monumentum requiris, circumspice') will often apply even with modern forms of communication such as email and texting.

Prime ministers without papers

In the case of some prime ministers there are very few papers. While for the vast majority of ordinary souls this is not so unusual, it is surprising and disappointing to discover about prime ministers. But their attitudes and behaviour have varied markedly, and as Graeme Powell observed: 'Their recordkeeping practices in fact could sustain a major study'.[5]

Taking Menzies as the first of several examples, he came to distrust diarists (especially if they were members of his Cabinet), and eleven years before his death wrote: 'My executors will do me a good service if they use the incinerator freely'.[6] By contrast, Whitlam came to distrust oral history ('much ... is no more than malice recollected in tranquillity'),[7] possibly with one exception. But he was obsessive about keeping and consulting documents. Between his time as a Pilot Officer in the Second World War and 2006 – as he told his biographer Jenny Hocking in a taped interview on 16 March 2006 – he recorded 16,000 flight log book entries.[8] An obvious beneficiary of these records, Hocking also described his habit of endlessly jotting ideas on backs of envelopes and scraps of paper, or utilising the ever ready pack of system cards in his jacket pocket. Yet he *and* Menzies left large collections of papers, admittedly of variable quality judged by the standard way historians assess primary source wealth.[9]

Malcolm Fraser, in his attitude to the past as in so much else, is both similar and a contrast to Whitlam. Margaret Simons, the co-author of *Malcolm Fraser: The Political Memoirs* explained in 'A Note from the Narrator' that 'repeatedly he declined to rely on his memory alone. He would proceed only when he knew the documentary proof was available.'[10] This he has accumulated in considerable quantity, and aged eighty, continues to do so.

What however if the attic is empty? This was the challenge facing Billy Hughes' biographer L F Fitzhardinge. Hughes' 'read and burn' practice has already been noted. As for any product from his own hand:

> Hughes did not pour out his mind on paper, like Gladstone or Deakin; indeed he seems to have been wary of writing, and preferred to do business by word of mouth and often through third parties. Nor did he bare his soul to

his intimates, who might have revealed the man as Boswell did Dr Johnson. His papers contain mainly letters to him, and few of his own have come to light elsewhere.[11]

This dearth was not just confined to prime ministers. In 1970 the eminent Australian historian and biographer Geoffrey Serle wrote, regarding his research on Victoria in the 1880s:

> Of about thirty-five Premiers of Victoria ... scraps of papers have been deposited in libraries only in four cases. None of their families (with one exception of a collection still held privately) cared enough to collect, cherish and pass on their papers to posterity, as for example the children of Alfred Deakin and Henry Parkes did. In several cases the papers were preserved and then wilfully destroyed by fools of the second and third generation who were too ignorant to care.[12]

Nevertheless, this lack can be overcome, and this is of course why the category of archival material *about* prime ministers should be emphasised. Thus Fitzhardinge explained that in Hughes' case his public persona was 'fully documented', enabling him to produce a huge two-volume biography 'almost wholly from external sources'.[13] John Robertson's biography of James Scullin overcame a similar difficulty,[14] while as if to prove the point, Alain Corbin famously chose his biographical subject precisely for the lack of documentation to write *The Life of an Unknown: The Rediscovered World of a Clog Maker in Nineteenth-Century France*.[15]

What's relevant?

Archivists know that, to quote a famous Deputy Keeper of the Public Record Office London, records are drawn up 'for purposes almost infinitely varying' and 'are potentially useful to students for the information they can give on a range of subjects totally different but equally wide'.[16] In other words, records arise from a vast array of human and business transactions, and future research angles are unpredictable. Accordingly there will be literally millions of 'about' collections to support millions of future research questions.

So what sources are relevant to studying prime ministers?[17] Whether one is writing a biography, drafting the acquisition policy for a prime ministerial library, producing an appraisal guideline for retention of records created in a minister's office, designing an exhibition, or preparing a guide to sources, what is 'in scope'? For example, to what extent and in what way is a prime minister's spouse and family (both from previous and subsequent generations) a proper focus? If their careers on leaving parliament are part of their story, what documentation of any new commercial activities should be contemplated? There are no absolute or neat solutions, and this guide interprets relevance widely including, for instance, both Thérèse Rein's student file and Bettina Gorton's staff file. The significance of the material it describes, however, can only be assessed against the overall pattern of prime ministerial documentation. Who are its custodians? Where is it concentrated?

Personal papers of prime ministers

Since Edmund Barton was commissioned to form government in 1901, prime ministers and their office staffs have been creating official and personal records of their activities. In the early decades a number came to office following established public careers in state politics, so existing personal and family papers already existed.

The Commonwealth National Library, one of the National Library's predecessors, took the first steps to ensure the preservation of prime ministers' papers. It had the advantage of links with the Parliamentary Library, and no competitor. The first government archivist was not appointed until 1944, thirteen prime ministers later. By the 1984 proclamation of legislation establishing a National Archives, giving it a mandate to collect and preserve official *and* personal papers of prime ministers, nine more had come and gone. The National Archives quickly made up ground at the very time the size of collections, prime ministerial power and the Prime Minister's Office were all expanding. This meant that while the two institutions between them account for the main collections of the first twenty-five prime ministers, the earlier collections tend to be with the National Library, the latter with the National Archives, though there is some overlap.

The Library has eleven substantial collections and five smaller ones, and accepted its first, the papers of Edmund Barton, in 1929. Most of the remainder are with the Archives. The only significant exceptions are personal collections of papers at university-based prime ministerial libraries which are discussed later.

Collections of prime ministerial papers are of course not confined to records created as prime minister. Some early prime ministers came to office with existing accumulations of papers. Indeed a surprisingly large number of prime ministers were in state politics, including as ministers (for example, Edmund Barton, Alfred Deakin and Robert Menzies). Two prime ministers (George Reid and Joe Lyons) were ex-Premiers, Reid also being a member of the House of Commons (1916–1918). And some, such as Andrew Fisher and S M Bruce, lived for considerable parts of their lives outside Australia. So while Australia's twenty-seven prime ministers are and will be remembered primarily because they held the highest office, their biographies cover not only their prime ministerial lives but their preceding generation and their pre- and post-parliamentary careers, and this potentially large canvas can be reflected in their papers.

Past practice in Australia, as with nineteenth-century British and American leaders, was a laissez-faire acceptance of prime ministers asserting their office papers were their private property. The 1983 *Archives Act* represented a stricter and more democratic and accountable approach, asserting their status as public records. This meant that some so-called personal collections held by the National Library (such as the McMahon papers) are now properly subject to official access rules. In turn, it would be wrong to think that all the National Archives' prime ministerial collections are exclusively official or political in nature.

This personal/official distinction has been a central issue where prime ministerial libraries have negotiated the transfer of personal components of collections held by the National Archives, although the line drawing has not only involved government archives. In the 1980s Bob Hawke's office files created while he was president of the ACTU were transferred to the Hawke Prime Ministerial Library at the University of South Australia, while the ACTU's own archives have been placed at the ANU's Noel Butlin Archives Centre. Here, of course, there is substantial documentation *about* Hawke and *by* Hawke while he was the Council's industrial advocate. Separations rarely excise everything relevant, just as personal/official distinctions in practice are not always black and white.

Archives about prime ministers

Documentation *about* is history's circumstantial evidence; the holster and ammunition pouch rather than the smoking gun itself. Marshalled *en masse* it can be highly persuasive, though rarely decisive in debates fraught with ideology and reputation. But it is central to the inferences drawn by historians and biographers, where a focus on factors such as a life and its times, its context and underlying conditions, have long been presumed to be essential to understanding.

The National Library and the National Archives are again pre-eminent in relation to archives *about* prime ministers, preserving collections of personal papers and series of government records which include extensive documentation about them.

At the Library, these collections include a heavy concentration of the papers of prime ministers' Cabinet and political colleagues, and other associates, containing letters from and references to prime ministers. Thus, in addition to the aforementioned Deakin papers, there are nearly forty complementary collections, over half including letters by Deakin.[18] Secondly there are collections of family members (for example, Deakin's son-in-law, Herbert Brookes), of wives (Dame Zara Bate, wife of Harold Holt, and Hawke's wife and biographer Blanche d'Alpuget), of staff (a Keating speech writer Don Watson) and of their biographers (John La Nauze and Allan Martin, biographer of Menzies). Finally, the Library obviously has a very large holding of relevant secondary sources including printed, electronic, audiovisual (including oral history interviews) and other material about all twenty-seven prime ministers.

At the National Archives, the interconnectedness of its personal holdings of prime ministers is readily evident; the point made earlier about relationships applies equally to the Archives, not only with Cabinet and political colleagues, but more widely as well. Even in regard to Frank Forde, who was prime minister for little more than a week (in July 1945), it can boast for example his notebooks from attendance at the War Cabinet and Advisory War Council, and radio interview transcripts, press releases and speech notes of his wife Vera. In terms of related material, it is also the custodian of Cabinet minutes and notebooks, and of the files of the original Prime Minister's Office (within External Affairs), and successive departments of the Prime Minister and the Prime Minister and Cabinet. When it comes to prime ministers, it is hard to think of more important sets of related records.

Prime ministerial libraries

In the 1980s, the *Archives Act* ratified the dual Library/Archives structure of the prime ministerial archival landscape, but the decade signalled change too. The reasons have yet to be seriously studied, but new prime ministerial structures, staffing and recordkeeping which emerged with the Whitlam government from the early 1970s were clearly factors. These were responses to the growing dominance of the prime minister in parliament, in Cabinet, their party and the media. In short, government was becoming 'Prime Ministerial Government'.[19] Secondly, during the 1990s the National Council for the Centenary of Federation campaigned to make us as knowledgeable of our prime ministers as Americans are of their presidents.[20]

Complementing this, biographies, documentaries, memoirs and musicals began to appear; concern was expressed about the upkeep of graves; and prime ministers' names began to appear everywhere, from commemorative walks, swimming pools and universities to electorates, dams and towers. And on the cultural heritage front, a new type of collector emerged: the university-based hybrid library/archives/museum, vaguely modelled on the US presidential library system. Most came to be described as prime ministerial libraries.[21] Drawing on public and private sector funds, their founders were determined to perpetuate the public memory and achievements of their prime minister and to promote the concerns and ideals which defined their public life. The first, in Perth, set the pattern:

> When the Western Australian Institute of Technology became Curtin University of Technology in 1987, there was a strong feeling that the new university needed 'a heart'. What better way to achieve that than to develop a centre which would focus on wartime prime minister John Curtin and the strength of his legacy to Australia. The first donation to the John Curtin Prime Ministerial Library (JCPML) archival research collection dated from that time and comprised significant historical material including books from John Curtin's personal library and bound volumes of the *Westralian Worker* newspapers annotated by him.[22]

Since 1987, in addition to Curtin, prime ministers Hawke (University of South Australia), Deakin (Deakin University), Whitlam (University of Western Sydney) and Fraser (University of Melbourne) have been chosen or agreed to be the focus of documentation. A sixth collection, the Menzies Virtual Museum, is outside the university sector and functions as its name suggests. It, and to varying degrees the others, have built collections by sourcing digital copies of original documents from other collections; Deakin, for instance, benefiting from the National Library's digitisation of the Deakin papers. All but the Menzies Virtual Museum have sought original material too – the Hawke, Fraser and Curtin collections include material transferred from the National Archives, as well as prime ministerial personal libraries, archival material from family members and political colleagues, oral history interviews and objects. Using these collections, they have encouraged scholarship, organised conferences, started their own digitisation programs and mounted exhibitions, all the time deepening their relationship with their prime minister and/or his family.

The prime ministers' portal

At the beginning of the new century, the picture was starting to appear uncoordinated and messy. There was no simple national search gateway into the collections building up around the country. The two university prime ministerial libraries in Perth and Adelaide were consolidating, and two more (Deakin University based in Geelong and the University of Melbourne, then holding Menzies' personal collection of 3,000 books and wanting to establish a Menzies Library) were seeking government support to follow their example. The government response was interesting.

During the twentieth century, governments had shown little interest in national documentation strategies. On the few occasions they seemed engaged, they confined funding to their own national cultural institutions and their programs. Small grants schemes for the preservation of community heritage, tax relief to donors of material, documenting multiculturalism and commissioning official histories and surveys marked the traditional limits of their (and their advisers') thinking. Almost by definition, however, documenting prime ministers presented a problem with no neat institutional solution.[23] The *Archives Act* and strict rules about the return of Cabinet papers by ex-ministers were in place, competition between the Archives and the Library had been resolved, while the universities seemed to be taking things into their own hands.

A comprehensive policy was yet to emerge when, early in the new century, the government agreed to support Deakin University's funding request (via Australian Research Council and Centenary of Federation avenues). Rejecting the University of Melbourne on Menzies, it explained that what Commonwealth funds were available for prime ministers would go to an initiative to benefit all. In the 2000–2001 budget it announced $1.6m would be spent over the following four years for the National Archives 'to make the official papers of former Prime Ministers more accessible to the public'. From the resultant Prime Ministers Papers Project came a portal website, *Australia's Prime Ministers*, with digitised documents and images, and published guides, documenting the existence of both official and personal collections of prime ministerial papers in the National Archives and other institutions.[24]

If the budget decision had a secondary aim to discourage the proliferation of university-based prime ministerial libraries, it quickly failed. In 2004, Malcolm Fraser decided to move his personal papers (and sought also his official papers) from the Archives to the University of Melbourne, where another composite collection documenting Fraser's entire life, and his forebears, began to take shape, including his large personal library. The Archives had no choice but to suffer the inconvenience up to a point, while its Advisory Council contemplated a dedicated prime ministerial archive and even a Hall of Prime Ministerial History.[25]

The Australian Prime Ministers Centre

All this coincided with, and in part influenced, the need to resolve what to do with Canberra's Old Parliament House once it was agreed in 2006 its largest tenant, the National Portrait Gallery, would move to a new permanent building beside the High Court overlooking Lake Burley Griffin. Though various personal and departmental agendas were in play, ultimately it was resolved – and so announced in May 2006 – to establish there a Gallery of Australian Democracy. The Gallery had a curious inclusion. Described as nothing more than an exhibition program and 'reading room and reference services' to support access to prime ministers' papers, it was called the Australian Prime Ministers Centre.[26]

In the past five years, this concept has been refined (the Gallery was renamed the Museum of Australian Democracy) and it and the Centre separately launched and officially opened. One of its first decisions was to fund an upgrade of the *Australia's Prime Ministers* website hosted by the National Archives. From the beginning too it reassured the long-established archives and libraries that it had no intention to compete for prime ministerial papers, but rather to encourage their deposit in the appropriate national institution, usually the National Archives.

For its own part, the Centre began to fill a gap in this specialist field of collecting, concentrating on material culture (e.g. political artifacts, portraits and caricatures), political ephemera such as how-to-vote cards and handbills, manifestos and policy statements, oral history interviews in an arrangement with the National Library, and published biographies and other relevant printed material. It has also endeavoured to develop a sense of common purpose among the national institutions and university collections, convening an annual Round Table of Prime Ministerial Research and Collecting Agencies. From 2007 there have also been exhibitions and an awards scheme for fellows and summer scholars to further the public's understanding of prime ministers.

The ANU collection

The *Australia's Prime Ministers* portal website amply illustrates that archival and other source material documenting individual prime ministers is held in libraries, archives, museums and other repositories throughout Australia. Others such as the National Museum, Australian War Memorial and National Film and Sound Archive also quickly began highlighting what they held on prime ministers for the portal. What it now shows, by literally mapping collection locations, is the extent to which prime ministers are represented in collections around the world. Taking Curtin as an example of one of the prime ministers who served during a world war, the portal shows relevant material can be found in Manchester, Cambridge, London, Maryland and Ottawa, as well as around Australia.

Because it is a portal, the limitations of the *Australia's Prime Ministers* website are inherent: it is dependent on contributing institutions and their diligence in updating information about relevant collections, and it can assist only indirectly by referring researchers on to the contributing library or archives. Once at their reading room (or online catalogue), the researcher might be overwhelmed with detailed lists and indexes pointing to numerous digitised documents highly relevant to his or her prime ministerial topic du jour – though probably not.

It has always been known that in the ANU's official archival records and in the collections of the Noel Butlin Archives Centre there were some documents about prime ministers, and brief descriptions of these were contributed to the National Archives' portal. It was also known that, until now, a systematic search had not been attempted, and it is this 'drilling down' that this guide addresses.

What it reveals falls entirely into the 'about' category: there are no collections of the personal papers *of* a prime minister at the ANU. Nevertheless, it describes archival and secondary resources about every Australian prime minister, and includes concentrations on two areas poorly covered elsewhere.

First, the ANU and our prime ministers are linked (and documented) in a surprising number of ways, well beyond any other Australian university. The ANU's official university archives are particularly important here, including as they do Council minutes with the Chancellor, Lord Bruce in the chair, John Gorton representing the Senate, Malcolm Fraser the House of Representatives, and Bob Hawke as both a student representative and a co-opted member, albeit at different times. There are photographs of Bruce, Chifley, Menzies, Gorton, Whitlam, Fraser, Hawke, Keating, Howard and Rudd on campus, and staff or student files for Bruce, Whitlam, Hawke and Rudd. The files of the *Australian Dictionary of Biography*, based at the ANU, reveal historians' debates about the lives of eighteen former prime ministers.

Secondly there is a wealth of material in the Noel Butlin Archives Centre's great collection strength, the documentation of Australian business firms and trade unions. Together with the University of Melbourne Archives, its only real equivalent in Australia, the Butlin represents the majority of the nation's business and labour archival heritage. It need hardly be said that these archives document many prime ministerial associations, and not only regarding Australian Labor Party prime ministers. The Maritime Dispute collection relates very much to John Howard's term in office, and all prime ministers have been lobbied by companies, industry associations and trade unions, directly through correspondence and delegations, and more obliquely through political campaigns. There are extensive resources of printed and other secondary source material with special concentrations on, for example, the peace, disarmament, anti-conscription, environment and labour movements.

Endnotes

1. G Powell, 'Prime Ministers as Recordkeepers: British Models and Australian Practice', in S McKemmish and M Piggott (eds), *The Records Continuum: Ian Maclean and Australian Archives First Fifty Years*, Ancora Press, 1994, pp. 99 and 106.
2. John La Nauze, *Alfred Deakin: A Biography*, 2 vols, Melbourne University Press, 1965.
3. L F Fitzhardinge, *William Morris Hughes: A Political Biography*, vol. 2, Angus and Robertson, 1979, p. 586.
4. See, for example, John Thompson, '"Let time and chance decide": Deliberation and fate in the collecting of personal papers', chapter 7 in Peter Cochrane (ed.), *Remarkable Occurrences: The National Library's First 100 Years 1901–2001*, National Library of Australia, 2001, pp. 105–21. The recordkeeping behaviour of novelists and poets are perhaps best known here, thanks to the work of literary biographers and of their family and friends via a classic study by Ian Hamilton, *Keepers of the Flame: Literary Estates and the Rise of Biography*, Hutchinson, 1994.
5. Powell, p. 93.
6. Allan Martin, 'Menzies the Man', chapter 1 in Scott Prasser, J R Nethercote & John Warhurst (eds), *The Menzies Era: A Reappraisal of Government, Politics and Policy*, Hale and Iremonger, 1995, esp. pp. 18–19.
7. Jenny Hocking, *Gough Whitlam: A Moment in History: The Biography*, vol. 1, The Miegunyah Press, 2008, pp. 89, 408; E G Whitlam, 'Go to the documents: An address on the role of historians', Whitlam Institute e-magazine, *It's Time*, issue 12, March 2003 at www.whitlam.org/news_and_ events/e-magazine/e-magazine/issues/2003.
8. Hocking, p. 89.
9. Convenient starting points for Menzies and Whitlam collections are at http://primeministers.naa.gov.au/findrecords/Menzies/ and http://primeministers.naa.gov.au/findrecords/Whitlam/.
10. Malcolm Fraser and Margaret Simons, *Malcolm Fraser: The Political Memoirs*, The Miegunyah Press, 2010, p. 6.
11. L F Fitzhardinge, *William Morris Hughes: A Political Biography*, vol. 1, Angus and Robertson, 1964, vi.
12. 'Notes' in *La Trobe Library Journal*, no. 5, April 1970, p. 27.
13. Fitzhardinge, vol. 1, vi.
14. John Robertson, *J H Scullin: A Political Biography*, University of Western Australia Press, 1974.
15. See Alain Corbin, *The Life of an Unknown: The Rediscovered World of a Clog Maker in Nineteenth-Century France*, Columbia University Press, New York, 2001, especially the Prelude: 'Investigating the torpor of an ordinary existence'.
16. Hilary Jenkinson, *A Manual of Archive Administration*, Percy Lund, Humphries and Company, 1966, p. 12.
17. Michael Piggott, 'Documenting Prime Ministerial Lives', *Limited Addition*, no. 25, June 2009, pp. 2–6.
18. http://www.naa.gov.au/naaresources/publications/research_guides/pdf/first_six/chapter_two_deakin.pdf.

19. See, for instance, Patrick Weller, *First Among Equals: Prime Ministers in Westminster Systems*, Allen and Unwin, Sydney, 1985 and James Walter and Paul Strangio, *No, Prime Minister: Reclaiming Politics From Leaders*, UNSW Press, 2007.
20. The Council found that 46% of Australians had not heard of the first prime minister Edmund Barton. The resultant First Prime Minister campaign showed ordinary Australians around the country trying to respond to the question: 'Who was the first Prime Minister of Australia?': http://pandora.nla.gov.au/pan/10492/20021115-0000/index.htm.
21. Though dated, an overview of university-based prime ministerial documentation programs was provided in a theme issue of *Australian Academic & Research Libraries* in 2005: http://www.alia.org.au/publishing/aarl/36.1/.
22. Lesley Carman-Brown, Kandy-Jane Henderson and Lesley Wallace, 'Australia's First Prime Ministerial Library: Past and Future', *AARL*, vol. 36, no. 1, March 2005: http://www.alia.org.au/publishing/aarl/36.1/full.text/carmen-brown.html.
23. It was little different concerning arrangements following their deaths. There was meant to be an official burial ground – the Prime Ministers Memorial Garden within Melbourne General Cemetery opened in June 1996 by John Howard who argued it was an appropriate location because Melbourne was for twenty-seven years the seat of government and Victoria was the birthplace of such a large number of former prime ministers. Victorian Premier Jeff Kennett went further, hoping it would become Australia's equivalent of the Arlington cemetery near Washington, DC.
24. See primeministers.naa.gov.au.
25. Hilary Golder, *A Necessary Safeguard: National Archives of Australia Advisory Council, 1984–2009*, Commonwealth of Australia, 2009, pp. 47–9. See also http://www.unimelb.edu.au/malcolmfraser/.
26. See http://moadoph.gov.au/research.

CHAPTER 3
Prime Ministers in the ANU Archives

The ten short narratives which follow draw on records held by the ANU Archives. They provide examples of how the records which are found in the University Archives and in the business and labour collections of the Noel Butlin Archives Centre can be used.

1. Three Labor dismissals
2. Hughes and conscription
3. Bruce the Businessman
4. 'Pig Iron' Bob
5. L F Fitzhardinge and W M Hughes
6. The IPA and three Liberal PMs
7. Bob Hawke and University House
8. Whitlam and Wave Hill
9. Heinz Arndt and Malcolm Fraser
10. The public face

1. Three Labor dismissals

Dismissals have been a constant in Australian federal politics, and one might argue they bookend the whole period of Federation. Even before Edmund Barton was commissioned to form an interim government and organise elections in 1901, the Governor-General Lord Hopetoun was obliged to correct a blunder and replace NSW Premier Sir William Lyne when he failed to form a Cabinet. Moving forward to June 2010, the ALP Caucus, through an enforced resignation, removed Kevin Rudd from his first-term prime ministership.

Before Rudd of course there had been party-room coups against Hughes, Menzies, Gorton and Hawke. The complete list is surprisingly long. Few Australians today have heard of John Christian Watson, the Australian Labor Party's first prime minister in 1904, let alone know that he was expelled for siding with Billy Hughes about conscription for overseas service in 1916.[1] Many more know that Hughes himself, and in the early 1930s Joe Lyons, 'ratted' on their party by leading non-Labor parties. Again, while most people are aware Gough Whitlam was 'sacked' by the Governor-General on 11 November 1975, fewer know about Joseph Cook's switch from Labor to the conservatives in the late 1890s or the story of the 1950s split and the rise of the Democratic Labor Party.

In fact there were a number of other expulsions. They took place in the industrial arena and followed on from the effects of bitter divisions in the ALP federally during World War I and in New South Wales under Jack Lang. Chifley and Hughes were each dismissed from their union, and Watson from a union-owned company: Hughes while he was prime minister, Chifley a decade before he became prime minister, and Watson over a decade after he had been prime minister. All three episodes are well documented in the collections of the Noel Butlin Archives Centre.

Watson

Though to some doubt still surrounds the date and place of John Christian Watson's birth,[2] all accord him the honour of leading the first national labour government in the world (April–August 1904). Nevertheless, such was the nature of parliamentary alliances in the nation's first decade his government was short-lived. After his government's defeat, he stayed on as party leader only until 1907 and resigned from parliament in 1910.

Watson ultimately became quite a success in business administration. In the 1920s and 1930s he held a number of directorships and became the national face of the NRMA. But in the years immediately following his parliamentary career he remained active within the labour movement, primarily through Labor Papers Limited, which published the Australian Workers' Union newspaper, the *Australian Worker*.[3]

Watson was elected its inaugural chairman of directors, and was heavily involved in arranging the construction of a headquarters building, MacDonnell House in Pitt Street, Sydney. In 1914 he became managing director and in a myriad ways ensured the company was well run and its publication flourished.

Watson publicly sided with Billy Hughes over conscription, an issue so divisive it split the federal parliamentary Labor Party and saw the creation of a new Nationalist Party and government in 1916. The industrial wing of the labour movement was strongly against conscription, and there was no question but that Watson's position became untenable. The minutes of his last meeting of the board of directors on 14 November 1916 read as follows:

> The attitude of Mr J C Watson in connection with the conscription issue and his position of Managing Director & Chairman of Directors was next considered. Mr Watson explained his view & stated he did not feel justified in voluntarily resigning but if the Directors considered it would be in the best interests of the Company to resign he would do so. Mr Lundie then moved & Mr T Hyett seconded: That in the best interest of the Company it was desirable for Mr Watson to resign his position as Managing Director & chairman of Directors. Carried.[4]

Minutes rarely convey a complete sense of a meeting's undercurrents, but in this case they mirrored the absence of bitterness which later faction fights and splits engendered. They also foreshadowed the response to Watson's death in 1941 when, as Ross McMullin wrote, 'Curtin contravened the ALP tradition of enduring hostility to defectors by honouring him with a warm obituary in both the caucus room and the House of Representatives'.[5]

Even at the November 1916 meeting, practicalities had followed the execution: 'In resigning Mr Watson suggested that a special audit of the books be made to the 15th November 1916 & that a report be obtained as to the suitability of the machinery & plant installed for publishing a morning paper up to 24 pages. The suggestions were agreed to.'

He had to go, but they were regretfully losing a most competent and courteous leader. At the end of the meeting:

> Mr Watson asked that his appreciation of the services rendered by
> Mr C Bamford the Business Manager, Mr H S Wynne the Engineer &
> Mr O E Foster, the Secretary, be placed on record. Mr Rae moved & Mr Hyett seconded: That the thanks of the Directors be tendered to the retiring managing director, Mr J C Watson, for his services while occupying that position. Carried.

Delegates to the 1900 Interstate Labor Conference include Billy Hughes and John Christian Watson (right) in the front row, both later 'dismissed' for their support of conscription (NBAC T39/74/26, K3808b)

Hughes

Commenting on Hughes' dismissal, Margo Beasley wrote in *Wharfies: The History of the Waterside Workers' Federation of Australia* that 'by this action the WWF earned the unique distinction of being the only trade union ever to expel a Prime Minister from its ranks'.[6]

For the two previous decades, this would have seemed impossible. Hughes was the driving force behind the formation of the WWF, foundation secretary of the Sydney Wharf Labourers' Union for seventeen years, and similarly served the Trolley, Draymen and Carters' Union. Following Andrew Fisher's resignation due to ill-health, Hughes was sworn in as prime minister on 27 October 1915, and the Federation Council's minutes recorded:

> That ....[it] desires to offer its most hearty and sincere congratulations to its President, the Hon. William Morris Hughes, on the occasion of his attaining the highest position attainable in the civic life of Australia, namely, that of Prime Minister of the Commonwealth.[7]

This meant a lot to Hughes: 'The President expressed his thanks for the motion and stated that of all the congratulations he received, he regarded those of the Committee of Management of the Waterside Workers' Federation with the greatest esteem'. The esteem continued. Just before he left for the United Kingdom in January 1916, he is recorded as receiving a payment of £72,[8] and a month after his return, he was re-elected the Federation president at the monthly meeting of 15 August 1916.

Within a fortnight, everything changed. On 30 August 1916 Hughes announced a referendum on conscription, and as he opened the 'Yes' campaign on 18 September, Cabinet, Caucus and the labour movement began to fracture. Whereas on 6 September the Sydney Wharf Labourers' Union had been discussing the butter shortage and had authorised him 'to represent the Union at the Price Fixing Board', at a 'Special Cease Work Meeting' of 14 September it resolved 'this Union emphatically protest against the introduction of Conscription of life as introduced by W M Hughes'. At the next special meeting, on 27 September:

> Mr McNeill said that he was pleased to see such a good roll up & moved the following motion 'That W M Hughes be expelled from this union'. Mr Serle seconded the resolution. Messrs Seale Bailey Thompson spoke in favour. Burrows & Woods Sands & Hunt against. Which being put to the meeting was carried by 160 vote[s] to 42 against.[9]

If Hughes had been there and misheard, the next motion confirmed the rejection: 'Moved that £5.0.0 be voted to the No conscription league'. By then however he had stopped attending their meetings. He was in the middle of six weeks of exhausting travel, public meetings and mounting vituperation, campaigning as he famously put it 'as though he were fighting for his very life'.[10] Before it was over, his other union, the Trolley, Draymen and Carters, had also rejected him, and his entry into the annals of Labor betrayal and treachery was confirmed.

35

Billy Hughes (centre) with other members of the Trolley, Draymen and Carters' Union committee in 1905 (NBAC Z277/86)

Chifley

In popular imagination, Ben Chifley is a pipe-smoking engine driver from Bathurst, and a dedicated member of his union, the Australian Federated Union of Locomotive Enginemen. During the Depression however, views about political and economic strategy were sharply polarised, and those who changed sides or stood for a middle path were attacked with equal vehemence. To many unionists and traditional Australian Labor Party voters, support for the 'Lang Plan' and opposition to the 'Premiers' Plan' were the litmus tests of true labour loyalty.

As economic conditions worsened, the Senate blocked treasurer Theodore's expansionary plans, and wages and employment fell, Chifley began to be singled out for blame. In January 1931 the Enfield branch told the Union's NSW general committee:

> That in view of Mr B Chifley's ineptitude and apparent laxity in the Federal House of Representatives towards the cancellation of our Federal Award, Enfield Branch demands from the General Committee Mr Chifley's expulsion from the Association.[11]

Chifley defended himself, and a motion 'that this Committee has the utmost confidence in the loyalty of Mr Chifley to the interests of members' was passed, but further trouble loomed. Elected by Caucus to join the Scullin ministry in March 1931, Chifley was compromised. To a growing number of the NSW branch of the AFULE, he quickly became one of those who 'had forfeited the confidence of the working class movement of this State' and 'had betrayed the trust reposed in them by the workers'.[12] Within a month of a speech in parliament in early July supporting the Premiers' Plan, the Bathurst branch of the AFULE resolved that: 'Due to his political actions Mr Chifley MHR has lost the confidence of members of this Branch, such resolution to be inserted in whichever local paper will publish same & the Labor Daily'.[13]

In October the expulsion move was successful, though Chifley appealed to the AFULE Federal Executive. Attitudes hardened within the NSW branch. It felt 'no good purpose' would be served by considering it. Support for the 'Lang Plan' was division policy; he 'merited expulsion from the Union' and 'abrogated the principles of unionism in opposing the union's policy'.[14] A showdown loomed, only to be resolved by Chifley withdrawing his appeal on 25 November, the day 'Stabber Jack' Beasley (the leader of the Lang Labor Party) voted with the opposition precipitating the fall of the Scullin government. In a final ignominy, Chifley was defeated as Member for Macquarie at the ensuing federal election by his former campaign manager and 'Lang Labor' candidate Tony Luchetti. Nine years were to pass before he regained the seat, and ten before he was readmitted to his union.

2. Hughes and conscription

During 1916 and 1917 the conscription debate dominates the *Australian Worker*, the weekly newspaper published by the Sydney branch of the Australian Workers' Union.[15] The ANU Archives holds an almost complete run of the broadsheet from 1903 to the 1970s. The newspaper covered local politics, international news, sports, and union news, and had regular columns, such as 'Our Women's Page, conducted by Mary Gilmore' with recipes, poetry and readers' contributions.

The newspaper ran a strong 'No' case for conscription with increasingly alarmist headlines such as 'Will the Farmers' Sons be Grabbed?', 'Look out, married men!', 'Women of Australia, be warned!' and 'A risk you cannot afford to take'. In the period leading up to the conscription referendum of October 1916, and again, in November–December 1917, the Union also published a twice-weekly 'No-Conscription Special' edition of the newspaper. It paid close attention to the conservative press such as the *Sydney Morning Herald* and regularly refuted statements quoted from other newspapers. There is also reporting of the court case against the Editor of the *Australian Worker* under the *War Precautions Act* for undermining the war effort through misleading reporting, and news from the front with black-bordered photographs of soldiers missing in action or killed on active service.

Prime ministers in this debate include not only Billy Hughes but former prime ministers, J C Watson, Andrew Fisher and Joseph Cook. The familiar description of Hughes as 'the Little Digger' is not used. Instead, he is described in terms such as 'our Little Nero', 'the Czar', 'the Welsh Kaiser' and 'the dangerous little tyrant'. He is depicted in numerous cartoons as small and aggressive, in ill-fitting formal attire (his top hat down to his ears), in league with rotund businessmen, and threatening violence against workers. He appears as a rat, but also as the Grim Reaper, a vulture, a monkey and a devil.

There is close reporting of Hughes' words with phrases extracted from speeches or remarks quoted out of context, such as 'I'll have you' (apparently a response to a heckler in Warwick) and 'one lie and I'll get you'. These phrases are used in cartoons and as boxed quotes to imply other meanings directly linked to the conscription campaign. Under the headline 'Hughes denounces conscription', quotations from earlier speeches and a biography are reproduced to contradict his current statements, though it is not clear if the quotations are Hughes' own words or his biographer's.

Trade union records reveal the split between the Hughes government and the union movement. The report of proceedings of the Australian Trade Union Congress in May 1916 'together with the Manifesto of the National Executive' refers to conscription as 'an instrument of working class subjugation' and 'a bludgeon to break down the standard of the industrial classes' (the latter comment, however, did not pass the censor).[16]

A circular memorandum was sent to all trade unions from the Australian Trades Union Anti-Conscription Congress in November 1916, shortly after the first referendum failed, outlining the need 'resting on the Labor Movement to hold to what has been gained, as well as prepare for any eventuality'. It is signed 'Yours fraternally, J Curtin, Secretary' (a future prime minister).[17] Trade unions sent delegates to a number of special trade union congresses on conscription and recorded the collection of payments from their members for an 'anti-conscription' levy.[18]

Caricature of Billy Hughes by Claude Marquet published in the *Australian Worker*, 17 December 1917 issue (NBAC S100)

A tactic of political campaigning at the time was the distribution of printed leaflets and pamphlets, often a single page or a small booklet. Their ephemeral nature adds to their rarity, but they are often found within correspondence files of trade unions and also in the personal collections of trade unionists and political activists. The identity of the organisations which produced them is not always clear, with names such as the Victorian Peace Society, the Australian Peace Alliance, and the Australian Freedom League.

Vida Goldstein, president of the Women's Political Association and the Australian Women's Peace Army, in a single-sheet open letter to 'the workers of Australia' takes issue with a speech by Hughes at the Bendigo Chamber of Commerce on 18 June 1917. Several paragraphs of the speech are reproduced with selective bolding of key sentences which are then analysed:

> Prime Minister's 'Organisation' means 'Preparedness' for Future Wars. The meaning of Mr Hughes' speech is clear – military and industrial conscription are aimed at … Mr Hughes is quite right. Organisation is needed, but it must be Voluntary Organisation, with the clear-cut, definite object of establishing a New Social Order, not Conscript Organisation backed up by Militarism to enforce allegiance to a dying social order.[19]

A leaflet headed 'Conscription and Single Men' takes issue with discrepancies between Hughes' statistics given in parliament in September 1916 and in another speech in Bendigo on 12 November 1917. Issued by the Anti-Conscription Campaign Committee, the leaflet counts the number of single men who enlisted or married in the interim period to prove that only 35,910 single men were available to be conscripted, not the 150,000 claimed by Hughes. 'Are we to believe what Mr Hughes said last year, or what he says now?'[20]

A small booklet, priced at 'One Penny' with the title 'Australian Conscription for Service Abroad Unnecessary and Unjust: A Reply to the Prime Minister' presents a direct response by 'W J Miles, Challis House, Sydney' to the arguments for conscription made by Hughes.[21] On the other side, for the 'Yes' case, a leaflet produced by the National Referendum Council is headed: 'Don't Scab: J C Watson, First Labour Prime Minister of Australia, talks to Australian Unionists on the Referendum' and continues:

> It is marvellous how, under the stress of controversy, so many men lose their sense of logic. The attitude of some of our trade-union leaders on the conscription issue may be instanced.[22]

The archives referenced here provide a different view from the mainstream press and are a sample only of sources on the conscription debates in World War I. Further material will be found by searching the records of individual trade unions and businesses.

3. Bruce the Businessman

Together with Keith Hancock's 'parties of initiative' and 'parties of resistance',[23] capital and labour represent two of the most enduring categories underpinning Australia's party political history. Remarkably, however, only one non-Labor prime minister had actual business involvement: Stanley Melbourne Bruce. Indeed his family investments and warehousing and importing business generated such wealth as to underpin another record. On his election in 1918 he was the first federal politician not to draw a parliamentary salary. This continued until he was appointed treasurer in the Hughes government late in 1921, when he resigned as managing director of Paterson, Laing and Bruce (PLB).

The Bruce family wealth, made and lost several times, was built by S M Bruce's father John. When his father died in 1901, S M spent what later might have been termed a 'gap year' with the Melbourne warehouse, then managed by his older brother Ernest. In 1907, following a Cambridge law degree and some legal work, Bruce became acting chair of the London board of PLB (confirmed the following year). He returned to Australia in 1914, briefly chairing the Melbourne branch, before enlisting back in the United Kingdom early in 1915. Returning to Australia in 1917, his business and political careers ran in parallel until the former ceased, as noted above, in 1921.

Though he was directly involved in business in total for only about a decade, in popular imagination Bruce was strongly identified as a businessman. Brian Carroll's *Australia's Prime Ministers: From Barton to Howard* reduces its subjects to a single stereotypical label: Gorton is 'The Wild One', Fraser 'The Prefect', and Whitlam 'The Crasher'. Bruce, however, is simply 'The Businessman'.[24] It was an identification, however, that Bruce himself cultivated, stressing it during his campaign as a Nationalist for the by-election which saw him elected as Member for Flinders in 1918, and his 'business acumen' was seen as a factor in this result.[25] Rumours that he was made treasurer by Hughes to appease the National Party's business donors added a more conspiratorial edge to the stereotyping.

Once prime minister from 1923, however, Bruce became known for his adoption of business processes in the management of Cabinet deliberations, and what he styled 'strict business principles' rather than ideology into policy proposals. He looked favourably on establishing independent boards to manage some government operations. His first budget as treasurer had foreshadowed borrowing for public works by the post office and appointing a board of businessmen to run it.

The Managing Director

Given the strong association of Bruce with business, it is hard to imagine a more valuable collection than the minute books of the Paterson, Laing and Bruce's Melbourne board of directors covering the period during which Bruce was its managing director (1917–1921). The general paucity of Australian business archives gives the minutes added significance, as well as the specific loss of the London office records of PLB from German bombing in the second world war.

The London records of Paterson, Laing and Bruce were destroyed in World War II – the location of the PLB office is marked with a white cross to the left of the building in the centre of this composite photograph (NBAC N29/130)

At first glance, Minute Book No. 1 seems to have little to offer. It lacks agenda papers, and the documents the minutes refer to, such as cables, balance sheets and reports, are absent. But it will reward careful scrutiny. Because the minutes record attendance and the minutes of previous meetings are signed and dated by the chair, the micro chronology of this critical period in Bruce's career can be plotted. For example his confirmation signature dated 14 December 1916 means we know he was by then back in Australia, not early the following year.[26]

The civilized capitalist

Bruce is almost always the only one of the three or four directors normally present at the board meetings who is mentioned: there are repeated references that: 'The Chairman indicated ...' and 'The Chairman reported ...' Whatever discussion and dissention might have gone unrecorded, it is reasonable to assume Bruce's position and standing invariably gave him the final say, even after his older brother Robert joined the board in March 1920.[27]

While the minutes respect hierarchy and favour brevity, a sense of Bruce's competency as a businessman can be readily gleaned. There are appraisals of how businesses in Victoria and other states which had been lent funds were performing and of others being considered as prospects. Bruce's nature as a manager and human being also emerges. He approved decisions such as that involving:

> The case of returned soldier H Fauvel ... This man was suspended on 13th February for gross misconduct. He was not discharged on that date, as being a returned soldier the matter had to be brought before the Board. After fully considering the reports by Mr Macrae and Mr Dickie, with regard to this man's conduct, it was resolved that, there being no extenuating circumstances, this man should be dismissed.[28]

As someone with war experience, Bruce was not always so unsympathetic.[29] Several instances are recorded of honouring undertakings given before staff had enlisted that they would be paid allowances when they were no longer in work after the war.[30] In another, which Bruce dealt with personally, additional factors were involved:

> The case of returned soldier J Grainger was considered, and the Managing Director reported having interviewed him on several occasions and that as a result of his observation during those interviews, he had come to the conclusion that the man had, unfortunately, been mentally affected by his experiences during the war. He also reported that he had arranged with Grainger that the Company should make him some allowance in fulfilment of their obligations to take him back into their employment, and after consideration, the Board determined on a compassionate allowance of £156, being a year's salary on the basis of £3 a week. At the time, this man was receiving 25/- a week.[31]

Bruce's earliest biographer has stated that he was one of the first to introduce profit sharing in Australia.[32] There is nothing in the minutes, although they do suggest he did care for his workers at a time when there was no compulsory superannuation and the Commonwealth aged pension, when introduced in 1909, was £26 per annum. PLB had their own staff pension scheme. In October 1919, the Melbourne board discussed:

> The retirement from the staff of Messrs M E Thomas, F Rookledge and J Pound … and … decided to place on record its highest appreciation of their past valuable services, and unanimously agreed to place their names on the pension fund list, carrying emoluments of £200, £200 and £150 respectively, payable at the Directors' discretion.[33]

Finally, there was the matter of industrial accidents where an enlightened view of occupational health and safety issues is apparent:

> It is regretted to have to record that an accident occurred in connection with our passenger lift, on the 14th inst., when it was bringing down a number of employes [sic] going out of the warehouse for lunch. Two sustained fractures and others severe jolts and shock. Those severely injured we are glad to say are progressing favourably. The Chairman, interrogating Mr Merry, the Lift Inspector, as to whether anything could be done to further safeguard persons travelling in the lift, was advised that the installation of the Governor Gear would have this effect. And this additional safeguard will be immediately installed.[34]

The Chancellor

In the 1950s, while he was the ANU's absentee Chancellor based in London, Bruce was constantly frustrated in his efforts to get to Canberra. Late in 1955, aged seventy-two, he wrote to the Vice-Chancellor Sir Leslie Melville explaining his planned trip had to be cancelled because he was 'unfortunately … somewhat preoccupied at the moment with the Bank of England and the Clearing Banks'.[35] Bruce was in fact involved in family and other business interests throughout his life, and to some, his role as prime minister was essentially that of 'the managing director of the national economy'.[36] Bruce's direct business experience, however, was relatively short. A crucial key to any comprehensive future assessment of Bruce the businessman will be the surviving records of the Melbourne office of Paterson, Laing and Bruce. The Bruce-related records in the university's archives are of similar significance, as Bruce reputedly 'destroyed all papers he received relating to his position as Chancellor'.[37]

4. 'Pig Iron' Bob

Worshipped or loathed, most Australian prime ministers came to be labelled as well as caricatured. Sobriquets ranged from the neutral ('the Doc' Earle Page) and the kindly ('Affable Alfred' Deakin and 'Honest Joe' Lyons) to the more judgemental ('Toby Tosspot' for Edmund Barton, 'Yes/No Reid' and 'Kerr's cur' for Malcolm Fraser). Sir Robert Menzies, befitting his long reign from 1949 to 1966, was known as 'Ming the Merciless'. While still a minister in the Lyons government before his first term as prime minister, however, he had become known especially in the left-wing press as 'Pig Iron' Bob.

Set against the deteriorating international situation of late 1938, a tired Lyons government and less than unified labour movement, the story behind the label remains one of Australian political history's more interesting mini dramas. Menzies' biographer Allan Martin saw him as valiantly defending, at some personal cost, a shaky government position not entirely of his own making, and one in which he showed a degree of physical courage.[38] Martin based his account essentially on newspaper sources, rejecting Rupert Lockwood's 1987 study as 'wild, partisan and inaccurate'.[39] In a footnote however he observed that:

> The intricate story of intra-union intrigue in this dispute has yet to be properly studied. It is clear the old story – on which the 'pig-iron Bob' fable is based – of an uncomplicated Government v. Watersiders clash, is unacceptably simplistic. That the Port of Kembla men's first vote against the Menzies proposals, against the recommendations of federal and local officials, was made on the urging of the State president of the union, Findlay, makes it clear that internal union conflicts were involved.[40]

To date, only labour historian Dr Greg Mallory has responded, combining oral history and research using some of the ANU archives collections to produce a chapter-length study in his *Uncharted Waters*.[41]

The journal of the Waterside Workers' Federation, the *Maritime Worker*, reports on the pig iron dispute in its December 1938 issue (NBAC S62)

Preconditions for a definitive account

Anyone producing a comprehensive account would need to examine relevant archives of all parties, not merely of the Lyons government and the Waterside Workers' Federation (WWF), but also of the Curtin federal opposition, BHP's subsidiary at Port Kembla the Australian Iron and Steel Company, the Federated Iron Workers' Association, the Seamen's Union, the ACTU, various Labor Party and Communist Party branches, the Commonwealth Steamship Owners Association, the Council of Civil Liberties, and religious organisations and prominent individuals who supported the wharfies' action such as Bishop Moyes of Armidale and the former Governor-General Sir Isaac Isaacs.

Such a project is amply provided for from various viewpoints via the holdings of the Noel Butlin Archives Centre. It has minutes and other papers of the two key union bodies, the Port Kembla (technically the South Coast) branch of the Federation[42] and the WWF Committee of Management (FCOM) and the general secretary Jim Healy.[43] It also holds the records of the Commonwealth Steamship Owners Association and the Australasian Steamship Owners Federation.[44] There are papers on the dispute in the archives of the Australian Council of Trade Unions.[45] They include rare documents like 'Mr Menzies' Statement', a six-page typescript which appears to be his address to the meeting he convened in Wollongong on 11 January 1939 with the Combined Union Committee – the day, according to some, that the police needed help from communists to guarantee his physical safety. In pencil on the verso it reads: 'Speakers Monk Crofts ACTU Healey Finlay [sic] Waterside Workers' and appears as if written up from notes or transcribed from a tape recording.

Though the Port Kembla branch documentation is also important – after all it was their action in refusing to load the SS *Delfram* carrying pig iron to support Japan's war in China which escalated the dispute to a national crisis – the WWF head office papers are exceptional. They include the general secretary's files of correspondence and telegrams on the dispute and the *Transport Workers Act* (the so-called 'dog-collar act') with the independent minded and Communist dominated Port Kembla branch, with the ACTU, and with Menzies' Attorney-General's Department.[46]

It is the Federal Committee of Management minutes, however, which take us to the very centre of the union as it negotiated with Menzies to see an end to the legislation which required wharfies to be licensed (thus permitting non-union labour) and to the port being reopened.[47] In January 1939 this had resulted in nearly 7,000 men being laid off. Fortunately for the historian, in October 1938 FCOM had begun one of its so-called 'half-yearly meetings'. More like an extended conference, it met off and on for forty-two days only ending two days before Christmas. Through its agenda papers, correspondence, telegrams (for example, from Menzies and to Curtin), records of phone calls, reports, letters of support and minutes of discussions of state representatives and federal office holders such as general secretary Healy and president Findlay one can track the progress of much of the 'pig iron' dispute. The relative weakness of the ACTU is on show, as is the tension between the Committee of Management's anxiety to contain and resolve the dispute and the South Coast branch's determination to endure.

5. L F Fitzhardinge and W M Hughes

Biography inevitably focuses attention on two people (subject and author), a fact which certainly applies to accounts of a prime ministerial life. Indeed the authors themselves can be part of the story: Lloyd Ross, Fin Crisp and Don Watson were directly associated with their subjects, Curtin, Chifley and Keating. And as more recent biographers such as Jenny Hocking and David Day have shown, researching and writing them can be fraught and challenging, regardless of whether or not the subject is alive. The collaboration between Meg Simons and Malcolm Fraser to produce a hybrid memoir/biography provides a further illustration and variation.

The biography by L F Fitzhardinge of W M Hughes broke new ground. The appearance of its first volume in 1964, and of John La Nauze's two volumes on Alfred Deakin the following year, heralded the arrival of large academic biographies on major Australian prime ministers and premiers based on primary sources from around the world.[48]

The job description

Shortly after Fitzhardinge joined the ANU in 1950 as Reader in the Sources of Australian History, he was asked by Hughes to write his biography. It was not the first time Hughes had sought a biographer, but the solution was unprecedented. Fitzhardinge was steeped in the sources of Australian history, having served for a decade from 1934 as a Research Officer and head of the Australian Section at the Commonwealth National Library. In 1940 he had helped Hughes collect material for a future biography or autobiography, and was considering a contract to write a biography.[49] He had also lectured in Australian history to foreign affairs cadets at Canberra University College.

The commission, which came with full access to personal papers, needed the ANU's approval; indeed the contract was between subject and university, not with the putative author. The Vice-Chancellor Douglas Copland and Hughes negotiated the terms of Fitzhardinge's release, and duly reported it to Council. It also came with £2000 over two years, the gift documentation being worded in general terms 'for historical research' so it would be 'free of income tax'.[50] Fitzhardinge's recollection of how he was 'lumbered with Billy', recorded in a oral history interview years later with the ANU official historian, makes hilarious reading even granted inevitable bias and a fading memory.[51]

The long march begins

From the very start there was tension about progress. Hughes, impatient and now aged 90 perhaps sensing he was mortal, seemed to think two years was all one needed. 'What I wanted, and must have,' he told Copland in July 1952, 'is Mr Fitzhardinge's full time services on my biography'.[52] In truth, the documentation suggests it was Vice-Chancellor Copland who gave the commitment, and the chosen author had to wear it.[53]

Up to the publication of volume one in 1964 and beyond, the rate of progress was an issue. After Hughes died late in October 1952, it was his wife Dame Mary Hughes' turn to express frustration, then the trustees and the ANU itself. Successive Vice-Chancellors, especially Copland's replacement Melville, were forced to get involved, in turn becoming defensive and exasperated. The Director of the Research School of Social Sciences, Sir Keith Hancock, wavered between support for one of his staff and maintaining pressure, reporting at one point he had 'urged' the biographer 'very forcibly to use his study leave in pushing ahead his work on Hughes'.[54]

Professor Keith Hancock welcomed at Canberra airport by Laurie Fitzhardinge, Ross Hohnen (behind), Professor Mark Oliphant and Vice-Chancellor Leslie Melville in 1957 (ANUA 225/511/6)

Fitzhardinge's critics had a point – which his reputation for 'frittering, pottering and gadding'[55] didn't help. In particular, he had a seemingly unquenchable need to talk: 'I must, however, admit', wrote Hancock, 'that he likes to settle down for a good talk'.[56] In addition, as Melville told Hancock, there was:

> Talk among responsible people in Canberra about Fitzhardinge's extra-mural activities ... he is said to take an active part in the running of a bookshop, which I understand is his property, and a farm which is his wife's. It is said that he serves in the shop upon occasion; that he keeps the books of the business, does the ordering and manages the enterprise; it is said that he personally delivers the produce of the farm and sells supplementary items of produce not from the farm. It is said that he devoted some significant part of his study leave to advancing his business interests.[57]

As the same file shows, Fitzhardinge was able to refute these charges, but his larger and quite plausible explanations about having to balance a number of work commitments, having to negotiate with the National Library over access to the

Hughes papers, and the need to consult new public archives becoming available both from the local Commonwealth Archives Office and from the United Kingdom and Commonwealth archives overseas were never fully accepted.

It might be right, but you can't publish it

It is not uncommon for a professional historian to want to thoroughly check all extant primary sources about someone who participated in some crucial world events. In an era before long-haul flights, email, digitisation and the thirty-year rule, this kind of research was not easy to rush, and Fitzhardinge's desire to do it strengthened after Hughes died (and thus was no longer available to answer questions and comment on drafts).

Added to Fitzhardinge's frustrations was the insistence of the Hughes estate's trustees that, as a condition of releasing the papers and funds, his manuscript be vetted to see if anything was defamatory. The university's legal advisers conceded up to a point; the vetting could proceed 'but only so Perpetual Trustees can take advice'. As Ross Hohnen the Registrar put it, the university must 'preserve … [its] independence of judgement on matters of scholarship'.[58]

In 1963, when the manuscript was finally produced, it was the way Fitzhardinge referred to Hughes' first marriage (to Elizabeth Cutts) that alarmed the Trustees. The surviving children from that 'union' could have grounds for defamation, and the trustees too might be potentially liable. On the other hand, the author did not want to be seen as negligent by failing to specify the marriage date and referencing documentary proof (such as a marriage certificate). Because no publisher would take the risk with the loaded term 'union', a compromise was needed which addressed both concerns.

Professor Geoffrey Sawer, the university's legal adviser, knew there must be no inference that the marriage wasn't valid: 'the prima facie validity of the marriage is so strongly established by law'. Expecting the absence of evidence to be taken as proof something didn't happen was 'being too insistent on "historical truth"'. The deal he brokered would have Fitzhardinge in effect implying there was a search and it failed; this 'confines the issue … to the question of the date of the marriage, which sufficiently conveys to the informed historical reader that the appropriate sort of searches have been made, but which does not ram home to the uninformed reader that it was lack of record in a marriage register that occasions the trouble.'[59] As published, the relevant footnote begins, 'I have been unable to establish exactly the date of this marriage'.[60]

In his Preface to volume one, Fitzhardinge tells something of the frustrations and difficulties he faced in writing about Hughes, and does so again in volume two, where he adds justification and a little self-satisfaction as having delay vindicated by newly released archives. In 1964, the scars were still fresh. When it came to acknowledgements, he nominated a special debt to Sir Keith Hancock and Professor Geoffrey Sawer. The files in the ANU Archives tell us some of the reasons why.

6. The IPA and three Liberal PMs

One enduring theme of Australian political history has been the relationships organisations promoting social and political beliefs have with political parties, their leaders and their policies. The obvious and perhaps clearest example is the industrial wing of the labour movement vis-a-vis the ALP. Some organisations have focused on ideas aimed at one or other of the major parties, while others have operated more like factions within a political party. They include the Fabian Society, the National Civic Council, the Socialist Left, *Quadrant* magazine and the Institute of Public Affairs.

The Institute of Public Affairs

Though the IPA is now a single organisation, it began in the early 1940s as two loosely affiliated branches formed in Sydney and then Melbourne. Later other state branches were established too. Its aim, expressed in reflections by the chairman to the Victorian branch annual general meeting in 1948, was 'in a nutshell … to combat socialisation and to advance the interests of free business enterprise in this country'.[61] Not surprisingly, its foundation Council included leaders of commerce and industry. Its chair was the retailing magnate Sir George Coles, with others, most later knighted, including Harold G Darling, Herbert Taylor, Charles Booth, Leslie McConnan, Geoffrey Grimwade and Walter Massy-Greene. In a sense, it was our first think tank, from 1947 publishing Australia's longest running political magazine, the *IPA Review*.[62]

THE IPA REVIEW

THE INSTITUTE OF PUBLIC AFFAIRS
289 FLINDERS LANE, MELBOURNE ● 63 6558

JANUARY-MARCH, 1966
Vol. 20 — No. 1

The Menzies Era

THE decade and a half, 1950 to 1965, has become known, inevitably, as the Menzies Era. The nature of the designation is unique. No other period in Australian history has been named after an individual; we do not talk of the Chifley era, the Lyons era, the Hughes era, or even the Deakin era. Doubtless this is partly because Sir Robert Menzies is the only Prime Minister who occupied the throne of leadership for a period of sufficient length to be dignified by the term "era". (Like Bradman's records, it is almost inconceivable that the 16-year period of Sir Robert's uninterrupted Prime Ministership will ever be surpassed.) But it is also because, over the entire period, Sir Robert exercised an unparalleled personal dominance in Cabinet, Parliament and in the country. He was in the minds of Australians more than just a leader of singular talents; he became a kind of national institution; it became increasingly difficult to envisage a Government without him as Prime Minister. Whether one liked or disliked him, agreed or fundamentally disagreed with him, the majority of Australians felt that nothing could go too seriously wrong while he remained at the helm. With others there was an element of risk; with him the risks were minimised; it was wise, therefore, to play safe.

But, paradoxically, the Menzies Era was, above all, a period of movement, of vast and significant change in every aspect of domestic affairs, in Australia's relationships with the rest of the world, in national attitudes and national thought. Over 16 years of rapid, bewildering transition it was Sir

The *IPA Review* headlines Robert Menzies' retirement in the January–March 1966 issue (NBAC Z714)

Menzies

It is Robert Menzies' role in the formation of the Liberal Party of Australia and his shaping of its early policies that makes the IPA (Victorian branch) of such interest. Historians are agreed Menzies was the ringmaster, and the party was, as expressed in the title of Gerard Henderson's book, *Menzies' Child*.[63] However, opinion on the exact nature of the IPA–LPA relationship has been sharply divided. From the beginning, some pointed to the IPA as evidence that the Liberals were stooges of the big end of town, while Chifley's biographer Fin Crisp called the Institute 'their satellite'.[64]

Most paint C D ('Ref') Kemp as the chief conduit of this influence. In the early 1940s he had been personal assistant to Sir George Coles, chair of the Institute's founding Council, and joined it as its in-house economist. In 1948 Kemp was appointed its first director, a post he held for the next thirty years. Most discussion about the alleged influence has concentrated on an early IPA publication, *Looking Forward*, which Kemp drafted. A seventy-page manifesto with a print run of 50,000 copies, its comprehensive agenda for post-war reconstruction appeared in October 1944, just in time for Menzies to quote with approval at the so-called Unity Conference in Canberra which led to the creation of the Liberal Party.

According to John Carroll, this was 'particularly influential ... in shaping the economic and social views of R G Menzies, then formulating the philosophy of the fledgling Liberal Party'. To the IPA's current executive director, John Roskam, Kemp 'wrote the manifesto that determined the economic policies of the Menzies government'. To the journalist Jason Koutsoukis, his 'pioneering work in the 1940s gave Sir Robert Menzies the intellectual framework to form the Liberal Party'.[65]

Such claims and others like them, made when Kemp died in 1993, contrasted with the appraisal presented in Chapter 3 of *Menzies' Child*. Here Henderson conceded that Kemp 'did have some influence on Liberal policy' and 'played an important role in the economic debate ... in the early 1940s'. But he then spent the remainder of the chapter arguing that the influence has been grossly exaggerated; Kemp was just a 'contemporary scribbler'.[66]

How does Henderson conclude, to quote one of his subheadings: 'Ref and Ming' – a myth demolished?[67] Firstly, by nominating how influence would be measured: there were so few Menzies letters to the IPA or Kemp, they only met twice, and Kemp had not received any government-initiated preferment. Secondly, by suggesting we should not read too much into Menzies' actual words in acknowledgement of Kemp and *Looking Forward*. And thirdly, by constantly shifting between the objects of the alleged influence: Menzies, Menzies' policies, Liberal policies and the Menzies' government.

To the archives …

According to *Menzies' Child*, it was writers such as J R Hay and Michael Bertram who (unlike the author) had examined the IPA archives and thus, by implication, were able to provide more balanced assessments. Ironically, Kemp's son David had also examined the archives for a University of Melbourne Bachelor of Arts Honours thesis on the first five years of the IPA (Victoria). For him at least, in regarding influence on the party and its policy at the time, 'the connection is certain and direct'.[68] But Henderson simply references the thesis, preferring to discount it by quoting recollections of the 77-year-old father recorded for the book in 1989.

Documentation of the IPA's varied and repeated interactions with the Liberal Party features heavily in the ANU Archives' IPA collection, including for instance a request from a key LPA organiser W H Anderson just prior to the inaugural Federal Council of the Liberal Party in late August 1945 'for assistance in drawing up the Liberal Party's platform'.[69] Menzies is undeniably there too. Thus the collection contains the report of IPA delegates, Kemp and the Institute secretary Captain A C Leech, written on return from the Canberra conference. They noted discussions with Menzies, his urging delegates to study *Looking Forward*, and his praise for it as a 'remarkable statement … by far the best that has so far appeared on fundamental political and economic questions in Australia'. Included too is evidence of a member of the Institute Council, Wesley A Ince, reporting in March 1946 on having consulted with Menzies about 'whether publishing Industrial Committee's report on forty-hour week would be contempt of court'.[70]

A definitive treatment of the IPA's relationship with the Liberal Party and Menzies in the 1940s has yet to be published. While it is perhaps unremarkable that the Institute's archives were ignored in Ian Hancock's history of the Liberal Party and Allan Martin's major biography of Menzies,[71] for any comprehensive study of the connection the IPA collection will be compulsory viewing. There are many clues to follow.

Holt and McMahon

Menzies aside, the IPA's archives include passing references to Arthur Fadden (later Sir Arthur), John Curtin, Frank Forde and Ben Chifley.[72] More noteworthy are traces of two additional future prime ministers which suggest the Institute's retreat from direct political engagement after the 1943 federal election was gradual and seemingly reluctant.

Billy McMahon joined parliament with Menzies' defeat of the Chifley government in 1949. As a new keen backbencher in 1950, he followed up an article in the *IPA Review* about the inadequacy of statistics on wages collected by the Commonwealth, sharing with Kemp correspondence he had had with the Statistician. In one letter, McMahon ended: 'If you feel I might be of any use to you in the future in connection with any statistical or economical matters, would you please let me know'.[73] McMahon's last letter came when he finally won the Liberal Party leadership in March 1971. Congratulated by the Institute president, Eric Lampe ('We have all gained much pleasure from our associations with you in the past through IPA dinners and in other ways'), McMahon thanked him, adding what today seems quaint, 'you may be sure I shall do my best to make a worthwhile contribution'.[74]

Though born the same year as McMahon, Harold Holt had already served as a federal minister by the time the IPA was formed. The 1940s, however, were wilderness years. Neither the moribund United Australia Party nor the fledgling Liberal Party had a federal secretariat, and the resources of opposition members and even the Parliamentary Library were limited. Help came in the form of a neighbour on the Mornington Peninsula, businessman Geoffrey Grimwade, who was a key foundation member of the IPA (Vic) and chair of its Industrial Committee.

As a result, Holt received briefings on current issues. There was for instance a paper on Bretton Woods (prepared by G R Mountain, a member of the *IPA Review* editorial committee and an 'official at National Bank'), and the loan of files of newspaper clippings (for example, on the exchange rate). In turn the IPA sought Holt's comment on the draft of the first issue of the *IPA Review*.[75] As noted, there are many clues to follow and, for the diligent and thorough scholar, they are potentially quite rewarding ones.

7. Bob Hawke and University House

Prime ministers have always been, almost by definition, public figures, and increasingly so now struggle to maintain their privacy. Inevitably their image becomes fixed in the popular imagination. Once established, it is repeatedly reinforced through documentaries, biographies, histories and exhibitions and can take generations to change. Caricature and myth envelops them. Bruce became little more than a toff who wore spats. Even in 2010, the National Archives' exhibition *Stanley Melbourne Bruce: Prime Minister & Statesman* called Menzies' 1962 assessment of Bruce ('probably the outstanding Australian of our time') as 'surprising'.[76] McMahon from the start was derided as a hapless ex-playboy of unbridled ambition who lost to Whitlam in 1972. As for mythology, prime ministers had affairs with their personal secretaries, were mugged by prostitutes in Memphis, fathered children out of wedlock, were ineligible by birth to stand for parliament, and spied for the Chinese. And then there's the one about Bob Hawke and the University House fishpond.

ANU doctoral student, R J L Hawke

In 1956 Bob Hawke won a Research Scholarship to begin doctoral studies in the law school at the ANU. Starting from the second term of 1956, he was also a part-time lecturer in Legal Method at the ANU's poor cousin, Canberra University College. His thesis, supervised by Professor Geoffrey Sawer, was a legal explanation of Australia's wage-fixing system. Sawer had a lot of time for the young tear-away, and was one of the few in Oxford or Canberra who recognised the importance of his research topic.[77]

At the end of February 1957 Hawke's first-born, Susan, was five weeks old. Single post-grads were required to live at University House, and this was where the newly married Hawkes lived too until Hazel became pregnant. They then qualified for a university flat nearby, but retained membership of the House. Hawke was popular, and active in the university cricket team. He was easily elected one of two student representatives of the ANU Council (the other being a New Zealand-born research student and future professor of economics, W P Hogan). He worked hard, and partied hard.

University House

Something happened at University House late Sunday and early Monday 24/25 February 1957 involving Hawke among others which became the stuff of legend. Common belief is encapsulated in a 2003 address by former University House Master Ralph Elliott:

> You probably all know by now the story of Bob Hawke's adventure in the gold fish pond. ... Early in 1957, ... a conference of Anglican bishops resided in University House. During the night a noisy, somewhat inebriated group of students stripped naked before the Episcopal eyes and proceeded to swim up

and down the length of our precious waterway. Legend has it that the chief culprit in this escapade was that future prime minister of Australia, Robert Hawke. He was certainly a happy participant.[78]

Versions like this had circulated for years, and were repeated officially, as recently as February 2004 by the Vice-Chancellor Ian Chubb in an address to the Founder's Day Cocktail Party.[79] A further variant added conspiracy. In 2006, the ANU published a collection of reminiscences about the Coombs Building. In it, the Pacific History scholar Niel Gunson, who was an ANU contemporary of the Hawkes, wrote:

> It was while I was on fieldwork in the Gilbert and Ellice Islands that one of my friends sent me a colourful first-hand account of the much vaunted episode involving the future prime minister's nocturnal adventures in the University House fishpond and related incidents for which he was sent down. I rather suspect ASIO has relieved me of that document as I have not been able to find it.[80]

At the time of the incident Professor Mark Oliphant was acting Master of University House (the Master Professor Dale Trendall was absent overseas) and as such he helped take evidence less than twenty-four hours after the events happened. During a toast speech to a dinner celebrating the 25th anniversary of University House, Oliphant recalled that:

> no-one but Trendall could have imposed the conditions of dress, and behaviour generally, which prevailed throughout the House. Of course there was horseplay. On one occasion a research student, Bob Hawke, now leader of the trade unions of Australia, was thrown in with the gold-fish.[81]

Multiple versions

And Hawke? When Jill Waterhouse wrote to him for her history of University House, he did not reply. She did have his 600-page *The Hawke Memoirs* which covered his time at Oxford, including the famous beer-drinking feat, although it dealt with the ANU years in a paragraph, and there is nothing on University House.[82]

His views can be roughly approximated through his cooperation with biographers, though there is nothing in Stan Anson's 1991 study *Hawke: An Emotional Life* – unfortunate, given its focus.[83] Around the time he was planning to enter parliament, however, Hawke had cooperated closely with two biographers. The broad outline of his account is clear. John Hurst's 1979 account referred to a 'wild party', and to Hawke as 'one of the revellers'. As to swimming, Hurst wrote: 'One of the professors, active in the Anglican Church, complained about the noise to Hawke ... [who] suggested that he might throw the professor into the ornamental fish pond'.[84]

Shortly following Hurst's book, Robert Pullan's biography appeared. He ignored the ANU incident while noting the earlier Oxford beer-drinking record. His comments are suggestive: the feat 'fascinated journalists in Australia for the next twenty years and greatly helped him to get publicity. Journalists sometimes said it was a world record, and by the end of the 1970s, Hawke was saying so himself.'[85]

Both Blanche d'Alpuget and Hazel Hawke wrote about Bob, the ANU years, and the pool incident. He was acknowledged as the principal informant for the former, and obviously, on 'the morning after the night before', for the latter too. Both women offered fascinating pictures of life in Canberra in the mid-1950s, although d'Alpuget's is based on extended interviews with others at the ANU as well as Hawke.

In *Robert J Hawke: A Biography*, d'Alpuget repeats the standard presumed facts – noise, drinking, threatening the professor, swimming, and the disciplinary consequences. While leaving the judgements to her informants, d'Alpuget herself does write that Hawke's 'high standing with the university establishment was swiftly and vigorously lowered'. Her account is insightful of him and sympathetic towards his young wife, noting this was 'only one of many escapades'.[86] In 1992 Hazel Hawke produced *My Own Life: An Autobiography*. About the escapade in question, it is understated, and, like her forgiving explanation, given all that was known then, let alone known now, poignant and incredibly loyal. She wrote:

> Our life was interesting and pleasant, except for the occasional ripple caused by alcohol-inspired revelling. The most notable of these led to Bob being told his services as student representative on the University Council were no longer required. He had jumped into the ornamental lily pond at University House late one night and upset a visiting bishop and, of course, the warden, with his loud, bawdy remarks.[87]

What happened (as far as we can know)?

What actually happened? Such truth can only ever be approximated. Unless we can conjure H G Wells' twin characters the Invisible Man and the Time Traveller, we will never know what happened late on 24 February 1957; never in any Rankean 'as it really was' sense.

In the 'Hawke-and-the-pool' case, we can get close. There are the official histories of the ANU and University House. The latter contains errors and is incomplete, but remains an excellent summary. There is also a surprising amount of relevant contemporary documentation now in the ANU Archives, including Hawke's extensive student file, draft minutes of the disciplinary committee of Council, and correspondence of its members such as Professor Mark Oliphant and the Master Professor Trendall.[88]

From the disciplinary committee especially we can derive the basic facts, not least because it began interviewing fourteen students the day after the incident. Its members – the Vice-Chancellor Sir Leslie Melville, Dr Bill Stanner, and Professors Mark Oliphant, Geoffrey Sawer, Leicester Webb, and Oskar Spate – included two eyewitnesses and one more than familiar with the presumption of innocence. At its second meeting two weeks later, Professors Ennor and Trendall were also in attendance.

Notes of Hawke's evidence to the Disciplinary Committee, the day after the night before (ANUA 34/2)

The picture of Hawke's role which emerges from its eleven pages (and other correspondence) is of (i) a repeat offender/ringleader, (ii) full of beer (and when that ran out, sherry), (iii) who was banging on doors, reducing female students to tears, and (iv) who used obscene language towards both students and teachers who tried to tell him to quieten down. For this he was fined, wrote a letter of abject apology to the Vice-Chancellor, was pressured to resign as one of the student representatives on University Council, and banned for six months from University House. But for the strong intercession of Sawer, it could have been worse, including dismissal.

As for the swimmer (to the extent one could actually swim in the shallow pool), it was not Hawke. There was only one, J M Roderick, and he was fined £10 and banned for a term from the House. We know of no documentary evidence either way that Roderick swam naked, just a line in the minutes of evidence from a postgraduate called Perry to the effect: 'After that to men's bathroom – swimmer apparently showered with much encouragement'.[89]

Aftermath

On 19 February 2010 Bob Hawke gave the inaugural Commencement Address to mark the new ANU academic year. In sharing recollections of his student years in Perth, Oxford and Canberra, inevitably he mentioned the University House incident. Following an injunction 'to drink hard', he told the assembled students that 'a few of us' were being 'exuberant'. They were confronted by a professor and some of his religious friends whose 'life experience' needed enhancing. Accordingly it was suggested 'playfully of course' they might have a 'dip in the pool … assisted by us'.[90]

And so the myth changes and endures; a new generation of students have been introduced to it directly via the memory of an eighty-year-old ex-larrikin student leader and ex-prime minister. It hardly mattered that he was simply wrong in telling them he was *the* student representative on Council at the time, and wrong too in saying 'I kept my position' though it 'didn't go over too well with the authorities'. The factual bedrock of the past is notoriously elusive. But even so, the extant contemporary document represents the limit of what can be reliably built on, and it is in the ANU Archives.

8. Whitlam and Wave Hill

Gough Whitlam seized a photo opportunity when he poured sand into Vincent Lingiari's hand to signify the return of a small portion of Wave Hill Station to the Gurindji people on 16 August 1975. While it is this photo which is remembered, it was the Fraser government which passed the Commonwealth *Land Rights (Northern Territory) Act* in December 1976 which ensured more significant gains for the Gurindji people.

Mervyn Bishop's photograph of Whitlam pouring sand into the hand of Vincent Lingiari is just one moment in a longer story documented in the Noel Butlin Archives Centre collections (Powerhouse Museum, Sydney © Mervyn G Bishop/Licensed by Viscopy 2010)

Prime ministerial actions such as these can only be understood fully in the context of what went before: the years that Vincent Lingiari lived and worked as a stockman on Gurindji land, leased by the British company Vestey's and run as Wave Hill Station, the regulations and awards that meant that Aboriginal workers were paid less than other workers, and the support that the Gurindji received directly or by lobbying by other organisations.

Justice delayed

The August 1966 walk-off from Wave Hill Station, led by Vincent Lingiari, occurred after a decision by the Commonwealth Conciliation and Arbitration Commission in early 1966 that equal wages were to be paid to Aboriginal stockmen, but from December 1968. The application had been made in 1965 by the North Australian Workers' Union to remove discrimination against Aborigines in the Cattle Station Industry (Northern Territory) Award.[91]

The delayed implementation was unprecedented and opposed by the Australian Council of Trade Unions and the North Australian Workers' Union who held a series of meetings with the Department of Territories, the Department of Labour and National Service, and the Northern Territory Cattle Producers' Council in 1966.[92] The ACTU files also include regular reports from NAWU official P Carroll on the strike at Wave Hill and other stations including negotiations with Vestey's over the introduction of full award rates. The NAWU also coordinated a fund to support the strikers taking contributions from other unions.[93]

The issue of wage inequality has a much longer history: in 1856 the Australian Agricultural Company drew up a list of all employees of the company at Port Stephens. Shepherds were paid 25 pounds a year (those indicated as an underage 'boy' received 20 pounds) plus rations, but the three shepherds under the heading 'Native Blacks' received half that amount. Similarly the Aboriginal stockmen received 20 or 24 pounds, while the non-Aboriginal stockmen received between 30 and 40 pounds a year.[94]

Many pastoral companies maintained separate wages books for Aboriginal workers which detail both wages and rations issued in lieu of payment. For Buddha Station near Narromine, NSW those for the 1870s survive and for Mt Eba Station (South Australia) those for the period 1879–1900. For Northern Territory stations, 'native wages books' are held for Victoria River Downs (the neighbouring station to Wave Hill) for 1932–1950, and Eva Downs, Creswell Downs, and Walhallow Pastoral Company for the 1960s.[95]

The evidence

The whereabouts of the wage records of Wave Hill Station itself is unknown, with differing anecdotal accounts that they were destroyed or returned to England at the time the Vestey Company handed back their lease. One significant record is held by the ANU Archives: an 'improvements book' maintained from the 1950s with regular updates to document the improvements made to buildings, stockyards, fences and bores on the station. An assessment was made of the condition of each structure and details of the costs of materials and labour were recorded. There are hand-drawn plans and often black and white photographs of structures.[96]

From this volume we can learn something of the living and working conditions of Aboriginal stockmen. There were separate dining rooms for Aboriginal and non-Aboriginal workers which are described in these terms:

> Men's dining room: Built of piping with sawn timber rafters & battens, corrugated iron roof, fibrolite walls and concrete floors. The shutter windows & the doors are gauzed.
>
> Aboriginal dining room: Built of bush timber with corrugated iron, walls & roof, earth floor … in fair condition [the photograph shows an open doorway].

Station labour was used to construct accommodation for Aboriginal workers. There are no photographs but the plans show rooms either 10 x 12 feet or 12 feet square and those constructed in 1959 are described as: 'Steel piping frame covered with second-hand galvanised iron and ant-bed floor'.

The records of the pastoral company, Goldsbrough Mort and Company Limited, which owned the neighbouring station Victoria River Downs, include maps showing Wave Hill Station. On these the dotted line of Wattie Creek and the location of waterholes and springs indicate where the Gurindji established their own settlement separate from Wave Hill Station.[97]

Trade union support

The files of the Australian Council of Trade Unions and of unions such as the Waterside Workers' Federation include the regular interaction between trade unions and organisations such as the Australian Aborigines League, the Council for Aboriginal Rights, the Federal Council for the Advancement of Aborigines and Torres Strait Islanders (FCAATSI), and Abschol (the National Union of Australian University Students Aboriginal Scholarship Scheme).

They also include union representations before the Commonwealth Court of Conciliation and Arbitration (later the Commission) arguing that Aboriginal workers should receive the same wages as other workers for the same work. For instance in the 1917 case, the Australian Workers' Union *v.* The Pastoralists' Federal Council on wages for station hands, the union's position was that all members of the Union should be covered by the award, countering statements by the other side, such as 'no man unless he is a lunatic would pay the same wages for an aboriginal as for a white man; it is never done'.[98]

In the Northern Territory in the early 1930s, the NAWU gathered evidence about the underpayment of Aboriginal drovers and reported to the ACTU on Aboriginal employment and conditions.[99] Representations were made to Lyons in March 1939 by the ACTU which related to the Cummeroogunga Mission in NSW, and a deputation to Senator Foll raised issues relating to health, education, water supply at the Jay Creek Aboriginal Reserve, and the Haasts Bluff Aboriginal Reserve.[100]

The Australian Workers' Union and the Seamen's Union had supported Aboriginal workers during the 1946 Pilbara Strike.[101] During the period leading up to the Wave Hill walk-off the ACTU passed regular decisions of congress on Aboriginal issues: in September 1951 (sponsored by J McGuiness, president of FCAATSI and an NAWU union official, and relating to discriminatory ordinances and citizenship rights), in 1963 (relating to equal pay and conditions, education, and opposing the removal of Aborigines from traditional lands) and in 1965 (relating to citizenship rights). It also received representations from state Labour Councils and other organisations about the conditions of work for Aborigines and the effect of atomic testing sites on their patterns of movement.[102]

Direct union action in the Gurindji land rights claim is evidenced in the circular letter Norm Docker of the Waterside Workers' Federation, supported by the Amalgamated Metal Workers' Union, the Sheet Metal Workers' Union, Teachers' Unions, Actors' Equity, and the Building Workers' Industrial Union, sent to other union officials on 17 July 1970, following a meeting held under the auspices of FCAATSI.[103]

Among the WWF files are reports on field visits to Wattie Creek sponsored by Abschol in 1969 and 1970, reporting on the water supply and building program and including photographs. There is also a transcript of an interview with Pincher Numiari on 29 November 1970, and a report of a meeting on 26 December 1971 where the question of taking a lease on land is raised and Vincent Lingiari is quoted:

> We don't want no lease. We don't belong to nowhere. We belong right here. We don't carry the lease. If I had come from big England then I should carry the lease, but I am on my own land.[104]

In November 1971, the WWF announced the provision of a $10,000 trust fund in support of the Gurindji. The file documenting the operation of the fund includes the original agreement where Vincent Lingiari signs by writing a cross, and receipts bearing the thumbprints of Aboriginal workers who received allowances.[105]

A substantial portion of the fund was spent on fencing supplies, and there are photographs and reports of this activity. There is also correspondence with the Angliss Group of 13 May 1971 indicating that Vestey's would not oppose land rights to land at Wattie Creek and copies of correspondence between Vincent Lingiari and Vestey's in March 1972 relating to a special purpose lease over 10 square miles – in perpetuity with no rent payable.[106]

Another view

The records of the Australian Woolgrowers' and Graziers' Council (a forerunner to the National Farmers' Federation) provide another perspective. They issued a press release in April 1968 objecting to the proposal to acquire part of the Wave Hill lease for 'a group of the Gurindji tribe':

> The issue in the Wave Hill strike of 1966 was wages, not land rights. The record is quite clear. When the strike was petering out with most workers back on Wave Hill and other properties, political action converted the issue to a land claim.[107]

The president of the Council Mr T B C Walker provides several lengthy quotations in the press release:

> Once this experiment is begun there is no end to it. There are on Wave Hill, and on many properties, more than one tribal group. Can the Government deny any such group what it does for you? ... Multiply this example in the North Territory alone by fifty – a conservative figure – and the Territory's welfare, police, health and administrative resources will be stretched beyond capacity ... If the aim is to see each aboriginal family properly housed with possession, if they wish it, of a garden with a fence round it, this does not need alienation of land.

5. In the event of the death of the said Norman Docker, the Federation shall have the right to appoint a substitute member to the Committee and thereupon such substitute member shall replace Norman Docker for the purposes of paragraph 4 hereof.

IN WITNESS WHEREOF these presents have been duly executed on the day and year first hereinbefore written.

THE COMMON SEAL of THE WATERSIDE WORKERS' FEDERATION OF AUSTRALIA was hereunto affixed on authority of a resolution of the Federal Council in the presence of CHARLES HENRY FITZGIBBON the General Secretary.

SIGNED by the said NORMAN DOCKER in the presence of:-

SIGNED by the said PETER EDWARDS in the presence of:-

SIGNED by the said JEAN SCOTT LEU in the presence of:-

SIGNED by the said VINCENT LINGIARI with his mark after the Agreement has been read over to him and he appeared perfectly to understand and approve the Agreement in the presence of us both present:-

VINCENT + LINGIARI

HIS MARK

The deed establishing the Gurindji Trust Fund is signed by Charlie Fitzgibbon and Norm Docker of the Waterside Workers' Federation and by Vincent Lingiari with his mark (NBAC Z432/24)

9. Heinz Arndt and Malcolm Fraser

'Prime ministerial studies' has not quite yet become an industry, and in the current context the term is unlikely ever to be used as John Howard deployed it during the 1996 election campaign in criticising 'the Aboriginal industry'. While biographies of prime ministers and their own memoirs have been popular for a generation, there has also been a mini boom in more analytical focused research, including investigation of personal characteristics, Cabinet and bureaucracy, political biography of spouses, eras and speechmaking.[108] Can a study of their overseas travel be far behind?

Very few impressions by ministers, staff, officials or others who accompany a prime minister overseas are published.[109] By contrast, reports filed by the journalists who accompany them are legion, some of them touching on what it is actually like to be travelling with the official group. On occasion incidents on tours themselves become genuine political news, as in the incident between Rudd and the RAAF steward recently reported.

Prime ministers' overseas trips tend to follow a standard pattern, at least in terms of documentation. There will be brief mentions in biographies and memoirs, and naturally in official records, communiqués and press items prepared by the accompanying media. Here Malcolm Fraser's trip in August–September 1980 is something of an exception. Its record is complemented by the observations of ANU Professor Heinz Arndt, who accompanied the official party as an expert adviser.

Arndt

Heinz Arndt was recruited from the University of Sydney to the Chair of Economics at the Canberra University College in 1950, and having turned 65, officially retired from the ANU in December 1980. At the time he was Head of the Department of Economics, Research School of Pacific Studies, having been long acknowledged as a world authority on international economic development particularly relating to Indonesia.[110]

Strangely, Arndt's earliest prime ministerial links arose directly from his 1950 CUC appointment. He was attacked within months via a question in parliament by a former student and then backbencher, William McMahon. He was accused of opposing the Communist Party Dissolution Bill, being a 'prominent and dogmatic' member of the Fabian Society, and for supporting the efforts of the 'Chifley Socialist Government' to nationalise the banks. In his official response, Robert Menzies wisely chose not to interfere. A press report filed on Arndt's ANU staff file couldn't have been clearer:

Three advisers to prime ministers at the relaunch of the journal *Asian Pacific Economic Literature* in 1992: Professor Ross Garnaut, Dr Peter Wilenski and Professor Heinz Arndt (ANUA 225/22/2)

> The Prime Minister, Mr Menzies, said yesterday that it was nothing to him whether a man appointed to an academic position were Labor, Liberal or Country Party. In these appointments he was in favour of academic freedom. 'I am not concerned with the politics of men appointed, so long as they have the academic qualifications,' he said. Mr Menzies had been asked to comment on the appointment of Mr H W Arndt as Professor of Economics at Canberra University College, which had been criticised by Government members of Parliament because of Mr Arndt's political beliefs. Mr Menzies said Mr Arndt was appointed by the College with the approval of the Melbourne University. The matter did not concern the Commonwealth. 'Even if it had been the National University to which the appointment was made I could not be called upon to examine the political position regarding it,' Mr Menzies added. 'However, if somebody raised the security aspect that would be a different matter,' he said.

In 1990 Arndt recalled his dubious welcome to the CUC when interviewed for the ANU's official history. He was bemused by his awarding McMahon a Distinction in 4th year Economics at the University of Sydney in the late 1940s, but saw equal irony in having supported bank nationalisation. Reading the transcript, one senses he was impressed by Menzies' refusal to interfere.[111]

The 1980 trip

At the August 1979 Commonwealth Heads of Government Meeting (CHOGM) in Lusaka, a Commonwealth Expert Group was established at the Fraser government's initiative to report on 'Constraints to Growth in the World Economy'. While technically the choice of the group's chair was Secretary-General S S 'Sonny' Ramphal's decision, de facto it was Australia's, having proposed the group. Fraser wanted Arndt, who said he agreed if the ANU did.

Certain courtesies apply when governments seek the services of an academic expert. Following a phone call from the Prime Minister's Department in late 1979, Arndt secured Vice-Chancellor Anthony Low's permission, and this was subsequently ratified by Council. The Vice-Chancellor did indicate that: 'PMs shd when convenient write to me formally – as they usually are good enough to do on such occasions' though there is nothing on Arndt's staff file nor in Low's papers to suggest they ever did.[112]

Appointed in August 1979, the Group of ten eminent economists delivered its report, *The World Economic Crisis: A Commonwealth Perspective*, in June 1980. Because Arndt was the Group's chair, Fraser asked that he join him at the regional meeting of CHOGM in New Delhi in September 1980 where it was to be discussed. Arndt's eighteen-page transcript 'Diary of Round-the-World Trip with Malcolm Fraser' covering 30 August – 10 September 1980 is the result. It is a small gem, and not surprisingly some extracts eventually appeared in print.[113]

Arndt seems to have been a natural diarist. This combined with the fact that he had relatively little to do on the trip and his insightful observations of those in Fraser's entourage gives his insider's account special interest. With Fraser at various stages were the foreign minister Andrew Peacock, two departmental secretaries, a number of advisers and staffers, other government officials, journalists (including Laurie Oakes), and wives such as Heather Henderson.

They departed from Melbourne for New Delhi in an RAAF Boeing 707 on 30 August 1980 via the United States and Rome. A nice sample of Arndt as Pepys came from his inclusion in a party attending the San Francisco restaurant Top of the Tower. 'At first conversation was slow, the PM finding little to say', Arndt wrote, having earlier described Fraser as 'shy'. He continued:

> But it gradually livened up, especially because Cathy [Quealy, private secretary] turned out to be an unabashed feminist, arguing her case with great aplomb. We talked about Imperial and Australian Honours (and the problem this presents: 'Tam does not approve of Honours, thinks they are a lot of nonsense'; I said my wife takes the same view).

The diary is full of such snippets. Arndt's comments cover tensions over policy approaches and tactics, and pen portraits and descriptions of the operating style of officials and staffers. Alan Griffiths, Dick Rye, Geoff Yeend, Owen Harries, David Barnett, Rob Merrillees, Roger Holdich and Peter Henderson are all mentioned. Henderson, secretary of the Foreign Affairs Department, he thought 'relaxed, deliberately low key'. Coincidentally Robert Menzies' son-in-law, Henderson had been one of Arndt's students when a diplomatic cadet at the CUC's hall of residence Gungahlin in the early 1950s.

A final illustration from the diary concerns a speech Fraser delivered during the trip at B'nai B'rith International, Washington. It was a major statement relating to the West's attitude to Soviet intentions particularly in the Middle East, and delivered in the presence of Ronald Reagan, soon to replace Jimmy Carter as US president. Arndt got on well with the speech's primary author, Owen Harries (during the flights, they passed the time over chess) and having been shown the draft by Harries, asked Fraser if he might arrange its publication. Arndt had in mind the monthly magazine *Quadrant*, as he was president of its sponsor, the Australian Association for Cultural Freedom and a regular contributing author too. According to the diary, Fraser said he'd be 'honoured'; his staff had other ideas:

> Another encounter with David Barnett about the Quadrant offprints. He said the PMs speech would be printed by the Government. When I said Quadrant would not be happy if too many copies had already been sent out, he said 'too bad' and objected when I said I would have another word about it with the PM. Later Geoff Yeend said he would try to sort it out. In the afternoon on the plane I tried to get to the toilet, but the PM was blocking the passage talking to a group of journalists. As I wondered whether to be allowed to pass by, Barnett shoved me away: 'You will have to excuse us.' Strange character.

10. The public face

The media's visual representation of Australia's first prime minister stands in stark contrast to today's image of the twenty-seventh. The technology of image capture, the degree of formality, the concept of 'photo opportunity' and the very idea of media management are among many differentiating factors. On the other hand, cartooning and an intrinsic public curiosity in what the prime minister of the day is doing have remained relatively constant. The Australian National University has been a convenient site for prime ministerial launches, openings and addresses from the mid-point of this change. Its official media resources amply attest to regular visits, while its collected archives of labour and protest offer another range of styles from savage campaign caricature to conference delegates awkward in stiff collars holding a pose.

On union business

Within the business and labour collections of the Noel Butlin Archives Centre, Labor prime ministers are those most commonly found. Fisher and Hughes sit side-by-side at the Waterside Workers' Federation conference in Melbourne in 1912, a fresh-faced Curtin (without his trademark glasses) is recorded as general secretary of the Timber Workers Union in 1914, Scullin poses on the balcony of the Australian Workers' Union building in Ballarat and lines up at the Australian Labor Party Conference in 1919, and Chifley is photographed in front of the Hotel Kingston at the 1951 Federal Labor Conference.[114]

Other photographs are unexpected: a photograph of Barton survives on a program for a farewell dinner, retained by the South Australian Typographical Society as a sample of printing techniques. Joe Lyons, as Tasmanian minister for railways, is photographed with members of the Tasmanian branch of the Australian Federated Union of Locomotive Enginemen by the official Tasmanian government photographer John Beattie.[115]

Later photographs of prime ministers in business and union collections are more spontaneous: Chifley accosted by picketing miners at Katoomba, John McEwen (later Sir John) visiting a tobacco-drying plant, Hawke snapped at ACTU and National Farmers' Federation events, and Fraser receiving his OK card after joining the Federated Engine Drivers' and Firemen's Association at the Parliament House site in 1980.[116]

Another source of prime ministerial images is trade union newspapers and newsletters. Apart from the printed images, some trade unions developed and maintained photographic archives to support their publishing activities so that their collections also include unpublished photographs.[117]

Malcolm Fraser was a regular target of cartoonists in the *Seamen's Journal* (NBAC N38/1080/6)

Union collections are also a source for alternative public images: the caricatures common to political cartoons which are found not just in newspapers and pamphlets, but on banners and posters, and in photographs of protests and demonstrations. Menzies was a popular target, easily caricatured by his prominent eyebrows and girth, and also as the longest-serving prime minister, and a Liberal prime minister, was the focus of many union campaigns.[118]

On campus

Prime ministers have been regular visitors to the ANU to lay foundation stones, open buildings, launch books, deliver addresses and to announce new programs and centres. Each time the official photographer recorded the event, and on many of these occasions the official speeches were also recorded or filmed. Many of the photographs, for the most part black and white, were published in the *ANU News* and later, the *ANU Reporter*.[119]

Photo opportunity: Bob Hawke examines Ben Chifley's pipe and stand, identified by the ANU's Forestry Department as made from Queensland Walnut (ANUA 225/526/1)

The first of these occasions was on 24 October 1949 when Chifley laid two foundation stones: one for the Research School of Physical Sciences and one for the John Curtin School of Medical Research, in the presence of Curtin's widow Elsie. When the JCSMR was opened by Sir Howard Florey in 1958, Curtin's son John and Menzies were present.[120]

Senator John Gorton was elected by the Senate as a member of the ANU Council in 1951 but resigned in June the next year. He attended the dinner held on 12 July 1951 to farewell the Interim Council and welcome the new Council. The future prime minister and minister for education is seated at the end of the table and is either omitted or obscured in the many photographs taken of the dinner. The Solicitor-General, H F E Whitlam, father of Gough, was another attendee at the dinner. In 1966, Gorton represented Menzies at the installation of Lord Florey as Chancellor and is photographed directly behind Florey in the academic procession.[121]

In October 1952, Bruce was installed as the first Chancellor and received an honorary Doctor of Laws degree: there are not only numerous photographs of this event but also a film entitled 'The First Chancellor'. Bruce's luncheon speech on the occasion of the conferring of an honorary degree on Dr Harold Macmillan is captured on audio tape, along with Menzies.[122]

Menzies was present at many university occasions during his long second term as prime minister 1949–1966, including the laying of foundation stones for the Haydon–Allen Building, the R G Menzies Building and the H C Coombs Building, and the opening of the John Curtin School of Medical Research, the Research School of Physical Sciences, and the R G Menzies Building. He received an honorary degree of Doctor of Laws in May 1966. There are photographs and audio tape of his speeches on most of these occasions, and film of the two Menzies Building ceremonies.[123]

While prime minister, Whitlam was a regular visitor and was photographed launching books and delivering speeches. His John Curtin lecture given in 1975 was recorded on audio tape. As a Visiting Fellow and a life member of University House, his presence on campus continued to be recorded, including his visit to the North Australia Research Unit at the ANU's Northern Territory campus in 1994. Malcolm Fraser was snapped as minister for education and science at the installation of H C Coombs as Chancellor and at the opening of Chemistry Building in 1968. Both Fraser and Hawke found themselves photographed as the focus of student demonstrations. Hawke opened a telescope at Siding Spring Observatory in 1984 and the J G Crawford Building in 1986, and Howard the Sir Roland Wilson Building in 1999.[124]

Kevin Rudd has been a regular visitor to the campus, opening the new John Curtin School of Medical Research and J G Crawford Buildings, delivering the

Burgmann College lecture and announcing the establishment of new programs. The photographs are now online, digital and in colour, and the speeches are transcribed or podcast for instant online delivery.[125]

The current Prime Minister has yet to visit the campus in an official capacity. Our only photograph of Julia Gillard appears in the pages of the student newspaper *Woroni* in 1983 when she was elected president of the Australian Union of Students. On the same page is a cartoon of Hawke and Fraser as Tweedledum and Tweedledee.[126]

Endnotes

1. A typical example where Hughes and Lyons are savaged but Watson is nowhere mentioned is Clyde Cameron, 'Labor leaders who betrayed their trust', *Labour History*, no. 53, November 1987, pp. 115–21.
2. Although Watson's genealogy has been clarified, a definitive identification of his parentage and date of birth remains elusive, given the lack of a birth certificate. See Bede Nairn, 'J C Watson, A Genealogical Note', in *Labour History*, no. 34, May 1978, p.102; Bede Nairn, 'John Christian Watson', in the *Australian Dictionary of Biography*, vol. 12, Melbourne University Press, 1990, p. 400; and Al Grassby and Silvia Ordonez, *The Man Time Forgot: The Life and Times of John Christian Watson, Australia's First Labor Prime Minister*, Pluto Press, Sydney, 1999, p. 13. Grassby and Ordonez claim that 'a record' of Watson's birth, but apparently not a birth certificate, is held by the Mormon Church at Santiago. See also Mark Hearn, 'John Christian Watson and "the instinct of self-preservation"', presented to the 11th Biennial National Conference of the Australian Historical Association, Brisbane, 3–7 July 2002, at: workinglives.econ.usyd.edu.au/watson.html.
3. Noel Butlin Archives Centre: Labor Papers Limited, N117/1534, Minutes of meetings of annual meetings of shareholders, 1910–1934.
4. NBAC: Labor Papers Limited, N117/1531, Minutes of monthly meetings of the Directors, 1910–1939.
5. Ross McMullin, 'John Christian Watson', in Michelle Grattan (ed.), *Australian Prime Ministers*, revised edition, New Holland, 2008, p. 62.
6. Margo Beasley, *Wharfies: The History of the Waterside Workers' Federation of Australia*, Halstead Press in association with the Australian National Maritime Museum, 1996, p. 43.
7. NBAC: Waterside Workers' Federation, T62/1/1, Council minutes, 16 November 1915, pp. 206–7.
8. NBAC: WWF, T62/29/1, Cash book, 1902–1924.
9. NBAC: Sydney Wharf Labourers' Union, Z248/98, Minutes, 27 September 1916.
10. L F Fitzhardinge, *William Morris Hughes: A Political Biography*, vol. 2, The Little Digger 1914–1952, Angus and Robertson Publishers, 1979, p. 194.
11. NBAC: Australian Federated Union of Locomotive Enginemen, E99/3/8, Minutes of general committee meetings, 11 January 1931.
12. NBAC: AFULE, E99/3/8, 26 April 1931.
13. NBAC: AFULE, Z154/417, Bathurst branch minutes, 2 August 1931.
14. NBAC: AFULE, E99/3/8, 22 November 1931.
15. NBAC: Australian Workers' Union, S100, *The Australian Worker*, 1903–1975.
16. NBAC: J C Coupe collection, P19/2/1, Report of proceedings of the Australian Trade Union Congress, 1916.

17. NBAC: Federated Furnishing Trade Society, T11/18, Anti-conscription campaign correspondence, 1916–1917.
18. Such as the Federated Furnishing Trade Society and the Operative Stonemasons' Society, see NBAC T11/18, E117/27, and E154/41/1.
19. NBAC: Normington-Rawling collection, N57/442, Anti-conscription leaflets and handbills, 1916–1917.
20. NBAC: FFTS, T11/18.
21. NBAC: Normington-Rawling, N57/1312.
22. NBAC: Les Barnes collection, P8/3, Leaflets re conscription, referenda, and union affairs, 1916–1946.
23. W K Hancock popularised the dichotomy in his seminal study *Australia* (Ernest Benn Limited, London, 1930, Chapters 10 and 11), though he was not the first to make it nor has it been accepted uncritically since. For an early, equally classic discussion, see Henry Mayer, 'Some conceptions of the Australian Party System 1910–1950,' in Margot Beever and F B Smith (eds), *Historical Studies: Selected Articles*, second series, pp. 217–39. An example of more recent discussion is in Chapter 1 of John Nethercote (ed.), *Liberalism and the Australian Federation*, Federation Press, 2001.
24. Brian Carroll, *Australia's Prime Ministers: From Barton to Howard*, Rosenberg, 2005. Others to stress this aspect of his biography include Colin A Hughes, *Mr Prime Minister: Australian Prime Ministers 1901–1971*, Oxford University Press, 1976 and Judith Brett, 'Stanley Melbourne Bruce', in Michelle Grattan (ed.), *Australian Prime Ministers*, New Holland, 2008, pp. 127–38. The latest Bruce biography, David Lee's *Stanley Melbourne Bruce: Australian Internationalist*, Continuum, 2010, emphasises not the two worlds of Australia and Britain but, as the subtitle suggests, a more integrated internationalism. While not a full biography, Lee's study did examine the PLB business papers and astutely observed that from his time as chairman of directors of the company's London board during 1907–1914, Bruce 'became attuned to adjusting supply to the ever-changing levels of demand in Australia and to minimizing costs, for example of labour, freight and insurance'. It was no small apprenticeship: 'He would later bring these perspectives with him to the task of leading the government of the Commonwealth of Australia, which he conceived of as Paterson, Laing and Bruce writ large' (p. 8).
25. Stuart Macintyre, 'Stanley Melbourne Bruce' in Graeme Davison, John Hirst and Stuart Macintyre (eds), *The Oxford Companion to Australian History*, Oxford University Press, 1998, p. 92.
26. John Connor, possibly following the *Australian Dictionary of Biography*, suggests it was January 1917. See *Stanley Melbourne Bruce: Guide to Archives of Australia's Prime Ministers*, National Archives of Australia, 2003, p. 14 and http://www.naa.gov.au/naaresources/publications/research_guides/pdf/bruce/bruce.pdf.
27. NBAC: Paterson, Laing and Bruce, 86/2/1, Minute book no. 1, p. 379.
28. NBAC: PLB, 86/2/1, p. 376, 27 February 1920.
29. In parliament, during a war loan debate, he said 'I have seen the effect on boys under twenty-one and on men over forty when they get into the firing line, and I say without hesitation that it is a grave blunder to send them in if it can possibly be avoided.' Cecil Edwards, *Bruce of Melbourne: A Man of Two Worlds*, Heinemann, 1965, p. 46.
30. For example, NBAC: PLB, 86/2/1, L W Lapthorne, meeting of 19 March 1920, p. 381; R Hepburn, 9 April 1920, p. 385.
31. NBAC: PLB, 86/2/1, 5 March 1920, p. 378.
32. Edwards, p. 33; see also Heather Radi's *Australian Dictionary of Biography* entry, http://adbonline.anu.edu.au/biogs/A070460b.htm and David Lee, email to authors, 22 April 2010.
33. NBAC: PLB, 86/2/1, 17 October 1919, p. 354.
34. NBAC: PLB, 86/2/1, 17 October 1919, p. 354.
35. Australian National University Archives: Central Records, ANUA 19, Staff files, 4.2.1.11A part 1, Sir Leslie Melville, Bruce to Melville, 9 December 1955.

36. Brett, p. 133.
37. John Connor, *Stanley Melbourne Bruce: Guide to Archives of Australia's Prime Ministers*, National Archives of Australia, 2003, p. 113.
38. Allan Martin, *Robert Menzies: A Life*, vol. 1, 1894–1943, Melbourne University Press, 1996, pp. 251–6.
39. Martin, p. 251 and Rupert Lockwood, *War on the Waterfront: Menzies, Japan and the Pig-iron Dispute*, Sydney, 1987.
40. Martin, p. 256, note 46.
41. Greg Mallory, *Uncharted Waters: Social Responsibility in Australian Trade Unions*, Boolarong Press, 2005.
42. NBAC: Waterside Workers' Federation, Z429, Records of the South Coast branch.
43. NBAC: WWF, T62, Records of the Committee of Management.
44. NBAC: Commonwealth Steamship Owners' Association, Z559, and Australasian Steamship Owners' Federation, E217.
45. NBAC: Australian Council of Trade Unions, N21/55, Subject and correspondence files, Miscellaneous file.
46. NBAC: WWF, T62/9/7/2, T62/24 and T62/25.
47. NBAC: WWF, T62/1/3.
48. The mid-seventies saw a small resurgence, with works by academics and contemporaries on Scullin, Curtin and Chifley, but biographies with the breadth and ambition of La Nauze and Fitzhardinge did not reappear until the new century.
49. ANUA: Fitzhardinge papers, ANUA 83, Folders of research material, 385, Biography of W M Hughes.
50. ANUA: Central Records, ANUA 53, Correspondence files, 9.1.5.2, Biography of W M Hughes, 1952–1973, Copland to Hughes, 13 June 1952.
51. ANUA: ANU History Project, ANUA 44, Transcripts and tapes of oral history interviews, interview no. 26 by Stephen Foster, 5 August 1992, pp. 14–17. He died just over a year later, on 31 October 1993.
52. ANUA 53/9.1.5.2, Hughes to Copland, 18 July 1952.
53. ANUA 83/392.
54. ANUA 19/9.2.2.4C, L F Fitzhardinge, Hancock to Copland, 3 February 1958.
55. S G Foster and Margaret M Varghese, *The Making of the Australian National University 1946–1996*, Allen and Unwin, 1996, p. 130 quoting Hancock.
56. ANUA 19/9.2.2.4, Hancock to Registrar, 17 November 1964.
57. ANUA 19/9.2.2.4C, Melville to Hancock, 31 January 1958.
58. ANUA: ANU Council, ANUA 198, Minutes of meetings, 14th meeting, 27 November 1953, resumed 18 December 1953; ANUA 200, Minutes of Advisers on Legislation meetings, 26 August 1953; ANUA 53/9.1.5.2.
59. ANUA 53/9.1.5.2, Sawer to Vice-Chancellor, 19 March 1963.
60. Fitzhardinge, vol. 1, p. 19.
61. NBAC: Institute of Public Affairs, N136/4.
62. A complete set is available for downloading at http://www.ipa.org.au/publications/index/type/12, however, some scanned pages have margins missing. A complete hardcopy set is held as NBAC Z714.
63. Gerard Henderson, *Menzies' Child: The Liberal Party of Australia 1944–1994*, Allen and Unwin, 1994.
64. L F Crisp, *Ben Chifley: A Biography*, Longmans, 1961, p. 307.
65. John Carroll in *Oxford Companion to Australian History*, p. 344; *The Age*, 17 and 13 July 2004 respectively.
66. Henderson, pp. 71, 83, 85.
67. Henderson, p. 87.

68. Copy at NBAC N136/112, pp. 21–2.
69. NBAC: IPA, N136/1.
70. NBAC: IPA, N136/105 and 56.
71. Ian Hancock, *National and Permanent? The Federal Organisation of the Liberal Party of Australia*, Federation Press, 2000, and Allan Martin, see endnote 38 above, and vol. 2, 1944–1978, Melbourne University Press, 1999.
72. Fadden correspondence (NBAC N136/1) and electoral material (N136/103), Curtin electoral material (N136/103), Forde and Chifley correspondence (N136/21, N136/1).
73. NBAC: IPA, N136/28.
74. NBAC: IPA, N136/20.
75. NBAC: IPA, N136/1 and 25.
76. *Stanley Melbourne Bruce: Prime Minister & Statesman*, National Archives of Australia, 2009, p. 1.
77. ANUA 44/6, p. 100.
78. ANUA: Jill Waterhouse papers, ANUA 235/1, Ralph Elliott, 'Some Memorable Moments in the History of University House', 3 pp. address presented on 23 April 2003.
79. University House Jubilee Speeches at http://www.anu.edu.au/unihouse/news/speeches.htm accessed 9 March 2009.
80. Niel Gunson, 'Hexagonal Reflections on Pacific History', in Brij V Lal and Allison Ley (eds), *The Coombs: A House of Memories*, ANU, 2006, p. 71.
81. ANUA 235/2.
82. Bob Hawke, *The Hawke Memoirs*, William Heinemann Australia, 1994, pp. 28–9.
83. Stan Anson, *Hawke: An Emotional Life*, McPhee Gribble, 1991.
84. John Hurst, *Hawke: The Definitive Biography*, Angus and Robertson, 1979, p. 25.
85. Robert Pullan, *Bob Hawke: A Portrait*, Methuen, 1980, p. 56.
86. Blanche d'Alpuget, *Robert J Hawke: A Biography*, Schwartz, 1983, p. 66.
87. Hazel Hawke, *My Own Life: An Autobiography*, Text Publishing, 1992, p. 70.
88. See ANUA 78/9.4.1.40 and 17.5.1.40, Student files, R J L Hawke; ANUA 34/2, Draft minutes of Council committees; ANUA 10/82, Oliphant papers; and ANUA 359, University House files, Trendall's correspondence, 1957.
89. ANUA 34/2, p. 74, Hawke 'did not go in pool'.
90. A podcast of Hawke's address can be found at: http://www.anu.edu.au/discoveranu/content/podcasts/2010_university_commencement_address/.
91. NBAC: WWF, Z432/24, Aborigines – Employment, FCAATSI, 1964–1966.
92. NBAC: ACTU, N68/2, Secretary's files.
93. NBAC: ACTU, N68/1.
94. NBAC: Australian Agricultural Company, 78/1/27, Despatches from General Superintendent in NSW to London Directors, no. 4, 8 November 1856.
95. See NBAC Z376/17; 8/212/2–7; 87/5; and Z200.
96. NBAC: Wave Hill Station, N182, Improvements book.
97. NBAC: Goldsbrough Mort and Company Ltd, 2/859/377, Victoria River Downs region (B290).
98. NBAC: Australian Workers' Union, N117/560, Transcript of proceedings, Mr Knox, p. 1204.
99. NBAC: ACTU, N21/48.
100. NBAC: ACTU, N21/60, N21/55.
101. NBAC: Michael Hess papers, Z522.
102. NBAC: ACTU, N21/662.

103. NBAC: WWF, Z432/24, Aborigines – Land Rights – Gurindji, 1970–1977.
104. NBAC: WWF, N114/490.
105. NBAC: WWF, Z432/24, Aborigines – Land Rights – Gurindji Trust Fund 1972–1980.
106. NBAC: WWF, N114/490.
107. NBAC: Australian Woolgrowers' and Graziers' Council, N92/843.
108. The literature includes, for example David Marr, 'Power Trip: The Political Journey of Kevin Rudd', *Quarterly Essay*, no. 38, 2010; Patrick Weller, *Cabinet Government in Australia, 1901–2006*, UNSW Press, 2007; Diane Langmore, *Prime Ministers' Wives*, McPhee Gribble, 1992; and James Curran, *The Power of Speech*, Melbourne University Press, 2004.
109. A partial exception is Don Watson's *Recollections of a Bleeding Heart*, Vintage, 2003.
110. ANUA 19/1922 parts 1–6 & C, Professor Heinz Arndt.
111. ANUA 19/1922 part 1. See also ANUA 147/7, ANU History Project binders of research notes, 'Staff'; Peter Coleman, Selwyn Cornish and Peter Drake, *Arndt's Story: The Life of an Australian Economist*, Chapter 10; and ANUA 44/13, Transcript of oral history interview.
112. ANUA 19/1922 part 5 and ANUA 55, D A Low papers.
113. ANUA: Heinz Arndt papers, ANUA 80, Reprints and photocopies of published articles, 13, Diary of round-the-world trip with Malcolm Fraser. Extracts appeared in H W Arndt, *Asian Diaries*, Chopmen Publishers, Singapore, 1987 and Coleman, Cornish and Drake's biography.
114. NBAC T62/63/2, K3833; T34/5/2, K3781; N117/1370 and T58/36/24, K2005; P94/50/2, K3932.
115. NBAC E216/18/11, K3972; T60/63/7, K2014.
116. NBAC E165/56/21, K2446; 110/8/1/2, K1354; N68, Z282A and N143/439; N72/706.
117. Examples of trade union newsletters include NBAC S100, *The Australian Worker* (Australian Workers' Union), S102, *Common Cause* (Australian Coal and Shale Employees Federation), S760, *The Lamp* (NSW Nurses' Association), S62, S984, *The Maritime Workers' Journal* (Maritime Union of Australia), and S187, *The Shop Assistant* (Shop, Distributive and Allied Employees' Association).
118. For example, NBAC P15/1/9 and 13, Phil Thorne collection.
119. ANUA 151, *ANU News* master set, 1950–1975 and ANUA 244, *ANU Reporter* master set, 1970 to present.
120. ANUA 15/27; ANUA 15/9.
121. ANUA 15/2; ANUA 225/405.
122. ANUA 15/6, 29; ANUA 191.
123. ANUA 15/3, 9, 13, 14, 111, 118, 143; ANUA 191.
124. ANUA 51/75002 and ANUA 240/3/5–6; ANUA 15/183 and ANUA 225/248; ANUA 226/303, 414; ANUA 226/788; ANUA 226/867.
125. For example, the opening of the new J G Crawford Building on 8 May 2010, http://news.anu.edu.au/?p=2138.
126. ANUA: ANU Students Association, ANUA 300, *Woroni* master set, 28 February 1983, p. 3.

CHAPTER 4
The Archives

The descriptions of records are arranged in alphabetical order by prime minister and then by record description. The creator of the records is identified, then the series or file title, followed by a highlighting of references to the relevant prime minister. The reference numbers needed to order the records in the Archives come after the text in brackets.

EDMUND BARTON, 1901–1903

Australian Agricultural Company records

William Parry's letterbook and despatches, 1824–1834

When William Parry arrived at New South Wales in December 1829 as Commissioner to the Company, Edmund Barton's father William had been the Company's accountant at Port Stephens for several years. As Pennie Pemberton explained (*In the Service of the Company*, vol. 1, ANU, 2005) Barton had been the senior officer in NSW and 'proved a difficult man to deal with – devising ever increasingly complex accounting methods and maintaining that his authority came directly from the directors in London. Finally, in July 1831 Barton and his family sailed for London where he was dismissed'. The Bartons returned to NSW in 1834, and promptly brought an action against Parry for libel and malicious prosecution. But more relevant for us, he began a new career in stockbroking and real estate, and his wife in young ladies' education. The eleventh of twelve children, Edmund was born in 1849. Parry's copied letters, addressed to recipients in New South Wales, include numerous mentions of Barton, and some are also addressed to him singly or as an addressee of a circular letter. They, and the copies of despatches to the directors in England, refer to finances, stores, personnel and related matters, but also testify to Parry's growing frustrations with his accountant. Parry's order books, mentioned in the 1834 trial, are also in the ANU Archives. (NBAC 1/38, 78/1/1–14; NBAC 1/14)

Australian Dictionary of Biography files

Edmund Barton, 1970–2009

This file covers the editing and production of a 5,000-word entry by Martha Rutledge which appeared at pp. 194–200 of volume 7 of the Dictionary published in 1979. At the time of commissioning, the author was Mrs M D Campbell, based at the ANU's Department of History, and working on Barton for Oxford University Press's Great Australians series. It includes correspondence with and notes by ADB staff, copies of source documents (such as birth, death and marriage certificates), and photocopies from newspapers and index cards from library catalogues. Of passing interest is the file's window into what happened after publication. While Rutledge judged an earlier biography (Reynolds' 1948 study) 'notoriously inaccurate', letters on file from A G L Shaw and Shirley Barton show that her own ADB entry attracted corrections, and there is also a sheet contrasting a dozen points of factual discrepancies between the published entry and Geoffrey Bolton's new biography published in 2000. Not for the first time however, the editors drew the line at conceding criticism received in 2006 that Rutledge had failed to mention Barton was one of the founding fathers of rugby union in Australia: this was addenda, not corrigenda. (ANUA 312)

South Australian Typographical Society records

Register of greeting, invitation and souvenir cards, 1885–1925

The register of printing samples compiled by the *Advertiser* Chapel includes an invitation featuring Barton's photograph. The invitation is to the Citizen's Farewell Banquet held at the Town Hall, Sydney on 26 April 1902 when Barton left to attend the Imperial Conference in London. (NBAC E216/18/11, K3972)

Edmund Barton depicted on the program for a banquet before leaving for England in April 1902 (NBAC E216/18/11, K3972)

STANLEY MELBOURNE BRUCE, 1923–1929

Amalgamated Postal Workers' Union of Australia records

Government and Parliamentary members' correspondence files, 1920–1952

The APWUA and its predecessor before it was formed in 1926 represented postmen, sorters and linesmen employed by the Postmaster-General's Department. The files record its lobbying, advocacy and pursuit of redress, participation in inquiries, submissions on legislative amendments and negotiations for increased pay and improved entitlements and working conditions. During Bruce's prime ministership, the union also campaigned as a member of the Joint Secretariat of the Arbitration Defence Committee of the Federal Public Service Unions. This was a time of industrial unrest and change, and the files also record the union expressing concern about such matters as legislation to change the Commonwealth public service arbitration system, the Commonwealth Employees Compensation Bill, the refund of fines, the 1926 and 1928 joint conferences, conditions of employment within the Commonwealth service, delays in operation and tabling of awards, superannuation and the discharge of temporary employees. (NBAC T35/22/5–6, 13, 15, 22–3, 30, 33, 42–3)

Australian Council of Trade Unions records

Correspondence files, 1924–1926

Includes an exchange of letters in January and February 1926 between Bruce's private secretary and the secretary of the Commonwealth Council of Federated Unions. They refer to previous and forthcoming meetings at which the unions wish to discuss amendments to the *Commonwealth Conciliation and Arbitration Act*. (NBAC N21/5)

Australian Dictionary of Biography files

John Munro Bruce, 1966–2006

Given his dates, Bruce's father John (1840–1901) appeared in the earliest sequence of ADB volumes, with J Ann Hone's 530-word entry appearing in volume 3 (1969) at pp. 276–7. The standard contents for an ADB file are in the file, documenting the results of preparatory research by ADB staff, comments on drafts, and copies of the usual certificates, though not the death certificate. It also records a number of factual points which needed correcting after the entry was published, and the very final folios, emails between Dr David Lee and more recent editors, relate to doubt about Bruce's cause of death. As Lee eventually showed, it was not diabetes as Hone thought and the ADB too readily accepted, but suicide. He also argues persuasively why this death, and by 1919 those of all bar one of his immediate family, influenced S M Bruce's sense of destiny, insecurity and melancholia so strongly. A tougher burden of proof required Hone to delete her mention that John Bruce 'became insolvent' in the 1890s, despite some primary evidence referred to on the file from the Union Bank Archives that he was 'turned out of the firm by Paterson as insolvent'. The general editor Geoff Serle noted for the file on 10 July 1967 that he was 'worried' about this. 'The evidence, though pretty reliable, is not conclusive,' he wrote, 'it could have been rumour. I don't think we should use it without confirmation from Archives. I shall get Mrs T to check. So hold.' There is no indication that this happened. Interestingly, in his new biography (*Stanley Melbourne Bruce: Australian Internationalist*, Continuum, 2010, p. 4), David Lee avoids the 'i' word, while stating Bruce lost 'nearly all the money he had made hitherto'. (ANUA 312)

S M Bruce, 1975–1978, 2003

This two-part file documents the commissioning, subsequent interactions and approval of Dr Heather Radi's 6,000-word biography of Bruce published in the *Australian Dictionary of Biography*, volume 7, Melbourne University Press, 1979, pp. 453–61. It includes details of Bruce's life, correspondence, drafts and readers' and editors' comments, mostly from 1978. The correspondence illustrates the author's struggle to capture a life. One exchange between Radi and the ADB's general editor Geoff Serle (13 August 1978; 3 October 1978) has her observing: 'There are just too many different comments, and often very conflicting ones, about the personality/character' and him replying: 'I sympathize with the difficulty of "catching" the personality. Write something in if you feel you can, but it's not essential. But shouldn't the spats be brought in somehow?' (ANUA 312)

Stanley Melbourne Bruce, the Businessman (ANUA 225/148/3)

Australian National University audiovisual material

Film and audio tapes, 1952–1972

A film was made of the installation of Bruce as Chancellor, including the presentation of greetings from representatives of other universities and the conferring of an honorary Doctor of Laws degree. There is also an audio recording of an after-luncheon speech by Bruce, following the conferring of an honorary degree on Dr Harold Macmillan in 1958. (ANUA 191)

Australian National University Chancelry records

Ceremonial documents, 1952–1956

A collection of documents primarily concerning Bruce's installation as Chancellor. Includes a copy of his honorary degree, scrolled greetings from universities and a list of universities that were represented at the ceremony. It also contains a copy of the program for the event, which was held in the Albert Hall, Canberra. (ANUA 63)

Australian National University correspondence files

Selection of Chancellor, 1951–1997

This three-part file documents the ANU's relationship with Viscount Bruce in the role of the ANU's first Chancellor and includes correspondence between him and various Vice-Chancellors. There are also cables and internal memoranda by, among others, the Registrar R A Hohnen and Sir Allen Brown, deputy high commissioner in London and the ANU's delegate in the United Kingdom. (ANUA 53/4.2.6.0C parts 1–3)

The Stanley Melbourne Bruce Fund, 1967–2000

In his will Bruce left a considerable sum to the university and this three-part file shows how his wishes were implemented. The fund was formally established in 1972, and by 1984 the income from investments began to be awarded to projects. (ANUA 53/4.5.0.63 parts 1–3)

Australian National University Council minutes

Minutes of meetings, 1951–1962

These minutes firstly cover meetings chaired by Bruce as the University's Chancellor on the few occasions he was present in Canberra. Secondly, they record the decision to approach Viscount Bruce inquiring whether he 'would be prepared to accept co-option to the Council with a view to becoming the first chancellor of the University' (1st meeting, 13 July 1951), an experiment as he noted in his response to Council's official welcome which followed UK practice where the Chancellor was 'less continuously active in University affairs that was the practice in Australia' (7th meeting, 24 October 1952). The minutes record subsequent interactions between the Chancellor and Council members such as the Vice-Chancellor Sir Leslie Melville and the Council chair in Bruce's absence, H C Coombs, covering matters such as the times when he would be in Australia to chair Council, attend graduations and his work in the UK on behalf of the ANU. By 1955 both Bruce and the ANU realised a London-based Chancellor was no longer practical nor to the ANU's advantage, the minutes tracking negotiations to renew his appointment while seeking a replacement. After several false starts, the problem was resolved, the minutes for the 59th meeting on 12 May 1961 noting 'that the Chancellor has submitted his resignation ... and that Sir John Cockcroft was willing to succeed him.' (ANUA 198/7–10)

Australian National University History Project records

Transcripts and tapes, 1990–1995

In 1990 Daniel Connell conducted an interview with the former Dean of Law Professor Geoffrey Sawer for the University's official history project. This came to fruition in 1996 under Stephen Foster and Margaret Varghese's names as *The Making of the Australian National University 1946–1996*. Sawer was questioned at one point about his memories of and contact with the Chancellor Lord Bruce. In the transcript (pp. 98–9) Sawer explains what 'led me to heartily dislike the man', and to write a poem about a Chancellor who 'never did come'. (ANUA 44/6)

Australian National University photographs

Envelopes of photographs of people and events, 1948–2005

Bruce was photographed many times at his installation as Chancellor and at the conferring of his honorary Doctor of Laws, 22–23 October 1952 (including Lady

Bruce), at the opening of University House by the Duke of Edinburgh, 16 February 1954, at the conferring of degrees ceremony two days later, and at University House with Sir Earle Page, following the conferring of an honorary degree on Dr Harold Macmillan in January 1958. (ANUA 15/6, 18, 20, 29, 55; ANUA 225/148)

Australian National University staff files

Lord Bruce, Chancellor, 1951–1958

Documents the administrative details and relationship management of Bruce's three terms as the ANU's first Chancellor. Especially noteworthy is the correspondence between the University and Bruce in London. It allows an insight into the perspective of Vice-Chancellors Copland and Melville on developments at the university, Bruce's on the financial developments in London and negotiations on an appropriate role for a Chancellor. (ANUA 19/4.2.6.1 part 1)

Sir Leslie Melville, Vice-Chancellor, 1953–1960

This multiple-part file includes a December 1955 letter from Bruce to Melville concerning arrangements to meet in London (in which Bruce refers to being 'somewhat preoccupied at the moment with the Bank of England and the Clearing Banks'). There are also copies of Melville's letters to Bruce written in June and July 1958 discussing among other matters Bruce's continuing as Chancellor. (ANUA 19/4.2.1.11A parts 1–2)

Australian National University Standing Committee minutes

Minutes, 1972

The minutes for the meeting of 21 December 1972 record that the second matter it considered under agenda item 'Urgent matters' was the Bruce Bequest. This was due to the fact that the funds he left the University following his death in 1967 ($71,000) were about to be received. It resolved to establish 'The Stanley Melbourne Bruce Fund' and use the anticipated annual income of $4,000 on awards supporting the application of science to industry. (ANUA 199/4)

Keith Hancock papers

Correspondence, 1947

The file comprises a small correspondence Hancock conducted in the UK during 1947 as he considered taking up an appointment with the ANU, though officially at the time he was just a member of its Academic Advisory Committee with Howard Florey, Mark Oliphant and Raymond Firth. Written in a 'my dear chap' style typical of men of the world at that time, it includes a signed letter from Bruce, and a copy of a letter to him about Bruce's 'recent honour' and the mistake of allowing him to return to the United Kingdom. (ANUA 77/8)

Paterson, Laing and Bruce records

Ernest Bruce's letterbook, 1907

In 1907 Bruce's eldest brother Ernest was chair of the London board of directors. The letterbook comprises copies of his 'out letters' to the directors of the Melbourne and Sydney branches, to specific individuals there and to others such as Australian banks. For our purposes, the volume's significance concerns several letters revealing Ernest's plan to convince others with stronger claims that 'Stanley' (as Ernest called him) be installed as chair of the London board, allowing the latter to go out to Australia. Of his younger brother (then only twenty-four), Ernest wrote on 20 September 1907: 'he is very smart, he is a good speaker, and has a good address, and also has the advantage of being trained by one of the very best Company lawyers and speakers in England, that is Mr Stephenson of Crisps'. The basis of the family's 20th century wealth began here too. Additionally, as David Lee explains (*Stanley Melbourne Bruce*, 2010, p. 7) through learning to manage sometimes difficult boards Bruce 'developed such a talent for chairing meetings that he would later be described as the best of the chairmen of committees of the League of Nations'. (NBAC 82/13/4)

Ernest Bruce's letterbook, 1908

The volume, though produced as a letter press book, contains pasted up carbon copies of typed letters and a few telegrams Bruce's eldest brother Ernest sent while running the Sydney office of Paterson, Laing and Bruce between April and November 1908. The cover label identifies the contents as 'E Bruce Private Correspondence', but in fact the letters are a mix of business and personal communications sent primarily to the directors collectively and individually in the London and Melbourne branches of the business. Among the letters are twenty-three to Bruce, who was acting chairman of directors of the London Office and during the year was officially appointed as chairman. As with the remaining letters, this mix of business and personal is a somewhat false distinction, as the Bruce family was in the process of regaining control of the business, and thereby beginning to re-establish the family's wealth. Though the letters offer only one half of their correspondence, they allow a glimpse of the relationships between two very close brothers, and through references to another (Robert), their sister Mary, and the management of the family estate (their mother dying midyear), the Bruce family. Clearly, Ernest helped set Stanley on his way. He successfully lobbied the Australian directors to secure Stanley's appointment despite his being only twenty-five. He provided background details on associates from his time in London, advised him on tactics and even forwarded pages of suggested text for his annual report to shareholders (letter of 29 August 1908). On 20 October 1908, he wrote of his pleasure that it had been 'a complete success' as: 'It was a great relief off my mind as I was frightened of some opposition from the Paterson family.' (NBAC 82/13/5)

Melbourne Board of Directors, minutes of meetings, 1901–1921

Bruce chaired approximately half the meetings of the Melbourne board of Paterson, Laing and Bruce in 1914 and most of the meetings on his return to Australia in late 1916 until 1921. From the minutes one can glean a sense of 'Bruce the Businessman' as explained in Chapter 3. (NBAC 86/2/1)

Melbourne Board of Directors, minutes of meetings, 1921–1928

Bruce chaired approximately half the meetings of the Melbourne board of Paterson, Laing and Bruce from 1921–1923, during the period he was a minister in the Hughes Nationalist government. His elder brother R L Bruce also continued to sit on the board. Bruce resigned on becoming prime minister in February 1923. For some meetings during periods he was absent overseas in 1921 and 1922, the minutes record receipt of letters and cables from him. (NBAC 86/2/2)

BEN CHIFLEY, 1945–1949

Amalgamated Engineering Union records

Alan Wilson letter, 1970

Inexplicably included with a bound set of the AEU journal *The Magnet* is this three-page letter dated 28 May 1970 from Alan Wilson to the National Librarian Sir Harold White. In it Wilson provides an appraisal of Chifley, interspersed with anecdotes and drawing on his three years with the NSW Railways as an engine fitter at Bathurst, 1924–1927, where Chifley was a 'loco engineman'. (NBAC Z102/200)

Amalgamated Postal Workers' Union of Australia records

Government and Parliamentary members' correspondence files, 1920–1952

The APWUA and its predecessor before it was formed in 1926 represented postmen, sorters and linesmen employed by the Postmaster-General's Department. The files record the union's lobbying, advocacy and pursuit of redress, participation in inquiries, submissions on legislative amendments and negotiations for increased pay and improved entitlements and working conditions. The union also campaigned as part of the Combined Federal Service Unions, and courtesy copies of its letters will also be found here. The union was in contact with Chifley when he was minister for defence, treasurer, and prime minister. He was lobbied in relation to matters such as the appointment of a Commonwealth Public Service Arbitrator, appointment of an Industrial Officer for the Commonwealth public service, conditions of accommodation in Canberra, post-war reconstruction of the public service, manpower planning conferences, payment of holiday periods, long service leave for temporary employees, preference for unionists, appointment of the chair of the Promotions Appeal Committee, the weekly payment of salaries and the 1943 promotions and transfers inquiry. (NBAC T35/22/4, 7, 9, 13–14, 16, 19, 25, 27–8, 30, 32, 37, 39–40, 43)

Australasian Coal and Shale Employees' Federation records

Coal Strike, 1949

These folders comprising papers on the 1949 coal strike were part of a larger deposit of Miners' Federation records collected by Edgar Ross (editor of the union's newspaper *Common Cause*) for research on his *History of the Miners' Federation of Australia*, published in 1969. Thus there are letters to him in response to requests for details about the strike, leaflets (printed and roneoed), clippings, telegrams of support, replies from police to the request for permission to march, logs of claims, copies of minutes of special meetings during June and July 1949 of the Coal Mining Unions' Council, letters to I Williams (general president, Australasian Coal and Shale Employees' Federation), report of proceedings of the conference between representatives of the Colliery Proprietors Association, combined mining unions and the Joint Coal Board on 30 May 1949 and a list of where meetings were held in Sydney in support of miners. Apart from thus providing important context to Chifley's involvement with the strike, the record series has a letter dated 14 June 1949 from Chifley promising to have inquiries made into 'an organised attempt on the part of major radio stations to prevent the Federation obtaining time on the air to state its case for the reorganisation of the Mining Industry'. (NBAC E165/3A)

Photographs, 1885–1965

In this collection Chifley is photographed 'flustered by the outspoken condemnation of young Western miners who met his car upon arrival at the Miners' Association meeting at Katoomba' in July 1949. Their placards refer to Chifley as a striker in 1917, now turned strike-breaker. (NBAC E165/56/21, K2446)

Ben Chifley confronted by striking Katoomba miners in 1949 (NBAC E165/56/21, K2446)

THE ARCHIVES

Australian Dictionary of Biography files

Ben Chifley, 1990–2005

In the early 1990s, the rise of serial prime ministerial biographer David Day still a decade away, the ADB editors debated who to commission to write its 6,000-word entry on Ben Chifley. As this file shows, it settled on Professor D B Waterson, allowed him another 930 words, and published it in 1993 at pp. 412–20 of volume thirteen. Waterson had access to the standard support of the editorial staff in documenting the basic facts about Chifley's life, the file thus incorporating photocopies of index cards, notes on earlier published studies, and copies of birth, death and marriage certificates. Beyond this expected and standard content, there is evidence from the correspondence, drafts and readers' comments of two disagreements. One arose from an old game, still played even by retired prime ministers, of their relative ranking. In an early draft, Waterson had made insightful comparisons of Chifley with Hughes, Curtin, Deakin and Menzies, and had opened not with birth details but the words: 'Of the Australian Prime Ministers, Chifley is not in the first rank. He lacked Curtin's intellect, passion and *fingerspitz gefühl*'. One reader thought this assessment 'highly debatable, unnecessary [and] not altogether consistent with what he goes on to say', and the editors convinced him to drop all except the comparison with Curtin, and to rename the third quality he lacked 'deftness'. The second phrasing to be negotiated centred on Phyllis Donnelly, in particular her title (Mrs or Miss) and role. Waterson agreed to drop 'Mrs' in the corrigenda, explaining to the then general editor Di Langmore he had 'probably been misled by some contemporary accounts bestowing a level of respectability', but despite David Day's 2002 biography (which suggested Ms Donnelly was Chifley's lover), she continues to be styled by the Dictionary, into the online era, as Chifley's 'personal secretary, confidante and affectionate companion'. (ANUA 312)

Australian Federated Union of Locomotive Enginemen, Bathurst Branch records

Minute book, 1919–1934

Chifley was a union man from his earliest days with the NSW Railways, first with the Bathurst branch of the Federated Engine Drivers' and Firemen's Association of Australasia and after 1920, the AFULE. He was also a Bathurst man, born and bred. If one document may be seen as the premier symbol of and source for both identities, it is this battered minute book. It reveals, firstly, Chifley's involvement chairing meetings, acting as a returning officer, signing minutes, helping audit the books and agreeing to join subcommittees, and above all, testifies to his diligent attention to mundane local branch concerns: 'Moved by Mr Chifley 2nd Burns [C H Burns] that water supply at Eskbank barracks be put in better order. When one tap is in use, all others useless owing to water supply being so very weak. Carried.' (14 January 1923). Simultaneously, the minutes track his emergence as a leader in the wider labour movement, representing his branch in Sydney and his state nationally. Also noteworthy is the membership's love–hate relationship with Chifley. He was regarded as very knowledgeable, often asked to explain legislation and industrial awards to the membership and in turn their working conditions to the Arbitration Court. But as the economy declined and the influence of Lang supporters grew, anger undermined respect for the loyal member of Scullin's Cabinet bound to support its conservative economic policies. Ominously, the 5 July 1931 meeting failed by a single vote to suspend standing orders 'to discuss whether Mr Chifley due to his political opinions should remain in Meeting', the blow coming on 2 August 1931 when: 'Due to his political actions Mr Chifley MHR has lost the confidence of members of this Branch, such resolution to be inserted in whichever local paper will publish same & the *Labor Daily*', as related in Chapter 3, 'Three Labor dismissals'. (NBAC Z154/417)

Australian Federated Union of Locomotive Enginemen, Federal Office records

Correspondence file, 1923–1924

The file includes letters Chifley wrote from Bathurst to A S Drakeford who was the Union's first general secretary when the union was formed in 1920. There are also copies of a number of long replies from Drakeford to Chifley. They discuss internal union matters, pre-strike seniority, NSW state branch concerns, who qualified for membership, federation rules and tensions with the Australian Railways Union. The file amply illustrates David Day's assessment (*Chifley*, HarperCollins Publishers, 2002, p. 224) that Chifley was 'almost a de facto deputy [to Drakeford], albeit a distant and occasional one'. (NBAC T60/17)

Federal award papers, 1924–1926

These twelve folders of papers are a by-product of a 1924 Union application for an award to the Commonwealth Arbitration Court seeking improvements in the federal award. There are also papers on a later submission to vary the award in December 1926. Chifley was personally involved in preparing the submission, which saw him take long service leave and travel to Melbourne to compile evidence about working conditions and appear before the Court. The files of primary interest here are two folders identified in faint red pencil as 'Originals of B Chifley' and in ink in Chifley's hand as 'J B Chifley NSW Evidence'. The former has tables of typed and manuscript data with notes explaining what they relate to, and papers including draft exhibits and letters to Chifley organised by clause within claim number aligning with the union submission. Many papers are signed by Chifley and witnessed by Tom Croft. The entire folder speaks of an era when 'cut and paste' meant literally that – typed paragraphs have been pasted up or pinned and interspersed with manuscript notes – and they illustrate in detail how thoroughly compiled the case was in assembling supporting evidence direct from the men. The second and larger folder has similar content but was clearly prepared closer to their appearance before the Court, being laid out and typed up for presentation. Here too however, Chifley's annotations are everywhere. (NBAC T60/27)

Federal award papers, 1924–1930

Despite the limited results of their application to the Commonwealth Arbitration Court in 1926, the Union maintained a precarious faith in that path over direct action and negotiation to achieve improvements, as these papers (envelopes of lists, claims and statements) show. It prepared for a federal award case in 1927–1928, again with assistance from Chifley both generally and personally as an actual example of hours and conditions. Included here are papers labelled by claim number, some annotated in Chifley's hand, typescript copies of memos from the NSW Railways, and details of hours of work. One of the latter states: 'On the 10–7–26 Driver Chifley signed on at Orange at 11.55 pm, off at Bathurst at 10.30 am. Total time in charge of engine 10.35 min.' (NBAC T60/28)

Australian Federated Union of Locomotive Enginemen, NSW Division records

Annual Delegates' minutes, 1913–1929

In 1913, when these minutes start, Chifley was twenty-eight, a fireman with the NSW Railways and qualified to be a driver when a vacancy appeared, still playing rugby union, and just starting to seriously court Lizzie McKenzie. And he was becoming increasingly active in his union, the Federated Engine Drivers' and Firemen's Association of Australasia; he appeared as a witness in an arbitration case and was accompanying Bathurst branch officials to negotiations with the railways. By their close in 1929, he had been through the scarring 1917 strike, had played a leading role in the creation of the AFULE (1920), was a seasoned union representative, witness and negotiator at the state and federal levels and had stood unsuccessfully (1925) and twice successfully for parliament (1928 and 1929). The minutes give us a detailed picture of the workings of a union, with complementing overviews provided by the secretary's annual reports. There are references to accidents, restoration of seniority, a 44-hour week, technical engine matters, appeals where a member had been disciplined or dismissed, tribunal and arbitration rulings, and the growing threat of Bruce's dislike of federal arbitration. Set against this is extensive detail on Chifley's involvements representing the western division on the NSW division general committee, which, along with the Bathurst branch minutes and in the absence of intimate diaries and letters, provide an idea of his mental world, its values, ideas of fairness, modes of address, organisational practices, worries about competition from the ARU, and approaches to dispute resolution. The union which sacked Chifley in 1931 appreciated and respected him in the 1920s. He played a key role in the creation of the new union in 1920 having been registered under the new *Arbitration Act* (a result of the Engineers' Case so famously won by Robert Menzies). He represented the NSW division at the special conference which established it, was a member of the subcommittee which had drawn up the new Constitution and Rules, and fought largely successfully for branch and division voting rights according to membership. Receiving his conference report, the Division agreed it was fortunate 'having a man of Mr Chiffley's [sic] capacity to represent it at the Conference'. A motion according him 'a hearty vote of thanks ... was carried by acclamation' (annual meeting of 24–25 September 1920, pp. 175–6). At the 23–26 September 1925 annual delegates meeting, noting they now had their own award, the minutes record: 'Our thanks are also due to Mr Chifley for the able assistance rendered by him in his capacity as witness on behalf of this Division' (p. 222). And when he was re-elected in 1929 as the Member for Macquarie, the secretary reported 'members will be pleased to note that our comrade and fellow-worker on the footplate, Mr J B Chifley, has been again returned with a greatly improved majority' (29 October – 1 November 1929, annual delegates meeting, p. 286). (NBAC E99/2/5)

Drivers Seniority Lists, c. 1921

Included in these half-dozen sets of folded sheets are the names of 'Strikers who returned after 11.9.17', men known as 'lilywhites' who were among the last to reapply for their jobs when the Great Strike of 1917 collapsed because of an abundance of scabs (also known as 'volunteers') and 'earlybirds' (those who returned before the strike officially ended). If those who held out to the end were fortunate enough to gain work with the NSW Railways again, typically experienced engine drivers like Chifley lost seniority and were demoted to firemen. The lists also record his number, the date of his promotion to driver, 18 March 1914 (a matter of debate among historians), and the date and time of his application for re-employment as 2.45 pm on 12 September 1917. (NBAC E99/39)

General Committee minutes, 1920–1925

The minutes allow another view of Chifley the active unionist, this time representing the western region in the NSW division of the newly formed federal union. He attended regularly in Sydney, and was clearly at the centre of the division's efforts to build its membership and influence, for example joining a deputation to the NSW premier to have the seniority of members who struck in 1917 restored. (NBAC E99/3/5)

General Special and Executive Committee meetings, 1930–1932

The minutes span years which are, in some ways, the worst of Chifley's career; he was expelled by his union, attacked by his own side in parliament and rejected by electors of Macquarie at the general election in December 1931. Once again he is prominent in the record as attending meetings, receiving expenses to attend, moving motions and joining discussions about the various work rationing measures introduced by the NSW Railways such as the guarantee provision (one week off in ten) and the rationing of work. After he had defended the 'Premiers' Plan' in parliament in early July 1931, references to him in the minutes become increasingly negative, culminating in his expulsion in October 1931, as related in Chapter 3, 'Three Labor dismissals'. (NBAC E99/3/8)

Australian National University Council minutes

Minutes of meetings, 1949–1951

Traditionally, convocation in relation to universities refers to the entire body of graduates. Very young universities, like the ANU in the early 1950s, need to apply transitional measures. Its 1946 legislation in fact allowed for the admission of 'graduates of other Universities' and 'other persons'. At the meeting of 8 June 1951 (just five days before he died) the Interim Council noted that the leader of the opposition Ben Chifley accepted nomination to Convocation. (ANUA 198/6)

Australian National University photographs

Envelopes of photographs of people and events, 1948–2005

Chifley laid two foundation stones on 24 October 1949: for the John Curtin School of Medical Research and the Research School of Physical Sciences, later known as the Cockcroft Building. Photographs of the ceremonies include Chifley, his wife Elizabeth and Elsie Curtin, widow of John Curtin. There are also two photographs of Chifley from the 1940s used to illustrate ANU publications and a large framed photograph of Chifley which hung in the foyer of the J B Chifley Building, housing the Humanities library, for many years. (ANUA 15/27; ANUA 225/216; ANUA 320)

Australian National University staff files

H C Coombs valedictory address, 1976

Coombs operated at the very centre of ANU affairs during its first four decades, being successively an Interim Council and Council member, Pro-Chancellor and Chancellor. Included with the University's multi-part staff file on him is another titled 'Chancellor and Visiting Fellow: Valedictory Address of 23/4/1976'. In the address, the departing Chancellor reminisced about Chifley, recalling a story from their interaction following the report of the 1943–1944 inter-departmental committee illustrating 'the quick and salty character of his mind'. The address reads, in part:

> The report had recommended a major expansion of Commonwealth participation in education ... Ben was sceptical. 'Education,' he explained, 'is linked in Australia with churches: and that means trouble for the Labour party.' 'But, Minister,' I replied, 'the Commonwealth is already involved in pre-schools and in universities.' 'Ah, yes,' Ben retorted, 'that's before they've got souls and after they've lost them.' (ANUA 19/4.2.1.30)

Australian Workers' Union records

Photographs, 1888–1986

In this collection there are photographs of Chifley and of his funeral procession in Bathurst in June 1951. (NBAC N117/1350, 1367)

Coal Mining Unions Council records

Minutes, 1946–1948

These are signed duplicate copies of minutes of the Coal Mining Unions Council. Formerly the Combined Mining Unions, the Council was a coalition of the Amalgamated Engineering Union, the Federated Mining Mechanics' Association, the Deputies' Associations, the Australian Collieries' Staff Association, the Australasian Coal and Shale Employees' Federation (the Miners' Federation), the Federated Engine Drivers' and Firemen's Association, the Blacksmiths' Society of Australia and the Maitland District Deputies' Association. The minutes are an excellent source of information on the industrial scene in the last years of Chifley's prime ministership. While they cover numerous bread and butter aspects of a miner's working life (e.g. dust and the mine workers pension allowance), the wider industrial and political dimensions are strongly represented. One can thus track the Council's letters, telegrams and deputations to Chifley, all in one way or another concerning the two entities designed to regulate the industry, the Coal Industry Tribunal and the Joint Coal Board. (NBAC E204/3)

Geoff McDonald collection

Photographs, 1916–1969

This collection includes a mounted photograph of Chifley with other delegates to the 19th Triennial Federal Labor Conference at the Hotel Kingston in Canberra on 1 March 1951. (NBAC P94/50/2, K3932)

Ian Turner collection

Coal strike, 1949

The collection of labour historian Ian Turner comprises political pamphlets, serials, books, press cuttings, interview notes, photographs, prints, maps and printed material about the peace movement and press cuttings on the Australian labour movement in the 1890s and on political and industrial matters 1946–1956. This latter component includes a good quantity of material on the Miners' Federation and in particular on the 1949 coal strike, and by extension helps document the context of a dispute which so dominated the final six months of the Chifley government. (NBAC P2/2/9/1)

JOSEPH COOK, 1913–1914

Australian Dictionary of Biography files

Joseph Cook, 1977–1984

The file documents the production of a 3,000-word article by Professor F K Crowley published in volume 8 of the *Australian Dictionary of Biography*, Melbourne University Press, 1981, pp. 96–9. It contains the usual evidence of the ADB staff's preparatory researches including photocopies of index cards, notes, extracts from sources, birth death and marriage certificates, as well as drafts of the article and correspondence between author and editors. Cook clearly didn't excite scholars in the 1970s. The ADB's first choice for biographer wrote to Bede Nairn in November 1977: 'I doubt if I could bear writing about the man', while a reader's report on a Crowley draft said: 'This is another of those dreary articles which is more about the ins and outs of politics than about the subject of the biography … [but] If you cut out the minutiae there is hardly an article left, yet as it stands the person Cook is obscured.' (ANUA 312)

Laurie Fitzhardinge papers

Folders of research material, 1941–1971

The folders include a small file documenting Fitzhardinge's production in August 1954 of a biographical entry on Cook for the UK Dictionary of National Biography. There is also an exchange of letters with Kenneth Binns, the retired Parliamentary Librarian about one of the drafts. In seeking his comments, unwittingly Fitzhardinge had anticipated later pessimism from the ADB editors by ending his letter of 12 August 1954: 'Some dullness is perhaps not inappropriate!' (ANUA 83/64)

Hartley District Miners' Mutual Protective Association, Lithgow Lodge records

Minutes, 1886–1899

Joseph Cook worked at the NSW Vale of Clwydd colliery from 1886 and, as miners organised themselves around the workplace, was a member of its lodge. He quickly gained its confidence, becoming the lodge's secretary, checkweighman and representative on the wider organisation's delegates board. By 1889 he was general secretary of the Coal Miners' Mutual Protective Association for the entire western district. Minutes for Cook's lodge for the time of his membership are not known to have survived, although those for the lodge centred on the nearby Lithgow Valley colliery have. Because the Lithgow and Vale of Clwydd lodges were branches of the same union, the Lithgow minutes inevitably if occasionally refer to matters from Vale of Clwydd, including several mentions of Cook – and of Cooke, a spelling he then still sometimes employed (see for example pp. 48, 104, 105 and 154). (NBAC E165/33/1B)

JOHN CURTIN, 1941–1945

Amalgamated Postal Workers' Union of Australia records

Government and Parliamentary members' correspondence files, 1920–1952

The APWUA and its predecessor before it was formed in 1926 represented postmen, sorters and linesmen employed by the Postmaster-General's Department. The files record its lobbying, advocacy and pursuit of redress, participation in inquiries, submissions on legislative amendments and negotiations for increased pay and improved entitlements and working conditions. It also campaigned as part of the Combined Federal Service Unions, and courtesy copies of its letters will also be found here. The Union corresponded with Curtin as both leader of the opposition and the federal Labor Party in the 1930s and as prime minister in the early to mid-1940s on such matters as the reintroduction of daylight saving, the payment of Commonwealth public servants in the militia, long service leave for temporary employees, and the 1943 Committee of Inquiry into systems of promotions and temporary transfers in the Commonwealth public service. (NBAC T35/22/1, 7, 16, 18, 25, 27–8, 30, 32)

Amalgamated Timber Workers' Union records

Printed material, 1915

The 32-page 'Official Report of the Twelfth Annual Conference' was published by the Amalgamated Timber Workers' Union of Australia. The conference was held in Melbourne between 6 and 12 April 1915 and represented the high point of Curtin's brief career as a union organiser, having been employed as secretary of its Victorian predecessor in 1911. By 1915 the timber workers had formed a nationally amalgamated union. As president, Curtin chaired the conference, and the official report has considerable evidence of his participation, including his president's address (p. 3), discussion of amalgamation with the Australian Workers' Union, asking questions and making rulings from the chair. Curtin also reported, representing the Victorian branch (pp. 17–18): 'Since I last addressed you in regard to Victoria, the *Workmen's Compensation Act* has become operative. Though it has been long delayed, it is, I think, the best Act of its kind in the world.' (NBAC T34/3)

Photographs, 1914–1915

John Curtin features in a group photograph in the official report of the 1915 annual conference as federal president and in a collage of photographs of 'Trades Unions' Officials 1914' as no. 39, general secretary of the Amalgamated Timber Workers' Union. (NBAC T34/3; T34/5/2, K3781)

Among the 'Trade Unions' Officials 1914', no. 39, a youthful John Curtin (NBAC T34/5/2, K3781)

Rule book, 1913

Mixed in with the NSW branch records are dozens of printed standing orders and rule books, including a 1913 rule book for the Victorian branch of the Amalgamated Timber Workers' Union of Australia. In one sense, they represent the parameters within which Curtin worked, for as the branch bye-laws show, he was the general secretary. (NBAC Z138/171)

Australian Dictionary of Biography files

John Curtin, 1991–2007

This file, both mundane and exceptional, documents the commissioning, subsequent interactions and approval of Geoffrey Serle's biography of Curtin published in the *Australian Dictionary of Biography*, volume 13, Melbourne University Press, 1993, pp. 550–8. It includes photocopies of entries from the relevant registers of births, deaths and marriages, newspaper clippings, a copy of Curtin's father's police staff file, book reviews, press articles by a former Curtin biographer Lloyd Ross, copies of journal articles, copies of library index cards, research notes from printed and original sources by ADB staff and edited drafts showing the evolution of the submitted text of 12,500 down to 6,800 words. The file holds additional interest for documenting exchanges between Serle (ADB general editor, 1975–1988), and the then editor Professor John Ritchie (general editor in 1990s) and others such as David Horner concerning Curtin's self-pity, cause of death and responsibility for military strategy (and thus casualties) in Balikpapan in 1945. (ANUA 312)

Australian National University correspondence files

John Curtin Memorial Lectures, 1970–1984

The file documents the establishment and administration of the lecture program. Some were subsequently issued by ANU Press, others issued less formally just by the ANU; some were directly on Curtin, others less so. The printed copies included on the file are:

- 1st – Lloyd Ross, John Curtin for Labor and for Australia, 1970
- 2nd – Kim Beazley (senior), John Curtin: An Atypical Labor Leader, 1971
- 3rd – Don Dunstan, Curtin, Australia and Now?, 1972
- 4th – Bob Hawke, The Economic Policies of Curtin and Beyond, 1973
- 6th – Gough Whitlam, Government of the people, for the people – by the people, 1975 (file also includes correspondence between Vice-Chancellor Low and Whitlam)
- 8th – Tom Fitzgerald, An Education for Labor Leadership: The Case of Curtin, 1977
- 9th – Alan Reid, Government, Employer and Trade Unions: The Shift of Power, 1979 (although not strictly on Curtin, it included some great anecdotes – it was initially to be delivered by Senator J R McClelland)
- 10th – Gareth Evans, The Politics of Justice, 1980

- 11th – J F Staples, Courts, Convicts and Labor Governments in New South Wales: From Cable to Dugan and Beyond, 1981
- 13th – Neil Blewett, Getting It Right: Some Thoughts on the Politics of Consensus, 1983
- 14th – H C Coombs, John Curtin: A Consensus Prime Minister?, 1984. (ANUA 53/10.2.2.47 parts 1–2)

Australian National University Instructional Resources Unit recordings

Audio and video tapes, 1972–1995

The following John Curtin Memorial Lectures were recorded on audio tape by the Instructional Resources Unit:

- 6th – Gough Whitlam, Government of the people, for the people – by the people, 1975 (ANUA 51/75002)
- 7th – Robin Gollan, The Labor Movement and Equality: 1890 and 1980, 1976 (ANUA 51/76012)
- 9th – Alan Reid, Government, Employer and Trade Unions: The Shift of Power, 1979 (ANUA 51/79018)
- 11th – J F Staples, Courts, Convicts and Labor Governments in New South Wales: From Cable to Dugan and Beyond, 1981 (ANUA 51/81074)
- 12th – G Harcourt, Making Socialism in Your Own Country, 1982 (ANUA 51/82024)
- 13th – Neil Blewett, Getting It Right: Some Thoughts on the Politics of Consensus, 1983 (ANUA 51/83034)
- 14th – H C Coombs, John Curtin: A Consensus Prime Minister?, 1984 (ANUA 51/84061)
- 15th – Bruce Grant, Australia in the Twenty-First Century, 1985 (ANUA 51/85082)
- 16th – Jean Blackburn, Changing Approaches to Equality in Education, 1986 (ANUA 51/86022–3)

Australian National University photographs

Envelopes of photographs of people and events, 1948–2005

John Curtin's widow, Elsie, attended the ceremony where Ben Chifley laid the foundation stone for the John Curtin School of Medical Research in October 1949 and she was photographed with Chifley and at the speeches which followed at the Albert Hall. Curtin's son John attended the opening of the John Curtin School of Medical Research in 1958 and is captured in several photographs. (ANUA 15/9, 27)

Australian National University Public Relations records

Speeches and lectures, 1984–1995

Printed copies of John Curtin Memorial Lectures are held in this collection of lectures and speeches: Diane Bell's lecture '1988: Still in Search of the Just Society', Peter Karmel's 1991 lecture 'Past, Present and Future: The Australian University into the Twenty-First Century' and Professor Eugene Kamenka's 1993 lecture 'Australia Made Me … But Which Australia is Mine?' (ANUA 158)

D A Low papers

Fifth Annual John Curtin Memorial Lecture, 1974

There is a typescript copy of L F Crisp's 1974 Curtin lecture 'Grave Diggers and Undertakers: Then and Now' in Anthony Low's papers as Vice-Chancellor. (ANUA 55/6)

ALFRED DEAKIN, 1903–1904, 1905–1908, 1909–1910

Australian Dictionary of Biography files

Alfred Deakin, 1977–1997

John La Nauze's two-volume 1965 biography of Deakin quickly became a classic and meant for decades he was the authority on Deakin. Inevitably asked to write the ADB entry in 1977, he declined nominating 'Norris Roe Shaw or Serle' though agreeing to be a reader. For reasons the ADB file does not explain, it asked Dr Ron Norris, the University of Adelaide author of *The Emergent Commonwealth: Australian*

Federation, Expectations and Fulfilment 1889–1910 (Melbourne University Press, 1975). He agreed, while admitting in a letter of 27 December 1978 to the general editor Bede Nairn: 'It's difficult to say anything original about Deakin, especially after La Nauze'. The file documents this back story and the subsequent preparation of a 6,000-word biography appearing in 1981 at pp. 248–56 of volume 8. It has the usual material, including edited drafts, correspondence between author and ADB editors, and copies of documents, clippings and other source material. Debate over suggested corrections dominates the file. One concerned whether Deakin was born in the Melbourne suburb of Collingwood or Fitzroy, and continued via proposed corrigenda from Barry Jones until 1997. A more substantive point arose from the perhaps inevitable disagreements between La Nauze and Norris. The central concern among the former's thirty-five pages of comments and queries were attacks on Deakin for forming a 'fusion' government with erstwhile enemies in 1909. Norris had written 'Lyne – never a friend of Deakin and now a foe – denounced his former leader as a "Judas", a charge which Hughes, at his vituperative best, believed slandered the disciple'. La Nauze commented:

> I must remark as D's biographer that I can't help regretting that the remark about Judas is inevitably quoted still, when at least notice ought to be taken of what I say on p. 569 of AD. After all, this was a 'political' attack, no doubt carefully prepared by a man with a reputation, to be maintained, for vituperation, and it seems a pity it shd be preserved in a Dictionary article when Deakin's remark about the 'tartshop' – for which he apologized – is not quoted (AD p. 378–9) – of course I quote Hughes at length, but ADB readers will not have the context given there (569 above).

Norris persisted. 'After much agonizing,' he told the Dictionary in a letter of 16 April 1980, 'I left in the Lyne/Judas/Hughes sentence.' He did make a slight amendment, reporting on 31 May 'vituperative' would become 'vindictive', but that otherwise it would stand as a:

> fair and accurate reference to one of the more dramatic scenes in fed. parl. In AD p. 569 La N says that Hughes's Judas reference has been quoted ad nauseam. I note that Serle's Dictionary of Biography makes no mention of the whole incident. On p. 19 of his comments La N says that the ADB entry on D will be all that most students read about D. Why then should they not be informed of this dramatic event & get a sense of the colour & bitterness of the occasion? Of course it was a political attack from Lyne & Hughes – politicians in parl. are inclined to make political attacks and I am not accusing D of being a Judas etc – I am merely mentioning that Lyne & Hughes did. (ANUA 312)

THE ARCHIVES

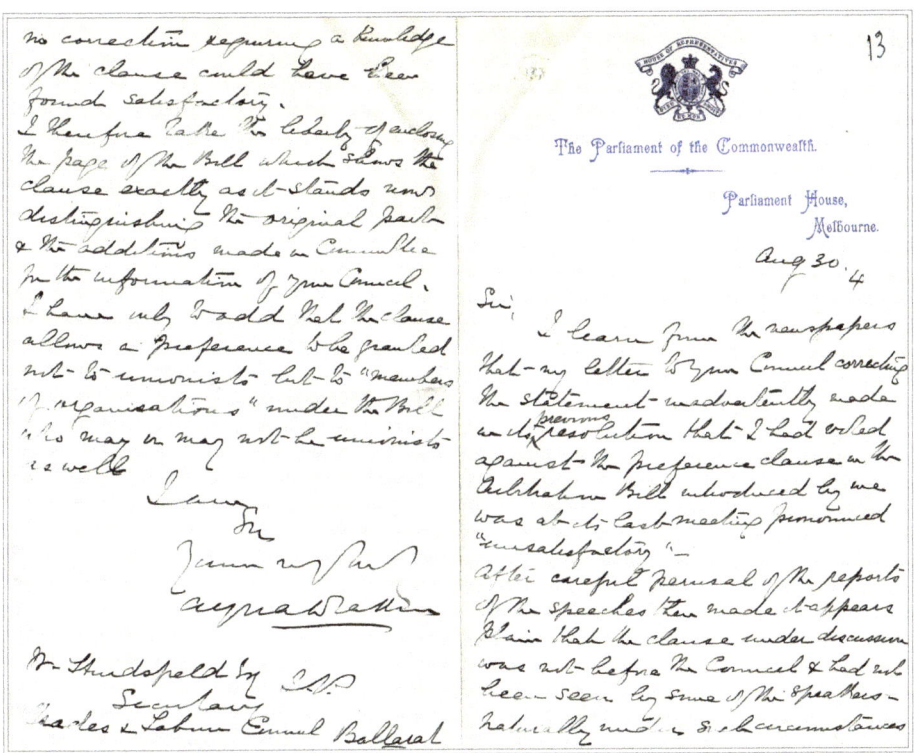

Alfred Deakin writes to the secretary of the Ballarat Trades and Labour Council in 1904 (NBAC E97/7/1904)

Ballarat Trades and Labour Council records

General correspondence, 1884–1923

Apart from a routine November 1888 acknowledgement letter sent to the Council on the chief secretary's letterhead replying on behalf of 'Mr Deakin', this small disparate collection has a folder of correspondence which includes four letters in Deakin's hand from the first years of federal parliament, where he was the Member for Ballarat 1901–1913. The first, dated 28 September 1903, thanks the Council on his becoming prime minister ('it gives me special pleasure both because of its terms & its place of origin. It is my best hope that at the close of my term of office my friends will be able to feel that I have devoted myself with single minded earnestness to the welfare of the Australian people'). In the second, dated 27 October 1903, he agrees to meet and discuss the Conciliation and Arbitration Bill ('introduced by me'). He resigned the following April in reaction to Labor's amendments to his draft legislation, ushering in the short-lived Watson government. When Deakin wrote the third letter to the Council, dated 30 August 1904, the Reid government had just

109

replaced Watson's, its fate also sealed in mid-August 1904 over amendments to the Bill concerning preference for unionists. The letter explains his views about 'preference' and refers to two attachments both of which are also filed here: an annotated page from the Bill and an earlier letter acknowledging a Council resolution on which Deakin had written: 'On this point I disagree, and continue to disagree, with the Ministry.' (NBAC E97/7/1904)

Frederic Eggleston papers

Notes and extracts on international affairs and Victorian politics, 1953

Included in papers possibly intended for a publication on international affairs by the lawyer, politician and diplomat Sir Frederic Eggleston is a seven-page typescript, with handwritten corrections headed 'Political Personalities. Alfred Deakin'. Eggleston knew Deakin, having a connection through his wife's family, and draws on first-hand observations to provide an insightful portrait of Deakin's career, personality and family life. (ANUA 107/16)

Laurie Fitzhardinge papers

Folders of research material, 1941–1971

One folder comprises a typescript copy of a long letter written on 23 August 1880 and headed 'from Crisp Papers' from Deakin to Christopher Crisp, almost certainly the editor of the *Bacchus Marsh Express*. Here Deakin discusses his views on religion and on the Catholic Church in particular. Among other points Deakin tells Crisp: 'I should like to break the neck of priestly authority if I could.' (ANUA 83/71)

ARTHUR FADDEN, 1941

Amalgamated Postal Workers' Union of Australia records

Government and Parliamentary members' correspondence files, 1920–1952

The APWUA and its predecessor before it was formed in 1926 represented postmen, sorters and linesmen employed by the Postmaster-General's Department. The files record its lobbying, advocacy and pursuit of redress, participation in inquiries, submissions on legislative amendments and negotiations for increased pay and improved entitlements and working conditions. It also campaigned as part of the Combined Federal Service Unions, and courtesy copies of its letters will also be found here. The Union corresponded with Fadden as treasurer in 1941 on the powers of the Commonwealth Superannuation Board and taxation deductions in relation to child endowment. (NBAC T35/22/1)

Australian Dictionary of Biography files

Arthur Fadden, 1992–1993

The file documents the commissioning, subsequent interactions and approval of Associate Professor Margaret Cribb's 3,000-word biography of Fadden published in the *Australian Dictionary of Biography*, volume 14, Melbourne University Press, 1996, pp. 123–6. It comprises papers such as clippings, copies of index cards, the will, birth and death certificates, Mackay newspaper reports, letters from contract researchers and comments on the draft by Allan Martin, David Lee and ADB editors Darryl Bennet and John Ritchie. There is also a classic expression of a biographer's frustrations and self-doubts which Cribb sent just over four months before her death ('I found him a very boring person but a very lucky one'). Noteworthy discussion focused on ensuring the complete accuracy of Fadden's birth date (needing correction in many published sources given the date of his parents' marriage), the duration of his term of government (less than forty days, yet allowed to stand as published), the nature of Menzies' appreciation for Fadden and his effectiveness as a campaigner. (ANUA 312)

ANDREW FISHER, 1908–1909, 1910–1913, 1914–1915

Australian Dictionary of Biography files

Andrew Fisher, 1978–2000

The file documents the commissioning, subsequent interactions and approval of Dr Denis Murphy's 4,000-word biography of Fisher published in the *Australian Dictionary of Biography*, volume 8, Melbourne University Press, 1981, pp. 502–7. It includes correspondence with Bede Nairn, ADB staff such as Jim Gibbney, notes on sources, index cards, copies of birth and death certificates, articles from journals and newspapers, and drafts. Of note are various papers on Fisher's death in 1928. The file copy of the death certificate records cause of death as '(a) Cardiac failure (b)

Influenza (c) Senile decay (Premature)'. The latter is annotated, probably by Bryan Gandevia: 'This is important to biographer, tho' not as cause of death'. Murphy's published entry avoids its cause altogether, stating Fisher 'returned to London in 1922 where he lived a quiet life in declining health until his death on 22 October 1928 at South Hill Park'. Also on file is a copy of the Fisher chapter from Brian Carroll's *From Barton to Fraser*, where it states that: 'His health by now was bad, his mental powers were failing.' (ANUA 312)

Waterside Workers' Federation records

Cash books, 1902–1938

Though Fisher's background was in mining, he was a member of the original committee established when waterside unions united in 1902. Accompanying its first cashbook are interleaved half-yearly balance sheets, showing from 1904 to 1908 signatures of two auditors, one being that of Andrew Fisher. (NBAC T62/29/1)

Minute books, 1902–1921

The minutes record deliberations of the WWF Council, and of monthly, special and general meetings and of committees such as the Printing and Publishing Committee which included Fisher. The very first meeting of 7 February 1902 records 'Mr Fisher MP … reported that the Maryboro Waterside Workers were willing to join about 20' (p. 12). He continued to attend intermittently as the branch representative for Gladstone and Maryborough for the next thirteen years, his last mention in the minutes being for the monthly meeting of 16 November 1915. The minutes record Fisher's presence at meetings, moving motions, being elected as auditor or trustee, reporting on strikes in 'Maryboro' (e.g. meeting of 23 August 1907, pp. 67–8) and commenting on others (e.g. minutes of special meeting 10 November 1909 re Newcastle strike) and acknowledging Hughes through motions and presentations. (NBAC T62/1/1)

Photographs, 1912–1950

This collection includes a photograph of delegates to the Waterside Workers' Federation conference in Melbourne on 30 October 1912, including Fisher and Billy Hughes, the president. (NBAC T62/63/2, K3833)

THE ARCHIVES

Andrew Fisher next to Billy Hughes with delegates to the Waterside Workers' Federation convention in 1912 (NBAC T62/63/2, K3833)

FRANK FORDE, 1945

Amalgamated Postal Workers' Union of Australia records

Government and Parliamentary members' correspondence files, 1920–1952

The APWUA and its predecessor before it was formed in 1926 represented postmen, sorters and linesmen employed by the Postmaster-General's Department. The files record its lobbying, advocacy and pursuit of redress, participation in inquiries, submissions on legislative amendments and negotiations for increased pay and improved entitlements and working conditions. It also campaigned as part of the Combined Federal Service Unions, and courtesy copies of its letters will also be found here. The Union corresponded with Forde as a backbencher (1928), leader of the opposition (1935), minister for the army (1942), deputy prime minister (1943), and as acting prime minister (1944, 1945) about such matters as adult male employees earning less than the basic wage, superannuation, the employment of military personnel for sorting mail and the establishment of special Military Postal Units, and wartime manpower regulations. Worthy of separate note are the papers on the 1929 inquiry into temporary employment in the Commonwealth public service. The Parliamentary Joint Committee of Public Accounts, which conducted the inquiry, took evidence from the Union's long-serving general secretary John V Dwyer. The file includes a copy of the report and a seven-page transcript of its questioning of Dwyer, which includes questions asked by Forde, a member of the inquiry. (NBAC T35/22/1, 13, 16, 35, 40–1)

Australian Dictionary of Biography files

Frank Forde, 2002–2006

The file provides the administrative background to the production of Malcolm Saunders and Neil Lloyd's 1,500-word entry on Forde published in volume 17 of the *Australian Dictionary of Biography* (Melbourne University Press, 2007), pp. 401–3. It includes letters and emails between the Dictionary staff and the authors, readers' comments, edited drafts, and a considerable quantity of background research material. Widely considered the third most powerful man in Australia during World War II, Forde was nevertheless a blip on the prime ministerial radar. His eight-day reign, squeezed between the giants Curtin and Chifley, is matched by the limited degree of interest offered by the file. The ADB liked the early draft they had commissioned with the exception of the authors' comment: 'An inveterate "joiner", in later life Forde was not one to decline invitations to the many functions he was asked to attend'. This it thought 'A bit snide & unworthy', wondering 'is this the strongest criticism to be made of Forde?' A further sidelight was the absence of a will, which after extensive commissioned research, the Dictionary concluded must have been retained by the Forde family. Only probated wills are on the public record, and as a result of Joh Bjelke-Petersen abolishing death duties in Queensland in 1977, there was no need for estates, particularly those with small assets or simply a family home, to be probated. (ANUA 312)

Institute of Public Affairs (Victoria) records

Correspondence files, 1944–1951

In late 1946, Forde was appointed Australia's High Commissioner to Canada. Here, in 1951 he assisted the IPA secretary C D Kemp on an overseas study tour, having been asked by Sir Hubert Gepp to arrange letters of introduction. The letters on file include several from Forde, and one dated 9 June 1951 from Kemp while still overseas reporting that 'Mr Forde was very good to us. Entertained us at lunch on

Sunday and his car drove us around Ottawa in the afternoon'. The details can be followed up in two of the Institute's files, one on the trip, the other of the director's correspondence, 1944–1951. (NBAC N136/21, 27)

MALCOLM FRASER, 1975–1983

Amalgamated Metal Workers' Union, National Office records

Subject Files: 'Various speeches, etc', 1974–1991

Includes a seven-page pamphlet published in September 1976 written by Lew Gibson entitled 'MILTON FRIEDMAN alias MALCOLM FRASER' and stating it was 'authorized by the National Research office of the Amalgamated Metal Workers' Union'. (NBAC Z102/990)

Heinz Arndt papers

Diary, 1980

'Diary of Round-the-World Trip with Malcolm Fraser' covering 30 August – 10 September 1980 is an eighteen-page typescript, accompanied by some off-prints of printed extracts from the diary. It represents a detailed insider account by Professor Heinz Arndt (at the time Head of the ANU's Department of Economics, Research School of Pacific Studies) of travelling with Fraser, together with Andrew Peacock, Geoffrey Yeend, Prime Minister's Department and Treasury officials, journalists such as Laurie Oakes, and Heather and Peter Henderson. It primarily relates to the Australian delegation headed by Fraser to the Commonwealth Heads of Government meeting in Delhi in 1980. Arndt explains at the beginning of the diary he had chaired an Expert Group whose report was on the agenda for the meeting. The diary is the subject of the story 'Heinz Arndt and Malcolm Fraser' in Chapter 3. (ANUA 80/13)

Australian Council of Trade Unions records

Subject Files: 'C'th Minister – Prime Minister', 1976–1979

Comprises press statements, ACTU union correspondence, extracts from Hansard, correspondence between Malcolm Fraser and ACTU secretaries Souter and Nolan and ACTU president Hawke on various issues which arose during 1976–1979.

There are also original signed letters from Fraser regarding, inter alia ACTU–Solo, wage restraint, construction of vessels for the Australian National Line, relocation of government departments, and the telecommunications industry. (NBAC N68/713)

Australian National University correspondence files

National Fellowships, 1980–1997

Though primarily about Gough Whitlam's selection in the early 1980s as the ANU's first National Fellow, the file shows Malcolm Fraser's name was also canvassed in the months following his loss to Bob Hawke in the March 1983 federal election. It includes memos from Department of Political Science head Professor Don Aitkin, who first raised the idea of an approach, from his director Professor Max Neutze, and notes by the Vice-Chancellor Peter Karmel. The need for policy consistency, the way things got done at the ANU and attitudes to Fraser are all on show. (ANUA 53/4.2.0.213)

Australian National University Council minutes

Minutes, 1964–1966

The minutes of 13 March 1964 record the attendance of Fraser at his first meeting as a member appointed on 3 March 1964. His resignation is noted in the minutes of 11 March 1966 'upon his appointment as Minister for the Army' on 26 January 1966. (ANUA 198/12)

Australian National University photographs

Envelopes of photographs of people and events, 1948–2005

Fraser was photographed on campus as minister for education and science at the opening of the Research School of Chemistry (ANUA 15/183, ANUA 225/83), the installation of Dr H C Coombs as Chancellor in September 1968 (ANUA 225/248, ANUA 226/221), and presenting a $10,000 contribution to the Florey Memorial Fund in September 1969 to Vice-Chancellor John Crawford (ANUA 225/405). There are also photographs of Fraser as prime minister at the 'Genesis of a Gallery' exhibition on campus in 1977 with protesting students waiting outside (ANUA 225/414, ANUA 226/303), with his wife Tamie and Dr Stephen FitzGerald on the Great Wall of China in 1976 (ANUA 225/414) and on the same occasion with John Shaw (ANUA 226/677). There are also photographs of Fraser and his 1980 Cabinet on the steps of Government House including John Howard and Peter Baume, later ANU Chancellor (ANUA 225/414).

Australian National University staff files

Professor Heinz Arndt, 1915–2002

Part 5 of this seven-part file complements the diary Arndt kept travelling overseas with Malcolm Fraser (30 August to 10 September 1980) while chairman of the Commonwealth Expert Group. Officially at the time Head of the Department of Economics, Research School of Pacific Studies, Arndt retired at the end of December 1980, having turned 65 in February. The file documents the process, begun in October 1979 by the Prime Minister's Department, to invite Arndt and in turn the steps he took to obtain approval within the university (involving Council and the Vice-Chancellor). A bonus for the researcher are the niceties and tensions which can arise in government–university relations thereby revealed. (ANUA 19/1922 parts 1–6 & C)

Wendy Brazil collection

Research files, 1980–1990

Accumulated by Brazil while a Research Officer with D J Hamer, Liberal Party Senator for Victoria 1980–1989, the files include a small 'subject file' folder on Malcolm Fraser, 1981–1986, comprising original and photocopied clippings. Most relate to press reaction to his speech at the launch of a book of his speeches in mid-1986. (NBAC Z372/23)

Colin Campbell collection

Transcripts and cassette tapes of interviews, 1988–2005

Transcripts and cassette tapes of interviews with Commonwealth public servants by Professor Colin Campbell, a political scientist from the University of British Columbia while based at the ANU. They were collected initially for a book with John Halligan, *Political Leadership in an Age of Constraint: Bureaucratic Politics under Hawke and Keating* (Allen and Unwin, 1992). Interviewees were senior officials who worked directly to Fraser, Hawke and Keating including Secretaries, Deputy Secretaries, First Assistant Secretaries and Prime Minister's Office chiefs: Tony Cole, Roger Holdich, Bernie Fraser, Pat Barrett, Andrew Podger, Chris Conybeare,

Peter Shergold, Ted Evans, Mike Codd, Dennis Richardson, Alan Rose, Pat Brazil, Allan Hawke and Max Moore-Wilton. Later interviews from 1994 to 2001 were conducted by Campbell to keep abreast of changes. (ANUA 316)

Federated Engine Drivers' and Firemen's Association of Australasia records

Photographs and posters, 1980–1982

In 1980 Fraser visited the construction site for the new Parliament House and was photographed being handed his OK card by a union official. The collection also includes a poster for the 1982 May Day parade 'Unite against Fraser'. (NBAC N72/706, 1775)

Goldsbrough Mort and Company Ltd records

Maps of pastoral properties, 1909–1957

Fraser records in his memoirs the sense of loss he felt when the family property 'Balpool–Nyang' near Moulamein on the Edward River in the New South Wales Riverina was sold while he was away at school. Two maps from the Goldsborough Mort collection relate to the subdivision of the original 'Nyang' station 'by the trustees of the late Sir Simon Fraser' in 1926. (NBAC 2/145/262; 2/859/116, D282)

Seamen's Union of Australia records

Cartoons, 1977–1981

Cartoons by Mick Gresham and Platton were used in the *Seamen's Journal* (S390) and include caricatures of Fraser particularly in relation to the Utah mining dispute. (NBAC N38/1079–80)

Waterside Workers' Federation records

Photographs, 1872–1992

This collection includes photographs of protests against Fraser such as the Labor Day protest in Brisbane in 1982. (NBAC Z432/86)

THE ARCHIVES

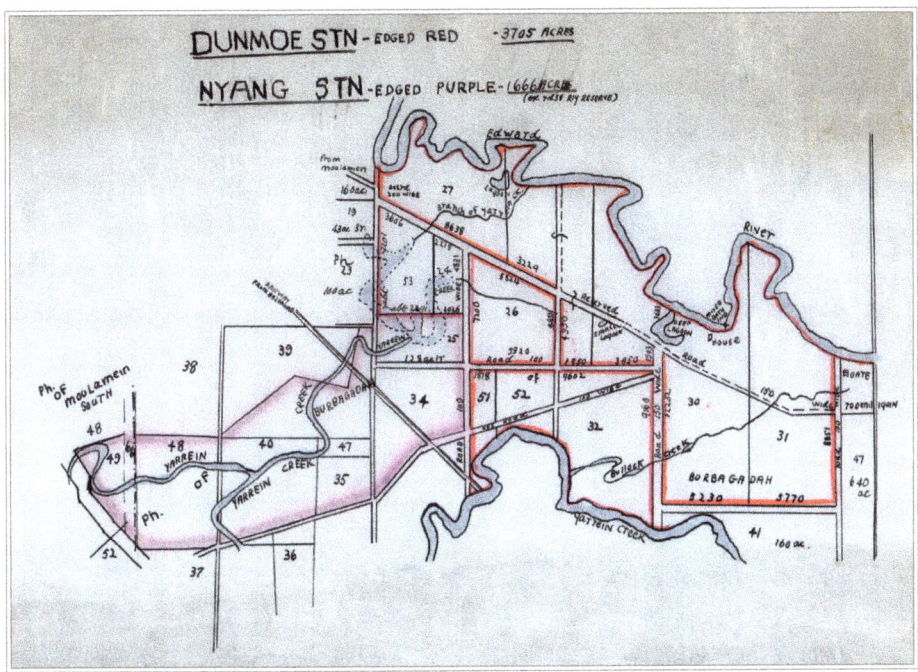

Malcolm Fraser's childhood home, Nyang Station, north-west of Deniliquin, NSW (NBAC 2/859/116, D282)

Serge Zorino collection

Publications, 1959–1985

Publications and other material used in anti-Fraser campaigns are found in the records of Federated Engine Drivers' and Firemen's Association union official Serge Zorino. (NBAC N177)

JULIA GILLARD, 2010–

Australian National University Students Association records

Woroni, 1983–1984

By 1983 Julia Gillard had moved from Adelaide to the University of Melbourne, and was incoming president of the Australian Union of Students. A number of the 1983 issues of the ANU students' newspaper *Woroni* published reports of AUS activities. They provide a view of the 1983 committee, including the president's speeches (e.g.

on 'Students and International Affairs', no. 11, p. 15) and activities (e.g. convincing Wollongong students not to leave the Union, no. 6, p. 21). Knowing all that happened next, the article 'A Left Alliance Report' written early the following year (1984, no. 2, p. 16) might also be highlighted:

> The dominant faction in AUS over the past few years has been the ALP leadership group which retains strong ties with the Socialist Left faction in the Victorian ALP.

A black and white photograph of Gillard on her election as president appears on page 3 of no. 1, 28 February 1983, underneath a caricature of Hawke and Fraser as Tweedledum and Tweedledee, accompanying an article on the federal election campaign. (ANUA 300)

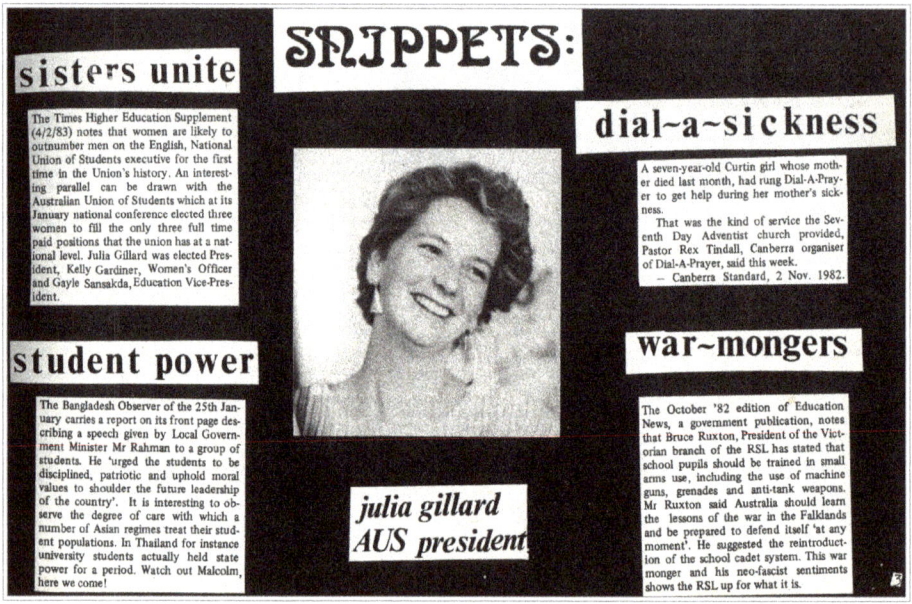

The ANU student newspaper *Woroni* reports Julia Gillard's election as president of the Australian Union of Students in the 28 February 1983 issue (ANUA 300)

JOHN GORTON, 1968–1971

Australian National University correspondence files

Registration for National Service, 1965–1972

Australia's involvement in the Vietnam War, conscription, anti-war protests and the ANU's relationship with the Holt, Gorton and McMahon governments form the backdrop to this multi-part file. Students were refusing to register for national service, those pursued by the authorities were finding sanctuary on campus, and funds were being collected for the National Liberation Front. The Vice-Chancellor at the time, Sir John Crawford, tried to maintain the university's independence, and the privacy of student information, but for a time faced proposed amendments to the *National Service Act* aimed at requiring the addresses of draft resisters to be supplied to the government. The file includes correspondence, press releases, newspaper clippings, telegrams and legal opinions. Inevitably, it includes references to McMahon who was minister for labour and national service and Fraser who was minister for education and science under Gorton, and to Holt and Gorton as well. (ANUA 53/4.0.0.22 parts 1–3 & C)

Australian National University Council minutes

Minutes of meetings, 1951–1954

In the minutes for the 1st meeting on 13 July 1951 it was noted that the Senate had elected John Gorton as one of its representatives on the new Council for a term of two years. The minutes for 27 June 1952 record his resignation on 5 June – the intervening minutes reveal that he had not attended any meetings of Council during his short term as a member. (ANUA 198/7)

Australian National University photographs

Envelopes of photographs of people and events, 1948–2005

Gorton was photographed as a new Council member at a dinner for the retiring Interim Council on 12 July 1951 at the Hotel Canberra, also attended by H F E Whitlam, Gough's father. At the installation of Howard Florey as Chancellor in 1966, Gorton represented Menzies and was photographed behind Florey in the academic procession. (ANUA 12/9; ANUA 15/2; ANUA 225/405)

John Gorton in the academic procession between Vice-Chancellor H C Coombs and the new Chancellor Howard Florey (ANUA 225/405/8)

Australian National University student files

Bettina Gorton, 1961–1983

Bettina Gorton's ANU student file incorporates her employment file and so documents her dual associations with the ANU. Both were decidedly part-time – her husband's ministerial duties, then accession in January 1968 to the prime ministership meant, as Gorton's biographer Ian Hancock wrote, that her own 'academic interests had to be placed on hold'. She was a part-time student, gaining a Bachelor of Arts (Asian Studies) in 1965, and undertook research supervised by Professor A H Johns on 'The life and times of Achdiat Karta Mihardja', qualifying to begin a Master of Arts in 1968. In 1970 she duly started a Master of Arts (Asian Studies), planning to undertake 'A study of the vocabulary prosody and style of Chairil Anwar'. From 1967 she worked as a part-time tutor and research assistant with a project to compile an English–Malay dictionary, and remained intermittently involved until it folded for lack of funding in 1977. The files contain correspondence, clippings, applications and other administrative papers. (ANUA 78/610079, 8258)

National Farmers' Federation records

Press releases, 1968–1970

As a national body whose aims including influencing government policies relating to farmers' interests, the Federation monitored statements issued by ministers on a broad range of economic, industrial, trade and other subjects. This thin file contains copies of five press releases issued while Gorton was prime minister. (NBAC Z135/17)

BOB HAWKE, 1983–1991

Australian Council of Trade Unions records

Basic Wage Case files, 1958–1959

Folders of papers documenting the 1959 case which sought an increase in the basic wage and restoration of quarterly adjustments. It was first led by Hawke, produced a favourable result for the union movement, and in some ways launched his industrial career. The main folder includes applications, ACTU publications, circulars, correspondence, telegrams, extracts of transcripts including a copy of Hawke's 28-page submission by 'R J Hawke, Research Office'. It also documents his use of witnesses such as Dr W E G Salter, Research Fellow in Economics, ANU and Eric Russell, Reader in Economics, Adelaide University. Hawke's impact on the union movement (and within the ACTU) is palpable in letters on file congratulating him on the result. This file is supported by related folders on the 1959 case, comprising exhibits, press clippings, statistics, employers' submissions, government reports and transcripts, a number with annotations in Hawke's hand. A further folder relates to the 1958 case and internal evidence suggests it was background for the 1959 case, and has manuscript notes possibly by Hawke. (NBAC N68/163–4; N21/2245–9A, 2251)

Basic Wage File, 1960

This is a folder of correspondence of the ACTU Basic Wage Committee, including position papers, correspondence of ACTU secretary Harold Souter (including copies of letters to Hawke) and press statements. Also includes a three-page manuscript titled '1960 Basic Wage Case – Interim report'. (NBAC N21/1013A)

Basic Wage Case files, 1961–1962, 1964

The ACTU records include files on several subsequent cases led by Hawke before he turned from research and advocacy to become its president in 1969, and include similar material to the earlier files. Two items may be separately noted. The first, the transcript from an application before the Commission in February 1962 to vary the basic wage, recorded Kirby, C J asking, 'Mr Hawke, have you any submissions to make?' Hawke replied, 'Your Honours, as hard as you may find this to believe, I wish to say very little. I have been instructed to make one or two brief submissions, which I think will take no more than five or ten minutes.' The second, concerning the 1964 Basic Wage case, includes a twelve-page document especially illustrative of Hawke's delivery style. It carries almost frenzied underlining, capitalisation and other prompts of emphasis. (NBAC N68/165; N21/2268)

ACTU Research Officer and Advocate, Bob Hawke (NBAC N68/1043)

Hawke's notes relating to the 1964 Basic Wage case (NBAC N21/2268)

Bourkes – List of Shop Stewards, 1971

The folder includes press statements, agreements, lists of shop stewards' names (for distribution of material about the store), copies of letters to suppliers from Hawke (then ACTU president) and Harold Souter (ACTU secretary) as directors of Bourke's Melbourne Pty Ltd and copies of letters by Souter to another director, Lionel Revelman. (NBAC N21/1022)

Correspondence files, Bob Hawke, ACTU President, 1971–1973

Letters, mostly handwritten, to Hawke as ACTU president (together with a few addressed to him as ALP president), half with attached copies of replies, and some carrying brief annotations by staff suggesting the nature of the reply. They cover a wide range of purposes including requesting help, financial advice, talks and settlement of outstanding bills; offering congratulations, birthday or Christmas greetings; making policy proposals and urging action on public issues (e.g. French nuclear testing, Israel and Lake Pedder); informing him what is happening in particular unions; and commenting on his television appearances. There is also a fine sampling of 'crank' letters. Correspondents include unionists, ALP members, pensioners, people Hawke had met, students, representatives of organisations and ministers of the Whitlam government who had taken action following Hawke's representations. (NBAC N68/1059–64)

Correspondence re the 1960 Basic Wage Case, 1960

The folder of Hawke's correspondence maintained while the ACTU's Research Officer and Advocate mostly refers to technical matters arising from the 1959 case. (NBAC N21/1013)

Maritime/waterfront dispute file, 1998

The ACTU supported the Maritime Union of Australia over the 1998 waterfront dispute, and drew on help from the ALP opposition, legal advisers and from Bob Hawke relating to industrial policy matters from his time as prime minister. Included among one of assistant secretary Greg Combet's files, largely faxes and press releases, are copies of papers sent to Hawke's office in April 1998, and references to other information 'provided to Bob'. (NBAC N160/9)

Photographs, 1960–1989

The publicity officer's records include many photographs of Hawke in his career as research officer and advocate, and then as president of the ACTU. He is photographed with Gough Whitlam, Sir John Moore, Sir Richard Kirby and trade union officials at the dinner celebrating the 50th anniversary of the ACTU on 3 May 1977. Hazel Hawke and Margaret Whitlam are also present. He is photographed in portrait shots, at various ACTU Congresses with union officials, at meetings and conferences, in his office, walking off a cricket field and on a tennis court with Hazel Hawke. (NBAC N68/956–1030, 1033–46, 1055; Z282A/448–50)

Recordings of ACTU Congresses, 1961–1992
Hawke's addresses to the ACTU Congresses in 1977 and 1979 were recorded as well as others such as that to the ACTU conference on manufacturing industry in April 1978. (NBAC Z282A/700–2)

Subject Files: 'C'th Minister – Prime Minister', 1976–1979
Comprises press statements, ACTU union correspondence, extracts from Hansard, correspondence between Malcolm Fraser and ACTU secretaries Souter and Nolan and ACTU president Hawke on various issues which arose during 1976–1979. (NBAC N68/713)

Subject Files: Hawke, R J, 1973–1976
The file of photocopies of clippings about Hawke includes an undated eighteen-page paper entitled 'Job Status and Income – R J Hawke'. (NBAC N21/2632)

Australian National University correspondence files

John Curtin Memorial Lectures, 1970–1984
This file documents the establishment and administration of the lecture program. The printed copies on the file include the fourth lecture by Hawke in 1973 entitled 'The Economic Policies of Curtin and Beyond' and a copy of the press release. (ANUA 53/10.02.2.47 parts 1–2)

Australian National University Council minutes

Minutes of meetings, 1955–1957, 1979
At its 29th meeting on 6 July 1956, the University Council minute taker noted Hawke's attendance as one of two new student representatives. He diligently attended the next four meetings. At the 34th meeting on 15 March 1957, however, the minutes record under 'Membership' and without elaboration, that 'it was resolved to accept Mr Hawke's resignation from the Council as from 15th March, 1957'. At its 161st meeting, on 2 February 1979, a month short of twenty-two

years after it had effectively removed Hawke from Council, it recorded that 'it was resolved to appoint Robert James Lee Hawke, AC, as a co-opted member of Council for a term of two years from 2 February 1979'. He had just completed five years as ALP president, was still ACTU president, and less than a year away from entering parliament. That year he also suffered a physical collapse. Understandably then, the pattern of attendance at Council was erratic. Thus the minutes show that following appointment, he was an apology on 9 March and then an attendee on 11 May. (ANUA 198/8, 23)

Draft minutes of Council and its committees, 1953–1977

The minutes include at pp. 64–74 the proceedings of what the minute taker termed '(Informal) Disciplinary Ctee'. An ad hoc committee of the most senior university men, it was chaired by the Vice-Chancellor to investigate an incident which occurred at University House late Sunday night 24 February 1957 and early the following morning. It met twice in the following fortnight, and took evidence from many involved, with Hawke's role being pieced together from his own and others' testimony. He was fined, banned from University House for six months and pressured into resigning as a student representative on Council, as related in Chapter 3, 'Bob Hawke and University House'. (ANUA 34/2)

Australian National University History Project records

Transcripts and tapes, 1990–1995

In 1990 Daniel Connell conducted an interview with the former Dean of Law Professor Geoffrey Sawer for the University's official history project. The project came to fruition in 1996 under Stephen Foster and Margaret Varghese's names as *The Making of the Australian National University 1946–1996*. As Hawke's doctoral supervisor, Sawer was naturally asked about the future prime minister. He commented with disarming frankness about the University House incident ('He was drunk of course, and he was quite frequently drunk'), his research ('He ... worked like hell ... and would undoubtedly eventually have turned in a quite satisfactory thesis if he'd persisted with it') and his decision to drop his research ('I strongly advised him to take this Trades Hall job because that was the family-dictated alternative, and as I hoped ... it would straighten him up.'). (ANUA 44/6, pp. 100–1)

Australian National University photographs

Envelopes of photographs of people and events, 1948–2005

As a regular visitor to the ANU Bob Hawke was photographed many times on campus. The earliest is from 1973 when he delivered the John Curtin Lecture as ACTU president. As prime minister, he addressed the 50th anniversary conference of the Australian Institute of International Affairs in 1983 and the ANZAAS congress in 1984. He launched the ANU Bicentennial project, the *Encyclopaedia of the Australian People*, in 1988 and volume 12 of the *Australian Dictionary of Biography* in 1990. In 1991, he was photographed with Chifley's pipe – the wood had been tested by the ANU Department of Forestry, and he opened the Research School of Biological Sciences Co-operative Research Centre in Plant Science. He delivered an address at a conferring of degrees in 1992 (ANUA 225/526). Hawke opened the Department of Astronomy's 2.3m telescope at Siding Spring in May 1984 (ANUA 226/788) and the J G Crawford Building, where there was a large student protest, in September 1986 (ANUA 226/414). He turned the first sod for the Australian Science and Technology Centre (which had developed from the ANU's Questacon) in May 1986 and presented the federal government's contribution to the Centre in March 1987 (ANUA 226/127). Hawke was also photographed with ANU academic Ross Garnaut, then Australian Ambassador to China, with a Chinese delegation on a visit to the Pilbara in 1985 and on a visit to the United States in 1985 (ANUA 225/432). Geoff Pryor, the *Canberra Times* cartoonist, was photographed drawing a caricature of Hawke at Orientation Week in 1985 (ANUA 226/339). There are also photographs of Hazel Hawke, then wife of the prime minister, addressing the ANU Club for Women in 1984, presenting certificates to students at the Communications and Study Skills Unit in 1989 and launching a Greening Australia publication in 1991 (ANUA 225/525 and ANUA 226/375, 382).

Australian National University student files

Bob Hawke, 1955–1960

These files concern Hawke's application for consideration for an ANU Research Scholarship, his application for a part-time lecturer's position in Introduction to Legal Method, and the 1957 University House incident. The first incorporates the original of Hawke's 1955 scholarship application sent from Oxford and supporting references from Professor K C Wheare at All Souls, E T Williams, the Warden of Rhodes House, and Professor F R Beasley, University of Western Australia Law School Dean. All of the references were unqualified: 'a really first class man'

(Wheare), 'plenty of common sense' and 'has great energy' (Williams), and 'lively and penetrating mind' (Beasley). Williams had added: 'I can recommend him without compunction. Personally, too, I like him', while Beasley's ended 'he will do work that will bring credit not only to him but to the University as well'. Later papers show, for instance, his request for an increased endowment when his first child was born and for extensions of the scholarship and thesis in 1958 and 1959 including a strong and revealing statement of support from Professor Sawer (e.g. letter of 6 August 1959). On the bid for a lectureship, there is correspondence between panel members Professor Herbert Burton, J Q Ewens and Professor J G Fleming, who agreed subject to the University of Melbourne's agreement to appoint Hawke for the 2nd and 3rd terms of 1956. Related papers cover his remuneration per lecture. Finally, there is the disciplinary matter, the subject of one of the Chapter 3 stories, 'Bob Hawke and University House'. The files include correspondence between Hawke and the University (the Registrar, the Vice-Chancellor and the Law Dean), and the University and University House (the Master) which allow us to reconstruct the aftermath of the incident. They include for instance the official letter to Hawke from the Registrar dated 27 February 1957, reporting the disciplinary committee's conclusions, including its opinion 'that your representation of students on the Council was no longer appropriate but must leave this matter to your discretion'. (ANUA 78/9.4.1.40 & C, 17.5.1.40)

Wendy Brazil collection

Subject files on Bob Hawke, 1980–1989

Part of a collection of research files from the office of Senator D J Hamer, these eight files include press clippings, press releases by and about Hawke and by Andrew Peacock and John Howard about Hawke, copies of the Liberal Party's *Current Political Notes*, a copy of Hawke's September 1973 John Curtin Memorial Lecture, press conference transcripts and extracts from Hansard. (NBAC Z372/23)

Colin Campbell collection

Transcripts and cassette tapes of interviews, 1988–2005

The collection comprises transcripts and cassettes of interviews conducted by Professor Colin Campbell, a Canadian academic based at the ANU, for a book with John Halligan, subsequently published by Allen and Unwin in 1992, titled *Political Leadership in an Age of Constraint: Bureaucratic Politics under Hawke and Keating*. The interviewees were senior officers in key departments such as Prime Minister and Cabinet, Treasury and Finance, many of whom describe working while Hawke was prime minister, and refer to his style of operation and decision-making. Later interviews from 1994 to 2001 were conducted by Campbell to keep abreast of changes. (ANUA 316)

CSR Limited records

Photographs, 1974–1985
Hawke is photographed at a CSR luncheon with Japanese executives in Melbourne in September 1985. (NBAC Z638/2815–17)

Jack Dwyer collection

Transcripts of speeches, 1970s
Jack Dwyer was a union delegate and official for the Federated Miscellaneous Workers' Union from the early 1940s until the mid-1970s. His collection of papers includes transcripts of speeches by Hawke as ACTU president and on Israel and the Middle East from the 1970s. (Z296/15–16)

Michael Easson papers

Subject file on R J L Hawke, 1972–1993
Comprises printed policy speeches as prime minister, transcripts of speeches, media interviews as ACTU president and as prime minister, and a November 1993 letter from Easson to Hawke. Also present is Peter Ryan's 'Is Bob Hawke a Curtin or a Hughes?' from the *Age* of 28 September 1987 and the uncorrected text of a speech Hawke gave on 24 August 1992 at the launch of Susanna Short's *Laurie Short: A Political Life*, clearly a vintage performance. At one point, recalling Colin Clark's rejection of his thesis topic when at Oxford, Hawke referred to the 'pernicious, more peasant doctrines pursued by Santamaria and Colin Clark'. (NBAC Z514/134)

ALP Victorian Branch, 1965–1984
This dossier-like folder of papers comprises correspondence, newspaper clippings, Labor Unity how-to-vote sheets, factional newsletters (*Spotlight* and *Socialist Objective*), and Easson's handwritten notes analysing unions and factional alignments. They convey a sense of the context in which Hawke rose to and held power within the labour movement, but also include more specific items such as material sent to Easson by Michael Danby (on the personal staff of Hawke minister Barry Cohen).

On a Clyde Holding electorate newsletter, Danby wrote: 'I was surprised that even Clyde would circulate this emotional claptrap (see attacks on Hawke pp. 15–17)'. (NBAC Z514/35)

ALP Victorian Branch, 1970–1985

The file covers the power plays of factions (the Participants, Labor Unity, Socialist Left, Centre Unity, and Centre Majority) within the Victorian ALP and union movement. It thus helps document the context to Hawke's battles as ACTU president and his entry into parliament and then The Lodge, a journey perhaps best summarised by an article in the file by Richard Farmer in the *Bulletin* of 28 February 1984 titled 'Hawke's power play: Crush the Victorian Left'. Subjects covered include the Combe/Ivanov Royal Commission, anti-uranium campaigns, re-affiliation of unions with the ALP, the Landeryou affair and ALP committee reports. In part accumulated from material sent to Easson by David Cragg from Senator Ray's office, it comprises letters, newspaper clippings, photocopies of journal articles, leaflets, circular letters, policy discussion papers and how-to-vote cards. (NBAC Z514/34)

Charlie Fitzgibbon papers

Unpublished autobiography

A legendary senior official of the ALP state and federal committees, the ACTU and the Waterside Workers' Federation, Charlie Fitzgibbon was described in an obituary as 'a key figure behind Bob Hawke's rise to power' (*Sydney Morning Herald*, 10 March 2001). His autobiography, a 324-page slightly annotated typescript, is not dated but from internal evidence was clearly prepared after Fitzgibbon received his AO in 1984. It includes numerous references to Hawke, such as the following: 'Bob decided to move the Executive proposition himself. It was the worst contribution he had ever made to that point of time in an ACTU Congress. The fact that he was right in what he was saying was secondary to the style of presentation which was combative and argumentative' (p. 265). The autobiography was never published, although shorter reminiscences are available as Fitzgibbon was interviewed in 1986 for a joint National Library and Labor Council of New South Wales oral history project. He was also consulted by Blanche d'Alpuget for her 1983 Hawke biography and many of her stories are complemented at length by the typescript autobiography. Thus her hilarious account of Hawke in 1973 suborning Fitzgibbon to stand for ACTU executive vice-president during a session with a bottle of Greek brandy is expanded on at pp. 197–8, the account ending: 'It seemed to be painless while we were drinking but I had an awful headache the next day and I had reluctantly agreed. Bob had thought then that it could be easily achieved. Maybe that was the Metaxas too.' (NBAC P102/91)

Audrey Johnson papers

Photographs, 1920s–1970s

Johnson was writing a biography of Tom Wright, federal secretary of the Sheet Metal Working Agricultural Implement and Stove Making Industrial Union of Australia, at the time of her death. Her papers include a photograph of Hawke with Tom Wright in the 1970s. (NBAC N162/196)

D A Low papers

Correspondence and reports, 1983

Includes a copy of a letter to Hawke on 22 March 1983 from Vice-Chancellor Anthony Low who congratulates him 'on your striking electoral victory and an excellent start'. It refers to Hawke's recent comments on the need to improve relations with Indonesia and urges action on the stalled Australian-funded Australian Studies Program at the University of Indonesia, Jakarta. (ANUA 55/128)

National Farmers' Federation records

Photographs, 1983–1990

This collection includes an envelope of photographs of Hawke as prime minister, both portrait shots and photographs of him addressing a National Farmers' Federation conference in November 1989. One photograph of Hazel Hawke is included. (NBAC N143/439)

Mark Oliphant papers

Correspondence files, 1949–1969

The files of Professor Sir Mark Oliphant, Deputy Master of University House and Director, Research School of Physical Sciences include some of the most important correspondence and related papers on the incident at University House in February 1957 involving Bob Hawke, arising from the fact that Oliphant was acting Master at the time. The correspondence includes communications with the Master Professor Trendall and captures the flavour of concerns, anxieties and rules surrounding the aftermath. (ANUA 10/82)

Sheet Metal Working Agricultural Implement and Stove Making Industrial Union records

Photographs, 1967–1969

In this collection of Tom Wright, NSW secretary and federal president of the Sheet Metal Working Agricultural Implement and Stove Making Industrial Union of Australia, Hawke is photographed with Tom Wright and others at a union dinner in December 1969. (NBAC E206/47, K2940)

University House records

Annual folders of papers, 1949–1975

The 1957 file in this collection documents the first University House Master's involvement in the aftermath of the incident of February 1957 including Hawke which led to disciplinary action against six students and a six-month ban on Hawke's visiting the House. Also includes correspondence between the University and the House concerning Hawke's request that the ban be lifted, including originals from Hawke himself. (ANUA 359/1957)

Governing Body minutes, 1953–1959

Includes minutes of a special meeting 1957/1 of 13 March 1957 at which two of Hawke's fellow revellers who were residents of the House were for 'misconduct ... on the night of February 24th, and on a number of occasions' banned from the House for the first term of 1957. Also includes minutes of meetings numbers 1957/7 (29 August) and 1957/8 (26 September) addressing the lifting of bans on various students, the September meeting minutes stating: 'It was decided to re-admit Mr R J L Hawke to Membership of the House.' (ANUA 207/1)

Jill Waterhouse papers

Research material for University House history, 2002–2005

Includes files on key figures from the 1957 incident involving Bob Hawke, such as Sir Mark Oliphant and Professor Ralph Elliott both of whom referred to it in subsequent addresses quoted by Waterhouse. The files also cover Francis West's earlier history, *University House: Portrait of an Institution* (1980), which in turn made guarded references to the incident. (ANUA 235/1–2)

HAROLD HOLT, 1966–1967

Australian Dictionary of Biography files

Harold Holt, 1992–1997

Holt's 4,000-word entry by Ian Hancock appeared at pp. 474–80 of volume 14 of the Dictionary. The file tells of its commissioning and editing, and follows the standard sequence of documentation, the first half comprising the notes, photocopies and other research material assembled by ADB office staff in preparation for the biographer. These include more than the usual number of birth, marriage and death certificates, given Dame Zara Holt's previous marriage and the circumstances of his death. The negotiation of changes to various drafts, for example their references to Holt's neighbour at Portsea Margaret Gillespie, are a feature of the file, perhaps explaining general editor John Ritchie's view as recorded on a file note of 11 September 1995 that the result was: 'One of the finest articles in Vol. 14'. (ANUA 312)

Zara Holt, 2001–2006

The file refers to the preparation, drafting and publication of a 760-word entry on Dame Zara Holt which appeared at pp. 546–7 of volume 17 of the Dictionary. Initially to be written by ADB editor Di Langmore, it was passed to Pennie Pemberton who in 2001–2002 was researching a comprehensive guide to sources on Harold Holt for the National Archives. Included here is a predictable sequence of documentation, the strongest concentration being photocopies of newspaper clippings and certificates recording Zara Holt's three marriages. The Dictionary could barely fault Pemberton's draft, John Ritchie writing in a 2003 file note: 'Impressive. She (subject and author) deserves more than 500.' Not for the first time, however, alluding to paternity required care. One reader noticed a logical inconsistency in the first draft reference to the then Mrs James Fell's visits from India back to Melbourne in the late 1930s. This was reworked to ensure the technical possibility of her second and third (twin) children being, as was finally published, 'probably Holt's sons'. (ANUA 312)

Australian National University correspondence files

Registration for National Service, 1965–1972

Australia's involvement in the Vietnam War, conscription, anti-war protests and the ANU's relationship with the Holt, Gorton and McMahon governments form the backdrop to this multi-part file. Students were refusing to register for national service, those pursued by the authorities were finding sanctuary on campus, and funds were being collected for the National Liberation Front. The Vice-Chancellor at the time, Sir John Crawford, tried to maintain the university's independence, and the privacy of student information, but for a time faced proposed amendments to the *National Service Act* aimed at requiring the addresses of draft resisters to be supplied to the government. The file includes correspondence, press releases, newspaper clippings, telegrams and legal opinions. Inevitably, it includes references to McMahon who was minister for labour and national service and Fraser who was minister for education and science under Gorton, and to Holt and Gorton as well. (ANUA 53/4.0.0.22 parts 1–3 & C)

Institute of Public Affairs (Victoria) records

Minutes of the Industrial Committee, IPA–Vic, 1944–1947

Though not in any formal sense affiliated, the Institute and the Liberal Party were a natural fit, both establishing their organisation and policy in the mid-1940s. In Holt's case, he was also well acquainted with Geoffrey Grimwade, an Institute founder and chair of its Industrial Committee, and used the Institute as a congenial forerunner to the Parliamentary Library research service. As noted in Chapter 3 ('The IPA and three Liberal PMs') and as these minutes vouch, Holt received briefings on current issues. There was for instance a paper on Bretton Woods (prepared by G R Mountain, a member of the *IPA Review* editorial committee and an 'official at National Bank'), and the loan of files of newspaper clippings (e.g. on the exchange rate). In turn the IPA sought Holt's comments on the draft of the first issue of the *IPA Review*. (NBAC N136/1)

Waterside Workers' Federation records

Photographs, 1947–1966

This collection includes photographs of protests against Holt in the mid-1960s, including placards reading 'Cost of Living Up, Down Holt' and 'Halt Holt in '66', and a Holt impersonator in diving gear, accompanied by a WWF member dressed as the US president, Lyndon Baines Johnson. (NBAC Z248/81–2)

A Harold Holt impersonator in the 1966 May Day parade in Sydney (NBAC Z248/81)

…and wharfie Owen Devitt as LBJ (NBAC Z248/81)

JOHN HOWARD, 1996–2007

Australian Council of Trade Unions records

Maritime/waterfront dispute files, 1997–2000

The first Howard government was determined to change industrial relations to reduce the role of arbitration and union-coordinated collective bargaining in favour of individual workplace agreements, famously coming to a head within the stevedoring industry in 1998. After Patrick Stevedores sacked its unionised workers and became insolvent, the ACTU became directly involved, successfully challenging Patricks in a series of court battles. The ACTU's files on the dispute present significant context to a dispute which helped define Howard's reputation and standing as a prime minister. Relevant files, while scattered through the record series, collectively provide evidence of the ACTU's growing involvement as the dispute developed, and in particular the work of its assistant secretary Greg Combet. They include affidavits, court exhibits, correspondence, newspaper clippings, media transcripts, faxes, press releases, legal and financial papers and copies of leaked documents including a 1997 letter from Howard to John Sharp, minister for transport and regional development. (NBAC N160/7–15)

Australian National University photographs

Envelopes of photographs of people and events, 1948–2005

John Howard was photographed on campus after delivering the inaugural Joe and Enid Lyons Lecture in September 1986 for the ANU Liberal Club, at the launch of the opposition's higher education policy, with protesting students in 1987 and at the opening of the Sir Roland Wilson Building in August 1999. (ANUA 225/582; ANUA 226/259, 313, 867)

John Howard with ANU Liberal Club students after presenting the Joe and Enid Lyons lecture in 1986 (ANUA 225/313/1)

Australian Society for the Study of Labour History, Melbourne Branch collection

1998 Maritime Dispute archive, 1960–2000

In 2005, Peter Reith told Paul Kelly for his *The March of Patriots* (Melbourne University Press, 2009), 'Margaret Thatcher's test came with the miners and with Wapping. Ronald Reagan's came with the air traffic controllers. John Howard's came with the waterfront'. The dispute set the scene for the October 1998 federal election and, wrote Kelly, was a dry run for 'the great showdown of 2005 over WorkChoices' (pp. 387–8). The Maritime Dispute archive thus provides invaluable background for students of Howard. It was the initiative of a group of Melbourne-based archivists and labour historians anxious to preserve material relating to the dispute while it was still available and memories of the dispute still current. It was adopted by the ASSLH and also drew support from the ACTU, the Victorian Trades Hall Council and the University of Melbourne Archives. Totalling over three metres of material, it includes copies or duplicates of publicity material, press cuttings, leaflets, ephemera, reports, union circulars, artefacts, and items of or collected by individuals such as parliamentarian Lindsay Tanner, historian Dr Peter Love and Mark Davis, an *Australian Financial Review* journalist. (NBAC Z592)

Jon Belmonte papers

Documents relating to the 1998 maritime dispute, 1997–1998

Belmonte was employed by Fynwest as a crane driver to work overseas under a three-year contract. He worked in Dubai, during December 1997 – February 1998, and on return was transferred to PCS Training Services under an Australian Workplace Agreement. This small record series adds to the contextual background of one of the issues which dominated Howard's first term as prime minister. It covers Belmonte's journey from enthusiastic employee, including 'Strictly Private & Confidential' contract details and letters concerning his training, through to disillusionment in the form of a letter of 16 June 1998 effectively sacking him from PCS Resources Pty Ltd, including an offer of $20k to keep the details confidential. (NBAC N183)

Wendy Brazil collection

Subject file on John Howard, 1984–1989

Part of a collection of research files from the office of Senator D J Hamer, this large subject file has clippings, media summaries, copies of addresses when Howard was leader of the opposition, Hansards and transcripts of media interviews. Interestingly, it includes a newspaper item reporting 'Howard's File on Keating' from the *Age* of 25 May 1986 which quotes from the list found in Brazil's 'Keating' file. (NBAC Z372/26)

BILLY HUGHES, 1915–1923

Adelaide Steamship Company Ltd records

Minutes of Directors meetings, 1920–1921

The minutes for the meeting of 14 September 1920 indicate earlier that month the company received a circular request from the Australasian Steamship Owners' Federation headed 'Proposed Testimonial to the Right Honourable W M Hughes'. No follow-up action or an amount donated is recorded, though we learn from his biographer Fitzhardinge that in late November 1920 a cheque for £25,000 raised from public and private sources in Australia and the UK was presented, a substantial proportion coming from 'the big business interests with which Hughes had been in contact during the war'. (NBAC Z535/16)

Amalgamated Postal Workers' Union of Australia records

Government and Parliamentary members' correspondence files, 1920–1952

The records of the APWUA show it lobbied Hughes on several occasions in support of its members (postmen, sorters and linesmen employed by the Postmaster-General's Department). He was approached as a member of the Bruce–Page government over the Commonwealth Employees Compensation Bill in June 1928, telling them that he was 'glad to do what I can along the lines suggested by your Union'. An earlier file on the public service arbitration system documents a meeting in Sydney on 12 July 1939 between the Combined Federal Service Unions (which included the APWUA) and Hughes, attorney-general in the Menzies government, regarding delays in hearing of claims by the public service arbitrator. The transcript shows Hughes as enigmatic as ever:

> Mr Dwyer: In our note to you about this interview, we mentioned that we raised the question of 40-hour week with Mr Menzies. Would you prefer that we took that up with the Prime Minister?
>
> Attorney-General: I should prefer that you took it up with anybody rather than with me. It is one of these things when if you do one thing, you wish you had done the other. (NBAC T35/22/5, 13)

Australian Dictionary of Biography files

William Morris Hughes, 1964, 1980–2007

The file concerns the commissioning and production of Laurie Fitzhardinge's 6,000-word biography of Hughes published in the *Australian Dictionary of Biography*, volume 9, Melbourne University Press, 1983, pp. 393–400. Like most ADB files, the Hughes file combines predictable papers, such as results of the prepared research of the ADB staff and evidence of the interaction between the editorial staff and the author, and some unexpected gems peculiar to this subject and author, starting with the choice of author. It shows that on 3 September 1980 the general editor Geoffrey Serle wrote to Fitzhardinge:

> It is quite a problem of policy as to whether we should invite the existing biographer or give someone else a go. It depends on several things: e.g. whether the existing biographer has revised his views to any extent, whether there are other worthwhile chaps eager to have a go, etc. (Actually both Bede and I would quite like to have a go, though we have enough on our hands.) John La Nauze refused Deakin and, though Norris has done very well, we wonder how happy John is with the result. In short, we consider we should offer it to you (rather than to Donald Horne!!).

The 'usual suspect' papers include original newspaper articles (1950s+), reviews of books on Hughes (e.g. by Donald Horne and W Farmer Whyte), copies of index cards (e.g. the *Melbourne Herald* and the *Sydney Morning Herald*), and copies of the will and birth certificate (the official government statist advice indicating that there was nothing held for Hughes' first marriage). The earliest papers comprise 1964 correspondence between the retired war historian Gavin Long (then at the ANU) with the National Capital Development Commission about the proposal of the National Memorials Committee to build 'small memorials in the suburbs in the Yarralumla valley' to commemorate prime ministers: 'The first of these, at Hughes [being] under construction'. Though Fitzhardinge was the acknowledged authority on Hughes, Fitzhardinge's draft did not go uncriticised, one report commissioned by the ADB in 1982 noting that it was:

> Very good though too restrained. There was a nasty side to Hughes which appears in the final summary but elsewhere does not feature. It showed up in his relations with his children as well as with his political enemies. Is there room for more of the famous anecdotes? I thought he only 'married' once?

This last question had dogged the biography too, and the file includes notes between the editorial staff deciding they had 'better leave things in their present vague state'. (ANUA 312)

Australian National University Advisers on Legislation minutes

Minutes of meetings, 1951–1958

The minutes for agenda item 11 of the meeting of 26 August 1953, Biography of Mr W M Hughes, note that the Executor for Hughes' estate had made his papers available to the ANU and had asked for an undertaking it would submit the draft to its legal advisers before publication to check whether defamation liability existed. The Advisers agreed to this, but only so Perpetual Trustees could take advice. (ANUA 200/1)

Australian National University correspondence files

Biography of W M Hughes, 1952–1973

Through memos, correspondence, file notes and opinions, the file documents the ANU's relationship with Hughes, Dame Mary and her legal representatives, the Perpetual Trustees, concerning the commissioning, funding, progress and vetting of Hughes' biography. Naturally discussions about all these within the University are well covered too, the Vice-Chancellors Copland and Melville, senior officials (e.g. R A Hohnen) and advisers (e.g. Professor Geoffrey Sawer) and Fitzhardinge himself each having a strong presence in the file. Several subplots are also revealed, including disagreement within the Hughes family about contributing to the ANU's costs, disagreement within the ANU about submitting the draft for vetting, and Sir Harold White's efforts to secure the Hughes papers and favourable access for the National Library. See also Chapter 3, 'L F Fitzhardinge and W M Hughes'. (ANUA 53/9.1.5.2)

Australian National University Council minutes

Minutes of meetings, 1951–1954

The minutes record reports provided at meetings of 9 October, 27 November and 18 December 1953 of arrangements between the ANU and Hughes' executors for L F Fitzhardinge to write Hughes' biography. Council was informed the executors 'had been furnished with an undertaking that the manuscript ... would be submitted before publication to allow the Executors to take advice on their possible legal liability for publication'. (ANUA 198/7)

Australian National University History Project records

Transcripts and tapes, 1990–1995

Stephen Foster interviewed L F Fitzhardinge on 5 August 1992 as part of the University's official history project, which came to fruition in 1996 under his and Margaret Varghese's names as *The Making of the Australian National University 1946–1996*. As noted in Chapter 3, Fitzhardinge's recollection of how he was 'lumbered with Billy' makes hilarious reading even granted inevitable bias and a fading memory. (ANUA 44/26)

THE ARCHIVES

Australian National University staff files

L F Fitzhardinge, 1934–1993

Documents the administrative details of Fitzhardinge's employment as an ANU academic (first as a Reader in Sources of Australian History, later Reader in Australian History and then a Professorial Fellow), including the various management issues relating to the production of the Hughes biography. Documented here are discussions with and about Fitzhardinge involving senior Chancelry officials, Vice-Chancellors, Sir Keith Hancock, Professor John La Nauze and others about progress with the biography, Fitzhardinge's overseas trips to undertake further research, use of the 'Hughes Fund', and the various factors such as access to Hughes-related material overseas and becoming available from the Commonwealth Archives Office which help explain the slow progress. (ANUA 19/9.2.2.4 & C)

Australian Workers' Union, Sydney Branch records

The Australian Worker, 1903–1975

The weekly newspaper of the Australian Workers' Union, the *Australian Worker*, features many articles about and caricatures of Hughes during his prime ministership, particularly relating to the conscription debate as related in Chapter 3, 'Hughes and conscription'. (NBAC S100)

Burns, Philp and Company Ltd records

Files regarding post World War One settlement of German New Guinea, 1915–1919

Burns, Philp and Company were plantation owners, merchants, traders, and shipping and travel agents with considerable interests in the south Pacific. In the aftermath of World War One Hughes' interests were aimed at ensuring Germany's former colonies were developed while remaining within Australia's responsibility. The extent to which these interests overlapped can be seen in letters, reports and telegrams to Sir James Burns, and his correspondence with BP managers, the acting prime minister W A Watt, government officials such as Prime Minister's Department secretary Malcolm Shepherd, and with Hughes himself. One such report, to Burns from his London Manager A K Mackintosh dated 28 May 1919, is instructive. It refers to a meeting with Hughes to discuss ideas for the creation of a company to foster the post-war development of 'the islands'. Hughes had apparently wanted such an entity to be formed privately, with the Commonwealth retaining 'a small interest'. According to Mackintosh:

> The reason for the Commonwealth desiring some interest is to be able to give the lie to any statement which might be made that the Government had given a monopoly of this trading over to such a Company as BP & Co. by stating the Government had an interest in the Company.

Told this would be seen as government interference, Mackintosh quoted Hughes saying:

> You know I am a Socialist and have been all my life and believe in Socialistic trading, but I am not foolish and unless Socialistic trading makes for profits it must be cut out. (NBAC N115/3)

Colonial Sugar Refining Company Ltd records

Subject files, 1912–1920

Included are files of papers, known as document sets within the company's file management system, covering its specific and more generic relationship to Hughes as follows: set 3 comprising mostly clippings from 1912 regarding Hughes' 1911 Referendum Bill relating to Corporations, sets 8 and 9 comprising notes of meetings between the Company's general manager E W Knox and Hughes, as well as telegrams, copies of letters from Hughes and agreements concerning the takeover of the Australian sugar industry in 1915, and set 17 which concerned the Company's donation of £100 in 1920 to a Hughes testimonial fund. (NBAC Z303/11)

Elder Smith and Company Ltd records

Walter J Young correspondence files, 1915–1917

The National Archives' prime ministers website tells us that: 'In an audacious coup, Hughes circumvented British wartime controls on shipping by secretly purchasing fifteen cargo vessels on behalf of the Australian government. These ships were to convey Australia's wheat and other commodities to British markets, and became the foundation of the Commonwealth Shipping Line.' The files of Walter Young (later Sir Walter Young), general manager of the Adelaide-based firm of Elder Smith and Company, help explain the background. They include correspondence with J Fred Downer, and H A Gerny of Elders' London office and provide a key insider's perspective on Hughes' negotiations to devise marketing arrangements for Australian wheat, wool and metals. There are equally important London office reports to Young on Hughes' discussions when in the UK in 1916. Earlier, Young had also received reports from W L Raws while Hughes was attorney-general in the Fisher government, specifically regarding his Energy Contracts Annulment Bill in May 1915. (NBAC 8/57/11–13)

Laurie Fitzhardinge papers

Folders of research material, 1941–1971

The folders comprise papers including research notes, correspondence, scripts, and newspaper clippings compiled while Fitzhardinge was Reader in Sources of Australian History at the Australian National University and working on a biography of Hughes. They include copies of minutes of and articles on the Waterside Workers' Federation of Australia, papers supporting the 1966 ABC television documentary by Professor Colin Hughes called 'Mr Prime Minister' for which Fitzhardinge was special adviser for the Hughes episode, papers about access to Hughes material at the Commonwealth Archives Office and the National Library, the Commonwealth Shipping Line and Hughes-related research in Australia, Ottawa, Toronto, the United States and the United Kingdom. There is also early 1950s correspondence with the ANU about the biography, with Dame Mary 1953–1955 about the progress of volume one, correspondence relating to the first – inconclusive – Hughes approach to produce a biography in the early 1940s, and notes for and drafts of the biography. The files also include a copy of a letter from Fitzhardinge to Vice-Chancellor Sir Douglas Copland after seeing Hughes in July 1952 and reporting him 'in bed with lumbago and in a particularly querulous and suspicious frame of mind'. (ANUA 83/383–99)

Correspondence file, 1963–1970

Comprises Fitzhardinge's correspondence with the Perpetual Trustee Company Ltd regarding progress of the biography. In a series of annual letters he explained the reasons for delay. In 1963 it was the requirement for vetting his manuscript, in 1967 he pointed to 'the complexity of Mr Hughes' activities, especially relating to the First World War' and 'the very scattered nature of the sources', and in 1968 he referred to frustrations with the Commonwealth Archives Office over access delays caused by processing and staff shortages. (ANUA 83/165)

Correspondence file, 1960–1971

The file documents Fitzhardinge's research on the Hughes project with scholars, librarians and others around the world. Most concern the author's search for information, although there are a few letters from others who sought advice about information in the Hughes papers; B A Santamaria in late 1965, for instance, working on a biography of Archbishop Mannix. (ANUA 83/103)

NSW Combined Colliery Proprietors' Association records

Correspondence file, 1909

The file comprises letters, telegrams and other papers of F Livingstone Learmonth from late 1909 on the Newcastle coal strike. Learmonth was president of the Northern Colliery Owners' Association (though his role as president of the Hunter River District Colliery Proprietors' Defence Association, Newcastle is also evident). The file provides a reflected view of Hughes' role in negotiations as self-appointed head of the combined Strike Congress representing the Northern Colliery Employees' Federation. The correspondence includes references to him and copies provided to the Association by the NSW Premier's Department of letters the NSW premier C G Wade sent to Hughes. There is also a fourteen-page verbatim record of a conference of 20 November 1909 between Hughes, Peter Bowling (leader of the Northern Miners' Association) and others comprising the Strike Congress and the premier. (NBAC E207/20)

NSW Typographical Association records

Photographs, 1891–1927

Included in an album of photographs of the Association is a group photograph of delegates to the Interstate Labor Conference held in January 1900. In the front row, Hughes in a straw boater is seated on the ground and beside him J C Watson in a bowler hat. (NBAC T39/74/26, K3808b)

Sydney Wharf Labourers' Union records

Membership ledger, 1891–1895

This large heavy volume, its ingrained dirt hinting repeated use, is of interest here for its record of Hughes' membership number 175 in 1894 on p. 129 and 1895 on p. 147. (NBAC Z248/1)

Minutes, 1896–1897

The Wharf Labourers' Union, 'smashed as a result of the Maritime Strike of 1890' as Fitzhardinge put it, can be seen here beginning to be rebuilt. Hughes emerges here too as a union leader. The records for a meeting on 27 July 1896 report him speaking 'at considerable length' and addressing another in November 'at great length on the great nessity [sic] of combining'. Inklings of the milieu and mindset he flourished in are captured too, the meeting of 22 September 1897 resolving: 'That this meeting indignantly protest against the conduct of the NSW police openly aiding and abetting the Employers to reduce Wages 2nd to attack civil Rights by the open dragooning Miners at Lucknow and The courupt [sic] use of power to proctet [sic] Blacklegs at the Bidding of Jews to in order starve The Workers.' (NBAC Z248/95)

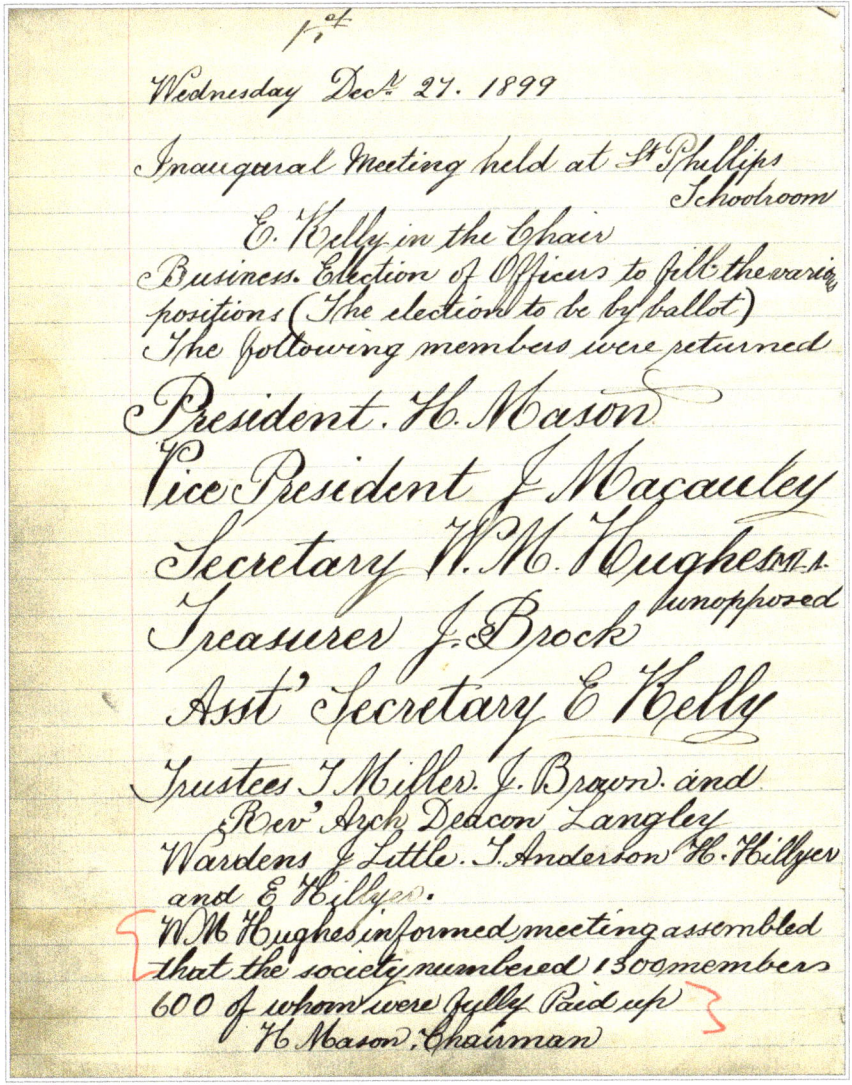

When the Sydney Wharf Labourers' Union reformed in 1899, Billy Hughes was elected secretary 'unopposed' (NBAC Z248/95)

Minutes, 1899–1902

These minutes begin on 'day one' of the new union, when at the inaugural meeting of 27 December 1899 Hughes was elected unopposed as its secretary. The discussions subsequently tell of rules development, membership counts and inherited debts and property. Hughes features regularly and prominently: on 3 January 1900 he gave a 'lengthy speech' re unionism, receiving a testimonial of £15 at the meeting on 13 February 1901, repeatedly being re-elected secretary, and engaged in mid-1901 in negotiations to affiliate with the nationwide Waterside Workers' Federation. Discussions about tactics and policy were often stormy, and often involved Hughes, the language rarely equivocal. Over the course of a year, speakers could state that a Hughes speech 'savoured of blackleg' and months later move motions that the union 're-affirms its unshaken confidence in Mr Hughes and wishes to place on record its deep sense of gratitude for his untiring efforts on behalf of this Union and for his services in the cause of Labour generally'. (NBAC Z248/95)

Minutes, 1902–1909

These minutes record Hughes' election as the union's general secretary (meeting of 9 April 1902) and his name is rarely absent from their pages, indicating participation in person or sending reports about industrial disputes, negotiations, conferences, arbitration, rule changes and so on. For someone who kept practically no private papers, something of the authentic Hughes voice is available here, the record of meetings usually including a fairly detailed summary of what he said. Thus the meeting of 29 October 1902 has very colourful exchanges with Hughes at the centre regarding treasurer Carstairs losing funds and skipping the jurisdiction, in the course of which Hughes was attacked and typically defended himself with gusto (pp. 108–10). More noteworthy is the detail of his report on return from his 1907 travel to attend the navigation conference in London, returning via the US and Canada. Thus we learn for instance that he 'addressed meetings of the Independent Labor party ... who gave him a very hostile reception because he stated that Australians at all hazards had decided to keep the Coloured Labor out' (17 July 1907, pp. 11–12). (NBAC Z248/96)

Minutes, 1909–1910

The minutes cover two years of great activity for Hughes industrially and politically. Here one can follow Hughes' organisational relationship to strikes, his attitude to boats 'coaled by blackleg coal', participation in mass meetings, provision of financial support for families of strikers and as a delegate reporting on conferences. His dominance of the union is obvious, more than once a motion (e.g. meeting of 4 April 1910) being passed that matters be 'left in the hands of Mr W M Hughes'.

His preference for negotiation over direct action is also clear, as at a 'Special Mass Meeting' of 15 November 1909 to hear a report of delegates to 'the Miners Conference' and to decide 'on the course of action intended to be taken in connection with the present Industrial Crisis'. Rather than strike, the wharf labourers passed motions that the branch 'cease work when ordered to do so by the Council of the Waterside Federation' and 'that this Union have complete confidence in their General Sec. Mr W M Hughes'. The minutes also record him being congratulated on re-election to parliament and his appointment as attorney-general. (NBAC Z248/97)

Minutes, 1910–1913

Hughes is very much a background presence during these years. Though he remained the Union's general secretary, being attorney-general in the Fisher government meant he was often in Melbourne and otherwise occupied. Occasionally he surfaces, for instance addressing members about a 'forthcoming conference' and being questioned about 'bag coke' (30 November 1910), representing the Union at the conference with the Ship Owners (10 May 1911) and addressing meetings and being consulted about donating to 'Labor Papers Daily' (1 March 1911 and 4 June 1913). The stark reality of capital versus labour surfaces too over the union's reluctance for health reasons to handle cement in unlined bags, the minutes for the meeting of 15 February 1911 noting a telegram from Hughes 'notifying that the members should continue to work the cement'. The matter of dust was discussed at further meetings, with Hughes in person at that of 26 April 1911 to address them about the issue. (NBAC Z248/97)

Minutes, 1913–1915

Judging by Hughes' record of attendance, correspondence and participation noted in the minutes, he was only intermittently involved in the union through this period, doubtless being based at parliament in Melbourne a factor. Nevertheless he was rarely far from union campaigns and Arbitration Court bids. The meeting of 25 February 1914 (p. 145) for instance dramatically conveys, despite the static and stilted medium of a minute book, Hughes' urgent plea to the Sydney branch to support a unified policy towards views via a ballot: 'I go into Court on Friday & must be able to state definitely what the position really is. I am not going to represent a Federation that cannot speak for all its members.' The rest is history: the 1914 Commonwealth award for waterside workers was acclaimed by historian Dr Margo Beasley as his 'greatest achievement as a trade union leader'. (NBAC Z248/97)

Minutes, 1915–1917

As its general secretary, Hughes continued to be mentioned in Federation minutes, despite his accession to the prime ministership following Andrew Fisher's resignation in October 1915. They provide for instance detail of financial support for a 'conversatzione' given in his honour by the West Sydney Labor League on his departure for the UK in early 1916 (meeting of 12 January 1916) and record his union's approval for him to 'represent the Union at the Price Fixing Board' (6 September 1916). Nevertheless it is his expulsion over conscription in late 1916 which dominates (see also Chapter 3, 'Three Labor dismissals'). A Special Cease Work Meeting of 14 September 1916 resolved that 'this Union emphatically protest against the introduction of Conscription of life as introduced by W M Hughes' (p. 238), and on 20 September, in his presence, foreshadowed discussion: 'That a special meeting be called for the purpose of considering the advisability of expelling W M Hughes' (p. 241). At that special meeting on 27 September 1916 (pp. 247–8), the minute taker recorded:

> Mr McNeill said that he was pleased to see such a good roll up & moved the following motion 'That W M Hughes be expelled from this union'. Mr Serle seconded the resolution. Messrs Seale Bailey Thompson spoke in favour. Burrows & Woods Sands & Hunt against. Which being put to the meeting was carried by 160 vote[s] to 42 against. (NBAC Z248/98)

Phil Thorne papers

Correspondence files, 1936–1940

Included in the papers of this left-wing solicitor are two folders of correspondence with Hughes connections, both resulting from Thorne's role as secretary of the Spanish Relief Committee from 1936 until it was disbanded at the outbreak of the Second World War. The Committee wanted the Lyons and, following his death, the Menzies government to change its policy of non-intervention in the Spanish Civil War, a cessation of the bombing and support for refugees. As Lyons' minister for external affairs and Menzies' attorney-general, Hughes was the recipient and author of correspondence, instances of which can be found here, some being courtesy copies of his correspondence with for example the International Peace Campaign and the NSW Council for Relief of Spanish Distress. In one letter to the president of the Council, Jessie Street, dated 29 August 1939, he explained why 'after discussing the matter with the Prime Minister' he decided against addressing one of their meetings:

I feel that in the present acute crisis in international affairs, when the fate of our country – and indeed of civilization – is hanging in the balance, I cannot accept your most kind invitation. Personally I am in sympathy with the efforts of your Council to help these unfortunate people, but in the present state of world affairs, I feel that my presence on the platform might be misunderstood. (NBAC P15/1)

Trolley, Draymen and Carters Union of Sydney and Suburbs records

Minutes, 1917–1925

As Fitzhardinge explains in *William Morris Hughes: A Political Biography* (vol. 1, p. 108), Hughes' involvement with the Trolley, Draymen and Carters Union was a natural complement to his work for the Sydney wharf labourers, and here too he served continuously as the foundation president from 1901 to his expulsion in 1916. While minutes for this period are not known to have survived, Hughes hovers just beyond mention in those for the years immediately following the November 1916 conscription referendum. At the 29 January 1917 meeting for example the union resolved that 'this body enters its emphatic protest against anyone representing Australia at an Imperial conference' (p. 3). Though the Imperial War Cabinet met between March and May 1917, Hughes did indeed not attend. During the second conscription referendum campaign, the union resolved at its meeting of 19 November 1917 (pp. 41–2) to place personnel and funds at the disposal of the Anti Conscription Committee. (NBAC Z277/74)

Photograph, 1905

Hughes is photographed at the centre of a group photograph labelled 'Committee – Carters Union – 22–4–1905'. (NBAC Z277/86)

Waterside Workers' Federation of Australia records

Agreements re awards etc, 1900–1956

The agreements include three folders with documents signed by Hughes (with others) in his capacity as president of the WWF, as follows:

(i) 'Branch industrial Agreements 1900 to 1914' includes several signed for the WWF with the union's seal, e.g. Commonwealth Conciliation and Arbitration Industrial Agreement 6 October 1911 (separate copies relating to the ports of Sydney, Burnie, Albany, Strahan, Launceston, and Devonport)

(ii) 'Copies of Agreements (Misc) 1911–25' includes a copy of letter from Hughes as president dated 17 December 1914 addressed to members seeking amendment to the rules as required by Mr Justice Higgins during 'the recent case before the Federal Arbitration Court'

(iii) 'Queensland Agreements 1911–38' which includes several signed by Hughes (and others) for the WWF with the union's seal, e.g. Commonwealth Conciliation and Arbitration Industrial Agreement 6 October 1911 (separate copies for the ports of Mackay, Gladstone, Bundaberg, Maryborough, Bowen, Townsville, Innisfail, Cairns, Rockhampton and Port Douglas). (NBAC T62/43/1, 3, 8)

Cash book, 1902–1924

The cash book covers the entire period Hughes was the Federation's president, from its inauguration in Melbourne in February 1902 until he was expelled in 1916. His intermittent appearances help fix some of the bread and butter facts, dates and income of his life during those years, as they record payments for his expenses from the mundane sending of telegrams to payments for editing and managing the *Waterside Workers' Gazette* and the presentation on 14 January 1916 of £72. (NBAC T62/29/1)

Minute book, 1902–1921

As the union's founding and long-serving president, Hughes features regularly and often prominently in the minutes of Federation Council, special, general and committee meetings. They record him proposing motions, chairing meetings, signing minutes as confirmed, reporting on industrial negotiations such as the Newcastle miners' strike in late 1909, and being presented with tokens of appreciation (on one occasion cash, on another a plate). He was re-elected president at the Federation's monthly meeting of 15 August 1916 (p. 217) but within a month the Sydney branch had expelled him over his stance on conscription. In contrast to previous references in the minutes, subsequent mentions are terse; those for the monthly meeting of 22 August 1917 recording: 'That the letter from the Prime Minister, Mr W M Hughes, be received and the General Secretary's action be endorsed' (p. 243). (NBAC T62/1/1)

Photographs, 1912–1950

Hughes is photographed as president with other delegates to the Waterside Workers' Federation conference in Melbourne on 30 October 1912, including Andrew Fisher, and at another early WWF conference in Sydney. (NBAC T62/63/2–3, K3833 & K2015)

PAUL KEATING, 1991–1996

Australian Council of Trade Unions records

Photographs, 1977–1991

Keating addressed the ACTU Congress in Sydney in September 1989. Photographs of the occasion, some of which also include Bob Hawke, are in this collection, and with other related material can also be found in the *ACTU Bulletin*. (NBAC Z282A/448; S18)

Recordings of ACTU Congresses, 1961–1992

This collection includes a recording of Keating's address to the ACTU Congress in September 1989 as prime minister. (NBAC Z282A/701)

Australian National University photographs

Envelopes of photographs of people and events, 1948–2005

As federal treasurer, Keating addressed the Tax and Equity conference held on campus in May 1985. He also addressed a seminar on the role of treasurers in 1991. Keating was photographed on campus at the launch of Tom Uren's book on the Burma Railway in 1993, at a lecture on Commonwealth and state relations in 1994 and with his then wife Annita, at the presentation of the Dr TT Tsui collection of Chinese art to the National Gallery in 1995. (ANUA 225/666; ANUA 226/466, 894)

Paul Keating at his ANU lecture on Commonwealth–State relations in 1994 (ANUA 225/666/1)

Wendy Brazil collection

Subject files on Paul Keating, 1984–1990

Part of a collection of research files from the office of Senator D J Hamer, these seven files include press clippings, press releases by and about Keating, media summaries, press conference transcripts, photocopies of magazine articles and extracts from Hansard. Of nostalgic interest, the files include an undated document running to fifty-five terms headed: 'Some examples of Mr Keating's Parliamentary Language'. (NBAC Z372/33)

Colin Campbell collection

Transcripts and cassette tapes of interviews, 1988–2005

The collection comprises transcripts and cassettes of interviews conducted by Professor Colin Campbell, a Canadian academic based at the ANU, for a book with John Halligan, subsequently published by Allen and Unwin in 1992, titled *Political*

Leadership in an Age of Constraint: Bureaucratic Politics under Hawke and Keating. The interviewees were senior officers in key departments such as Prime Minister and Cabinet, Treasury and Finance, many of whom describe working while Keating was prime minister, and refer to his style of operation and decision-making. Later interviews from 1994 to 2001 were conducted by Campbell to keep abreast of changes. (ANUA 316)

JOE LYONS, 1932–1939

Amalgamated Postal Workers' Union of Australia records

Government and Parliamentary members' correspondence files, 1920–1952

The APWUA and its predecessor before it was formed in 1926 represented postmen, sorters and linesmen employed by the Postmaster-General's Department. The files record the union's lobbying, advocacy and pursuit of redress, participation in inquiries, submissions on legislative amendments and negotiations for increased pay and improved entitlements and working conditions. As illustrated in the records described here, it also campaigned as a member of the High Council of the Commonwealth Public Service Organisations and the Combined Federal Service Unions. In particular, the files evidence Union contact with Lyons in his roles as postmaster-general (1930), treasurer and prime minister (1932–1934, 1937–1938) about such matters as furlough for Commonwealth public servants, Douglas Social Credit proposals, restoration of salary cuts, amendments to the *Public Service Act*, adult pay below the basic wage, a five-day working week, Christmas holidays, preference for unionists, long service leave for temporary employees and the weekly payment of salaries. (NBAC T35/22/1, 3, 6, 14, 19–21, 25, 28, 37, 39)

Australian Dictionary of Biography files

Joe Lyons, 1983–2008

Documented here is the commissioning and editing for publication of Philip Hart and Clem Lloyd's 4,000-word entry on Lyons which appeared in 1986 at pp. 184–9 of volume 10 of the Dictionary. There is correspondence between the authors and ADB staff including general editors Bede Nairn and Geoff Serle, drafts, readers' reports, copies of birth death and marriage certificates, the will, clippings, articles and book reviews and copies of cards from the *Sydney Morning Herald* index. As ever, the editors worried over the right phrase, ever cautious not to allow their authors to stray too far beyond verifiable and essential facts. Lyons' cause of death was edited to delete mention that he had suffered a series of heart attacks over several days. While his officially stated cause of death was a coronary occlusion and arteriosclerosis, the published reference became 'Lyons died in Sydney Hospital on 7 April 1939 from coronary occlusion'. The file also shows the blue pencil at work on Hart and Lloyd's description of Lyons' final break with the Scullin Cabinet. Lloyd wrote of his support for national unity to fight the depression, 'Lyons was shouted down and information was leaked that he wanted a coalition government'. There was no Laurie Oakes in 1930, however: 'information was leaked' was transformed into the vaguer 'rumours were spread that he wanted'. (ANUA 312)

Australian Federated Union of Locomotive Enginemen records

Photographs, 1920s

Lyons, as Tasmanian minister for railways, is photographed with AFULE officials, E M Cunningham, W Drewett and J Fleming, by John Beattie, the official Tasmanian government photographer. They have each signed the back of the mounted photograph. (NBAC T60/63/7, K2014)

Australian National University correspondence files

Canberra University College – establishment of a National University, 1933–1938

This ANU file incorporates a top-numbered Canberra University College file from the 1930s, combining clippings, correspondence and other papers. Reflected in them one can sense the Lyons government's reservation concerning a proper university for Canberra; in today's language, he had 'no appetite for it'. As an item on file from the 11 April 1938 issue of the *Canberra Times* reported: 'The Prime Minister, Mr Lyons declared at a University of Melbourne luncheon yesterday that Canberra should move warily toward setting up a university. Mr Lyons said he had very grave doubts about the wisdom of pressing on with it.' (ANUA 53/14.1.0.77 part 1)

THE ARCHIVES

Joe Lyons, Tasmanian minister for railways, with officials of the Australian Federated Union of Locomotive Enginemen (NBAC T60/63/7, K2014)

Institute of Public Affairs (Victoria) records

Secretary's correspondence, 1943–1950

In the early 1940s, the various state branches of the IPA were still deciding whether to become directly involved in party politics. The August 1943 federal election was the last time they explicitly took sides, while it marked the beginning of Dame Enid Lyons' public career, as she won the seat of Darwin for the United Australia Party. As documented in this file of the secretary Captain A C Leech's correspondence, the Victorian branch negotiated the screening of a campaign film featuring Dame Enid in Hoyts, Union and Metro–Goldwyn theatres in Victoria and elsewhere. Also evident here, she had made inquiries of them concerning political broadcasts on radio stations 3DB concerning the Workers' Rights Association and 3GL featuring the Political Rights Association. (NBAC N136/56)

Phil Thorne papers

Correspondence file, 1936–1938

Included in the papers of this left-wing solicitor are two folders of correspondence, both resulting from Thorne's role as secretary of the Spanish Relief Committee from 1936 until it was disbanded at the outbreak of the Second World War. The Committee wanted the Lyons government to change its policy of non-intervention in the Spanish Civil War, a cessation of the bombing and support for refugees. The first folder, 'Commonwealth government correspondence, Oct 1936 – Jul 1938' includes copies of three letters to Lyons. (NBAC P15/1)

Waterside Workers' Federation records

Commonwealth Attorney-Generals, 1934–1939

This WWF head office file records interactions between the Federation and Lyons government ministers (Menzies and Hughes), and Lyons himself, on the discussions which preceded the refusal of the Port Kembla waterside workers to load pig iron for shipment to Japan, including the contentious *Transport Workers Act*. It includes correspondence between Lyons and the newly elected Federation general secretary Jim Healy. There is also a telegram dated 23 May 1938 sent to Lyons from a chairman representing a public meeting ('This meeting of Melbourne citizens held Imperial Theatre') to Lyons supporting the Federation. (NBAC T62/25)

JOHN McEWEN, 1967–1968

Australian Dictionary of Biography files

Sir John McEwen, 1997–1998

This small file documents the commissioning, subsequent interactions and approval of Clem Lloyd's 3,000-word biography of John McEwen published in the *Australian Dictionary of Biography*, volume 15, Melbourne University Press, 2000, pp. 205–8. The research material the ADB made available to authors is there in the form of notes, references, articles and copies of the will, AIF enlistment papers and birth, marriage and death certificates. The final draft, delayed because P Golding's *Black Jack McEwen* appeared as the entry was being finalised, drew the general editor's approval. 'Marvellous, a gem from start to finish', John Ritchie wrote on 10 February 1997. The only other reaction recorded was a Dictionary reader who felt references to

McEwen's role as party leader and his electoral base needed strengthening, and added that 'Canberra insiders spoke of McEwen as a "pants man"' and asked 'Has Clem Lloyd opted not to evaluate and/or comment on his reputation with women?', below which another hand had written 'Alleged womanizing: Ask author for comment?'. Clearly neither understood the ADB's policy about hearsay. (ANUA 312)

Federal Chamber of Automotive Industries records

Correspondence, 1958

The folder comprises firstly copies of letters sent out announcing that the secretary of the Chamber, James ('Jim') R Murray, had resigned due to ill-health and secondly replies to the vice-president R M Jacka but mostly to Murray wishing him well. Murray had served as secretary for many years and from the replies, had clearly developed a large network of contacts and friends within the industry and in political circles, and was well respected. The folder includes several letters from McEwen as minister for trade, not surprising given the role of the Chamber. (NBAC Z171)

Goldsbrough Mort and Company Ltd records

Photographs, 1873–1954

When Queen Elizabeth and the Duke of Edinburgh visited the Goldsbrough Mort Melbourne office in 1954 they were accompanied by McEwen who was photographed at the rear of the official party. (NBAC 2/622/84, K3655)

National Farmers' Federation records

Press releases, 1966–1970

As a national body whose aims including influencing government policies relating to farmers' interests, the Federation monitored statements issued by ministers on a broad range of economic, industrial, trade and other subjects. These two files cover McEwen's period as minister for trade and industry and deputy prime minister in the Holt and Gorton governments and comprise about sixty copies of transcripts of interviews, printed ministerial statements, national addresses and press releases. Several were also issued while he was acting prime minister. (NBAC Z135/17, 58)

New Zealand and Australian Land Company records

Photographs for staff newsletter, 1958–1959

McEwen is photographed at the opening of the Victorian Tobacco Growers Cooperative Society tobacco drying plant in Melbourne. (NBAC 110/8/1/2, K1354)

BILLY McMAHON, 1971–1972

Australian National University correspondence files

Registration for National Service, 1965–1972

Australia's involvement in the Vietnam War, conscription, anti-war protests and the ANU's relationship with the Holt, Gorton and McMahon governments form the backdrop to this multi-part file. Students were refusing to register for national service, those pursued by the authorities were finding sanctuary on campus, and funds were being collected for the National Liberation Front. The Vice-Chancellor at the time, Sir John Crawford, tried to maintain the university's independence, and the privacy of student information, but for a time faced proposed amendments to the *National Service Act* aimed at requiring the addresses of draft resisters to be supplied to the government. The file includes correspondence, press releases, newspaper clippings, telegrams and legal opinions. Inevitably, it includes references to McMahon who was minister for labour and national service and Fraser who was minister for education and science under Gorton, and to Holt and Gorton as well. (ANUA 53/4.0.0.22 parts 1–3 & C)

Australian National University History Project records

Binders of research notes, 1990–1996

Compiled during research to produce Stephen Foster and Margaret Varghese's *The Making of the Australian National University 1946–1996*, the record series includes a binder on 'Staff'. The notes in part cover the recruitment of academic staff irrespective of political affiliations, which became a public issue when on 11 October 1950 McMahon raised in parliament doubts about the appointment of Heinz Arndt to Canberra University College. (ANUA 147/7)

THE ARCHIVES

Transcripts and tapes, 1990–1995

In 1990 Daniel Connell conducted an interview for the University's official history project with Emeritus Professor Heinz Arndt, who was recruited from the University of Sydney to become foundation Professor in Economics at the Canberra University College in the early 1950s. At one point he was questioned about a fourth-year economics student at Sydney, Billy McMahon. Arndt told Connell he had supported bank nationalisation in the late 1940s, though he would 'now be horrified'. In the interview he relates that shortly after, when McMahon the keen backbencher asked Menzies:

> whether he was aware that the latest person appointed to the Chair of Economics in Canberra was a socialist ... Menzies of course had never heard of me and .... said that it was not the practice of the government to interfere in academic appointments. (ANUA 44/13)

Institute of Public Affairs (Victoria) records

Director's correspondence, 1950, 1971

As noted in Chapter 3 ('The IPA and three Liberal PMs'), the IPA files include correspondence with McMahon in 1950 as an eager young backbencher and on his gaining the ultimate political goal in March 1971. (NBAC N136/20, 28)

Audrey Johnson papers

Photographs, 1920s–1970s

Johnson was writing a biography of Tom Wright, federal secretary of the Sheet Metal Working Agricultural Implement and Stove Making Industrial Union of Australia, at the time of her death. Her papers include a photograph of McMahon and Menzies with Tom Wright and other union officials in the 1950s. (NBAC N162/182)

National Farmers' Federation records

Prime Minister's speeches, 1971–1975

As a national body whose aims including influencing government policies relating to farmers' interests, the Federation monitored statements issued by ministers on a broad range of economic, industrial trade and other subjects. The file on McMahon includes copies of transcripts of interviews, printed ministerial statements, national addresses and press releases. (NBAC N18/538)

Speeches and press statements by the Prime Minister, 1972–1977
Though relating largely to Whitlam's terms as prime minister, the file includes statements, press releases and related documents covering the final months of McMahon's period as prime minister. (NBAC Z135/59)

ROBERT MENZIES, 1939–1941, 1949–1966

Adelaide Steamship Company Ltd records

Meetings of shareholders minutes, 1901–1928
As the principal defendant in the Engineers' Case, in which Menzies represented the plaintiffs, the Company obviously felt bound to keep its shareholders informed. At the ordinary general meeting of 21 September 1920, one can sense the annoyance Menzies had caused, the chairman Mr M G Anderson asking 'when are we to get finality as far as the powers of the Arbitration Court, States Rights, etc are concerned, if after a comparatively short period the High Court reverses its decision, as has been done in the case?' (NBAC Z535/10)

Amalgamated Postal Workers' Union of Australia records

Government and Parliamentary members' correspondence files, 1920–1952
The APWUA and its predecessor before it was formed in 1926 represented postmen, sorters and linesmen employed by the Postmaster-General's Department. The files record its lobbying, advocacy and pursuit of redress, participation in inquiries, submissions on legislative amendments and negotiations for increased pay and improved entitlements and working conditions. It also campaigned as part of the Combined Federal Service Unions, and courtesy copies of its letters will also be found here. They wrote to Menzies when he was attorney-general and prime minister about such matters as public service arbitration and long service leave for Commonwealth public servants who had enlisted. In the case of the forty-hour week, the files document the Union's deputation to meet him when he was attorney-general in December 1938. (NBAC T35/22/1, 5, 17)

THE ARCHIVES

Australasian Coal and Shale Employees' Federation records

Sketches, 1940s

Menzies was often caricatured as a wealthy banker in cartoons for the Federation's newsletter *Common Cause* (NBAC S104), including one by Noel Counihan. (NBAC E165/58/4, K3919)

Noel Counihan's 1940 cartoon of Robert Menzies for the Miners' Federation newspaper *Common Cause* (NBAC E165/58/4, K3919)

Australian Council of Trade Unions records

File titled 'ACTU Miscellaneous File – Judgements, Speeches, Pamphlets, Reports, Wages, Logs etc', 1930s–1940s

Though testifying to less than optimal records management practices, the file's contents provide both context and direct documentation to the Port Kembla dispute and Menzies' role in its resolution. Two papers are especially relevant. The first, titled 'Mr Menzies' Statement' (undated six-page typescript) is almost certainly Menzies' address, made in highly charged circumstances, to wharfies at the Wollongong Town Hall on 11 January 1939. It is annotated in pencil on the verso 'Speakers Monk Crofts ACTU Healey Finlay [sic] Waterside Workers' and opens

'Gentlemen, I am obliged to you for coming up here'. Occasional gaps in the typed original have been filled in by pencil, suggesting the transcript was checked against notes or a tape recording. The second document of note is the transcript of the meeting of 17 October 1938 in the Commonwealth Offices, Melbourne between Menzies and E J Holloway and a deputation from the ACTU, WWF and Seamen's Union seeking the repeal of the *Transport Workers Act* (i.e. the infamous 'dog-collar' Act). (NBAC N21/55)

Australian Dictionary of Biography files

Robert Menzies, 1993–2001

This file covers the commissioning and editing of Allan Martin's 6,000-word entry on Menzies which appeared in 2000 at pp. 354–61 of volume 15 of the Dictionary. All the standard papers are here: copies of the key certificates, newspaper cuttings of obituaries, reviews of existing biographies on Menzies, and correspondence with editors. When sending the first draft, Martin wrote on 7 July 1996 explaining to the general editor John Ritchie that:

> It is frankly interpretive, but this is the Menzies I've come to know and believe in, and I want to see him treated fairly. His political opponents, Curtin and Chifley get a good if not unbiased run and Evatt is bound to enjoy the same. So it seemed a good idea to try to dispel some left-wing myths about RGM.
> I do believe everything I've written here.

ADB office staff liked it too, one noting of a later draft: 'Of course, a masterly summary by an unrivalled authority – appropriately sympathetic but covering most of the accusations of his enemies.' The only negative note was struck by everyone failing to catch a mistaken reference to there being an election in 1939. It was pointed out to them by A G L Shaw in 2001, who suggested its correction in corrigenda. The general editor apologised to Martin ('I have egg on my face'), who in turn wrote that he was puzzled as to how it had crept in, while speculating:

> I suppose I exaggerated because I was particularly miffed that the promise to Menzies was never honoured [i.e. that Lyons would hand over leadership to Menzies, thus contesting the 1937 and '1939 election'], which is particularly rich given that Dame Enid was mostly such a bitch to him! (ANUA 312)

Australian National University audiovisual material

Film and audio tapes, 1952–1972

Menzies' laying of the foundation stone for what was to be named the R G Menzies Building in 1961 was captured in a silent film with a separate audio recording of speeches at the event. The opening of the building by Queen Elizabeth, which Menzies attended, was also recorded and filmed. Other audio recordings include Menzies' speeches at the opening of the Cockcroft Building for the Research School of Physical Sciences in 1952 and the opening of the John Curtin School of Medical Research in 1958, and an after-luncheon speech following the conferring of an honorary degree on Dr Harold Macmillan in 1958. (ANUA 191)

Australian National University correspondence files

Opening of R G Menzies Building of the University Library, 1963

The multi-part file covers the arrangements for and speeches at the opening of the R G Menzies Building on 13 March 1963. (ANUA 53/18.1.1.10A)

Australian National University Council minutes

Minutes of meetings, 1949–1951

Traditionally, convocation in relation to universities refers to the entire body of graduates. Very young universities, like the ANU in the early 1950s, need to apply transitional measures. Its 1946 legislation in fact allowed for the admission of 'graduates of other Universities' and 'other persons'. At the meeting of 8 June 1951 the Interim Council noted that the prime minister Robert Menzies accepted nomination to Convocation. (ANUA 198/6)

Australian National University History Project records

Transcripts and tapes, 1990–1995

In 1990 Daniel Connell conducted interviews with, among others, the former Director of the Research School of Physical Sciences Sir Mark Oliphant, the former Vice-Chancellor Sir Leslie Melville and the former Dean of Law Professor Geoffrey Sawer for the University's official history project. This came to fruition in 1996 under Stephen Foster and Margaret Varghese's names as *The Making of the Australian National University 1946–1996*. All three commented on Menzies' support (though not open-ended) for the university, the relative lack of political interference, and the forced amalgamation with the Canberra University College. On the latter issue, Sawer for instance was asked if Menzies 'in a sense, forced it on the university'. He replied:

> Oh yes, he did, there's no question about that. Indeed Bunting told me afterwards ... This thing had been around and finally, and this was the way in which he decided many things, he demanded that a paper outlining all the arguments for and against shortly should be prepared and delivered to him on a Friday and he'd take it home and read it on the weekend. And he read it on the weekend and came back on the Monday morning and said, 'It's on, they're going to be married'. (ANUA 44/6 Sawer, 44/1 Melville, 44/2 Oliphant)

Australian National University Library records

Papers relating to opening of R G Menzies Building, 1962–1963

These two files of University Librarian J J Graneek relate to preparations for the opening by the Queen on 13 March 1963 of the R G Menzies Building of the University Library. There are speeches, a press kit, the order of proceedings, and memos. Menzies had laid the foundation stone in 1961, and Graneek's speech notes from that occasion are also included. For the Queen's opening speech, the University's draft had suggested, in part: 'How appropriate that the name Robert Gordon Menzies, indelibly identified with the defence of scholarly standards and the development of learning, should dignify this bastion of scholarship'. We learn from the second of the two files she actually said: 'I am delighted that it is named after my Prime Minister who has done so much to advance the universities and to maintain the standards of scholarship in Australia'. (ANUA 85)

Photographic portrait, 1963

This large framed portrait of Menzies hung in the foyer of the R G Menzies Building for many years. (ANUA 303)

Visitors' book, 1963–1975

The visitors' book for the Menzies Library includes the signatures of Queen Elizabeth, the Duke of Edinburgh, Menzies and other dignitaries. (ANUA 319)

Australian National University photographs

Envelopes of photographs of people and events, 1948–2005

As prime minister at the time of the University's early building program, Menzies attended many ceremonies on campus, often accompanied by his wife Pattie, including the opening of the Cockcroft Building in 1952 and the John Curtin School of Medical Research in 1958 (ANUA 15/3 and 9) and the laying of foundation stones for the Haydon–Allen Building in 1959 (ANUA 15/13) and the Coombs Building in 1962 (ANUA 15/118, ANUA 226/435). He laid the foundation stone in 1961 for what was to be later named the R G Menzies Building. In one photograph, Gough and Margaret Whitlam can be seen in the crowd behind him (ANUA 15/111). Menzies was also photographed at the opening of the building in 1963 with Queen Elizabeth and other dignitaries (ANUA 15/14, ANUA 226/396), at the installation of Sir John Cockcroft as the second Chancellor in 1962 (ANUA 15/11 and 55), during various inspections of Physics research facilities (ANUA 15/52, 54A), at a presentation of books honouring his seventieth birthday in 1964 (ANUA 225/848), at the conferring of his honorary Doctor of Laws in 1966 (ANUA 15/143), and as Chancellor of the University of Melbourne, with ANU Chancellor Sir John Crawford and Vice-Chancellor H C Coombs at a conference on the role and responsibilities of governing bodies in May 1969 (ANUA 15/151, ANUA 225/848).

Australian National University staff files

Sir Leslie Melville, 1951–1978

As might be expected for someone who was its Vice-Chancellor for seven years (1953–1960), the University's file on Melville is extensive, in parts confidential, and has more to offer than just the mechanical documentation of personnel and financial transactions. Melville's recruitment to chair the Tariff Board in 1960 for instance provides an excellent illustration of how the Menzies government interacted with the university, particularly the copies of letters reporting on discussions with the prime minister by H C Coombs, Pro-Chancellor at the time. An earlier sequence of letters from Melville while overseas to acting Vice-Chancellor Trendall include a number of references to Menzies, who was clearly interested in the university budget, and through departmental representatives on Council such as Allen Brown and later John Bunting, in large equipment purchases. (ANUA 19/4.2.1.11 parts 1–3 & C, 4.2.1.11A parts 1–3, 7227)

House for Professor Mark Oliphant, 1948–1950

As encouragement to become foundation Director of the Research School of Physical Sciences, the ANU agreed to build a house for Professor Oliphant, to a design and location of his choice, which he would then purchase. The file records these sometimes rocky negotiations. Due to cost overruns, he ended up renting rather than buying. When the ANU needed additional funds to bring it to fruition, the Interim Council appealed directly to Menzies (letter of 7 January 1950), who as the signed original letter of 18 January on file shows, was happy to agree. (ANUA 19/12.1.2.4A)

Professor Oliphant's confidential correspondence and documents, 1948–1988

Reflecting a time before the ANU had proper archival arrangements, Oliphant's staff files include an envelope stamped 'Confidential', and a file of original and photocopied documents from official files entitled 'Professor Oliphant Personal Early Correspondence'. Included are several letters from the University to Oliphant sent before he arrived, about the new house and Menzies' intervention, one from the Registrar Ross Hohnen explaining that 'Mr Menzies is administering the University Act personally ...' (letter of 18 January 1950). Once in Canberra Oliphant was in regular contact with Menzies. In a confidential 'Note for Archives' initialled and dated 25 August 1953 and which began: 'During a discussion with the Prime Minister on August 25th', he set down Menzies' opinions he judged significant and confidential. In what today might be termed a 'spray', Menzies told the nuclear scientist for instance how little regard he had for the architect of University House, and the extent to which he supported the ANU. He said, wrote Oliphant, 'he, personally, had saved the University from complete extinction', and that 'the "security boys" had reported adversely on a number of members of staff, while the continued publicity given to new appointments had engendered in cabinet an impression that the place was snow-balling extravagantly'. (ANUA 19/8.2.1.4C & CA)

Canberra University College Council records

Minutes of meetings, 1938–1940

Early in 1939 the Council approached Menzies, then attorney-general and soon to be prime minister, to present an occasional address. The minutes of meetings in February, March, May and October 1939 provide the detail of the approach and the subsequent printing and circulation of the address. (ANUA 133/2)

Lectures and addresses, 1946–1960

Included in this small collection are a printed program for the foundation stone laying ceremony for the College's new Arts building, later named the Haydon–Allen Building, on 12 October 1959, and a roneoed copy of Menzies' speech. Doubtless on the day the guests followed his every word, not least as the decision on whether the College and the ANU would amalgamate was, as he teased, only a week or two away. Otherwise, judged by the text, there are some light witticisms and platitudes about higher education which amount to three pages of nothing. On the other hand, reflecting on his life at the conclusion of a two-volume study published in 1999, Allan Martin referred to Menzies' 'expository gifts' and, quoting Howard Beale that he was always a delight to hear, cautioned that written reports rarely caught the feel of his speeches. (ANUA 67)

H C Coombs papers

Confidential correspondence, 1946–1972

A cover note to the correspondence by ANU official historian Stephen Foster explains Coombs passed it to him in 1993, having withheld it from his own papers at the National Archives and from the ANU's official files. Coombs operated at the very centre of ANU affairs during its first four decades, being successively an Interim Council and Council member, Pro-Chancellor and Chancellor, and inevitably received sensitive documents. One letter, to 'Dear Nugget' from Professor R D Wright dated 26 August 1955, is worth quoting at some length:

> The Government, especially the PM, is prepared to interfere directly in policy and appointments at the University and to lead attacks on members of the staff who offend by expression of opinion adverse to the Government. Of course the Government provides the money but the Council is the governing body of the University. It is impossible for policy, appointments and discipline of staff. I myself have been annoyed at the apparently authentic story I have heard of RGM's personal participation in the appointment of the VC. I would expect any discipline of people such as Webb and Fitzgerald to be left as a matter for the Council – I have had personal conversation with RGM and expressed the view that if a member of staff published inaccurate information he was open to be shot at by the appropriate department, but if it was an expression of opinion it should be treated with respect and refuted with evidence, not ex cathedra polemic – but obviously RGM held the view that, while the government provided the funds, the members of the University should keep out of matters of public policy.

The correspondence also includes copies of letters between the Vice-Chancellor Leslie Melville and Menzies, 1954–1955, concerning ANU funding such as Professor Mark Oliphant's proton-synchrotron project. (ANUA 71/1)

Hugh Ennor papers

Confidential papers, 1965–1966

Professor Hugh (later Sir Hugh) Ennor served as Dean of the John Curtin School of Medical Research from 1953 to 1967, and during the last years of this term, also Deputy Vice-Chancellor. His papers include a number of references to Menzies, clearly indicating the extent to which he was interested in the ANU. There are for instance extracts of minutes of the ANU's Finance Committee meetings regarding a deputation to Menzies in July–August 1961. Also included are papers covering Menzies' receipt of an honorary Doctor of Laws degree in 1966. (ANUA 29)

Federal Chamber of Automotive Industries records

Correspondence, 1958

The folder comprises firstly copies of letters sent out announcing that the secretary of the Chamber, James ('Jim') R Murray, had resigned due to ill-health and secondly replies to the vice-president R M Jacka but mostly to Murray wishing him well. Murray had served as secretary for many years and from the replies, had clearly developed a large network of contacts and friends within the industry and in political circles, and was well respected. Menzies for instance wrote on 19 February 1958 to 'My dear Murray' that: 'It is a source of very real satisfaction to me that I can conduct negotiations with people like yourself, knowing that any disagreement on matters of policy will not endanger our happy personal relationships.' (NBAC Z171)

Laurie Fitzhardinge papers

Correspondence, 1938

The file includes a six-page typescript carbon copy of a speech Menzies gave to the Annual Dinner of the Royal Institute of International Affairs, London on 21 June 1938. An attached letter to Fitzhardinge from Peter Heydon, who had travelled with Menzies as his private secretary, explained the speech had 'caused a furore'. (ANUA 83/373)

Institute of Public Affairs (Victoria) records

Committee minutes and correspondence files, 1944–1969

Though not in any formal sense affiliated, the Institute and the Liberal Party were a natural fit, both establishing their organisation and policy in the mid-1940s. Accordingly, their records provide background and context to Menzies' role in establishing the new Liberal Party of Australia in the mid-1940s, developing a new political philosophy and presenting a cogent anti-Labor anti-socialist narrative. Menzies is referred to repeatedly here in minutes, speeches and reports, and more directly, in a small amount of correspondence. In short there is no 'smoking gun' document and no conspiratorial link to be documented, as discussed in Chapter 3, 'The IPA and three Liberal PMs'. There was on the other hand warm affection on both sides. The eleventh Annual Report reproduces Menzies' address to the April 1954 dinner thus: 'I would like to say to George Coles, and I would like to say to my friend Kemp, that the publications of the IPA have to me, and I don't doubt to many other people, been beyond value'. (NBAC N136)

Audrey Johnson papers

File on B A Santamaria, 1964–1984

Audrey Johnson was a left-wing social worker, university administrator, research assistant and the author of two works of biography. Among her papers is an unidentified file which suggests she compiled a dossier on B A Santamaria containing a small number of photocopies of speeches, pamphlets and clippings, as well as original newspaper articles and reviews. Included in the photocopies is a letter signed by Menzies to Santamaria dated 12 October 1976 offering support for *News Weekly*, mentioning an enclosed cheque, and ending: 'Your own Broadcasts, which are re-produced in the journal, are, as I have told you, full of the clearest political thinking which comes under my notice.' (NBAC N162/399)

Photographs, 1920s–1970s

Johnson was writing a biography of Tom Wright, federal secretary of the Sheet Metal Working Agricultural Implement and Stove Making Industrial Union of Australia, at the time of her death. Her papers include a photograph of Menzies and McMahon with Tom Wright and other union officials in the 1950s. (NBAC N162/182)

Geoffrey Sawer papers

File of correspondence with R G Menzies, 1966–1967

The file documents assistance the ANU Law Dean Geoffrey Sawer provided Menzies when the latter was reworking for publication the text of seven lectures he presented to the University of Virginia in 1967. In particular, Sawer assisted with the lecture on the famous 1920 Engineers' Case which made constitutional history when the 25-year-old Menzies won for the Amalgamated Society of Engineers with what his biographer Allan Martin called 'a series of brilliant moves' before the High Court, and which 'put a seal on what was already a promising practice'. In a long letter of 2 May 1966 Sawer suggested four lengthy additions to the lecture, and a careful comparison with Chapter 3 of the published version, *Central Power in the Australian Commonwealth* (Cassell, 1967) shows the extent to which Menzies adopted them. At the beginning of the book, Sawer is acknowledged for 'suggestions', but this letter, read side-by-side with the book, reveals the extent to which Sawer's actual phrases and sentences are repeated word for word as Menzies' own. Of course this was not plagiarism but, when one knows the actual origin of a sentence which begins 'I am under the impression, I may be wrong, that ...' (p. 29) hindsight may judge some of it as patently disingenuous. (ANUA 7/27)

Seamen's Union of Australia records

Federal election campaigns, 1941–1958

The file comprises letters, clippings, leaflets and speakers' notes directed to the defeat of the Menzies government at the federal elections of 1954 and 1955, the 1951 referendum and (though the links with Menzies are indirect) the 1943 federal election. There are also a few references to the 'Out Menzies' campaign. (NBAC E183/26/44)

'Out Menzies Campaign 1953' file

A file of papers comprising copies of letters sent by the secretary, Seamen's Union and the Out Menzies Deputation, correspondence with unions making contributions, copies of leaflets, lists of names for mail-outs relating to campaign activities, fund-raising, petitions, and a deputation to Canberra in March 1953. This campaign is also referred to elsewhere as the 'Oust Menzies' campaign. (NBAC Z263/42)

Phil Thorne collection

Publications, 1922–1957

The activist Phil Thorne's collection of socialist publications includes booklets such as *Guilty Men Again* by Len Fox and *Robbing your Pay Envelope* by R Dixon, president of the Communist Party of Australia, with caricatures of Menzies from the early 1950s. (NBAC P15/1/9, 13)

Waterside Workers' Federation records

Campaign material, 1952–1961

The WWF records include two folders of clippings, correspondence, leaflets, minutes, how-to-vote cards, single issues of union newspapers, mailing lists and other miscellaneous papers from several 1950s (primarily electoral) campaigns. Menzies is a constant thread: the sobriquet 'Pig Iron' is much in evidence, and there is material of the 1953 Combined Unions 'Oust Menzies' Committee, a comic titled 'Bob and his weird mob' and WWF and Communist Party campaign material urging defeat of the Liberal Party at the 22 November 1958 federal election. (NBAC Z248/67A)

Federal Committee of Management minutes, 1938–1939

As noted in the item on Menzies in Chapter 3 ('Pig Iron' Bob), the Federation's files provide important documentation of the context to Menzies' role in the industrial action at Port Kembla in 1938–1939 to stop the export of pig iron to Japan. Through the minutes of the Federal Committee of Management one can track the course of the dispute and negotiations. Providing almost a daily picture, the minutes also include copies of letters and telegrams such as the 'Urgent wire' from Menzies dated 29 November 1938 which threatened to apply the so-called 'dog licence' measures, and its reply which opened: 'Intended action of Government deplored by Committee Management Waterside Workers' Federation action of our members is not inconsistent with principles of democratic freedom stop'. (NBAC T62/1/3)

Photographs and cartoons, 1949–1966

The WWF collection includes photographs and cartoons which were used to illustrate the *Maritime Worker* (NBAC S62). Menzies features in caricature on WWF banners including at the May Day parade in 1954. There is also a photograph of 'The Lair' Smith, a regular Menzies impersonator and photographs of the 'Out Menzies' protests of the mid-1960s. A cartoon poster by Mickey Rooney headed 'Menzies'

Jungle Law' has Menzies say in reference to a WWF figure and the Stevedoring Bill: 'Never mind the Court of Enquiry – let's hang him first'. (NBAC Z248/81–2; P56/280/5)

Secretary General's files, 1932–1940

Included in the files of the WWF head office is correspondence documenting the national perspective of the Federation and thus relevant context to Menzies' crucial role in representing the Lyons government's position. The files include 'ACTU correspondence, 1932–1940', 'Correspondence, March 1936 – Jan 1940 w South Coast Branch' and 'Correspondence C'th A-Gs 1934–1939'. The latter provides a perspective on the long build-up to the Port Kembla dispute and the contentious *Transport Workers Act*, including letters and telegrams from Menzies sent to the Federation in 1935 and 1938. (NBAC T62/9/7/2, T62/24–5)

South Coast Branch minutes, 1931–1939

As noted in Chapter 3 ('Pig Iron' Bob), the Federation's files provide important documentation of the context to Menzies' role as attorney-general and minister for industry in the Lyons government in ending the industrial action at Port Kembla in 1938–1939 to stop the export of pig iron to Japan. The minutes of the Port Kembla branch, as it was commonly known, include those for a series of 'special meetings' held in November – December 1938 and January 1939. Of special note are references to the 'proposed visit of Menzies & the arrangement that are in hand' (meeting of 10 January 1939), a report on negotiations with Menzies '& the subsequent formula' (16 January 1939) and the motion of 17 January 1939: 'Mov E Roach & W Midgley that we recommend the acceptance of the proposals & furthermore that in the event of a future attempt being made to ship any further contracts that we emphatically refuse to handle it.' (NBAC Z429/53)

EARLE PAGE, 1939

Amalgamated Postal Workers' Union of Australia records

Government and Parliamentary members' correspondence files, 1920–1952

The APWUA and its predecessor before it was formed in 1926 represented postmen, sorters and linesmen employed by the Postmaster-General's Department. The files record the union's lobbying, advocacy and pursuit of redress, participation in inquiries, submissions on legislative amendments and negotiations for increased pay and improved entitlements and working conditions. The union also campaigned as part of the Combined Federal Service Unions, and courtesy copies of its letters will also be found here. Page attracted the union's ire over his comments from the backbench in 1929–1930 concerning the federal service arbitration system, citing the tone of its letters as his reason for refusing to meet them. There is other correspondence on file involving Page as treasurer (1926, 1928) regarding the weekly payment of salaries, the Commonwealth Employees Compensation Bill and the discharge of temporary employees. (NBAC T35/22/5, 13, 37, 42)

Australian Dictionary of Biography files

Earle Page, 1985–1990

Dr Carl Bridge's 4,000-word biography of Page appeared at pp. 118–22 of volume 11 of the Dictionary published in 1988. All the expected papers are there: copies of certificates of birth, death and the two marriages, clippings, obituaries, index cards, drafts, readers' comments and correspondence about drafts and corrigenda. Reading the file, concern about reputation and truth emerge as the main subtext. It includes for instance an itemised list of the factual errors and inconsistencies in Page's autobiography *Truant Surgeon* (1959). As for Bridge's earliest draft, the editors allowed some strong appraisals ('Having destroyed Hughes in 1922, Page now tried to destroy Menzies'), but were careful too, as general editor Geoff Serle implied in his letter of 6 April 1987 ('I've incorporated a number of changes suggested by the family and by your various readers'). The family issue concerned the first Mrs Page. Although Bridge's draft had in effect shown that separation is not necessarily estrangement, later he had also written: 'Ethel had moved up from Sydney to help her son and remained with her husband until he re-entered politics'. The editors added 'at Boolneringbar', the family property near Grafton to avoid, as Serle explained, 'the suggestion that Page & his wife separated in anything but temporary physical terms once he re-entered politics. The family is very sensitive on that point.' (ANUA 312)

Australian National University photographs

Envelopes of photographs of people and events, 1948–2005

Page attended the installation of Bruce as Chancellor on 22–23 October 1952 and was photographed at that event. He was also later photographed with Bruce at

University House in his robes as Chancellor of the University of New England on the occasion of the conferring of an honorary degree on Dr Harold Macmillan in January 1958. (ANUA 15/6, 55)

Canberra University College Council minutes

Minutes of meetings, 1930–1938

At its meeting of 2 April 1935, under item 7, Establishment of a National University at Canberra, the Council received a report from George (later Sir George) Knowles, at the time Solicitor-General and a foundation member of the Council. He told the Council that he 'had had an interesting talk with the Acting Prime Minister (Dr Earle Page) regarding the prospects of establishing a University in Canberra, and Dr Page had stated that he was convinced of the necessity for taking steps in that direction at once'. (ANUA 133/1)

GEORGE REID, 1904–1905

Australian Dictionary of Biography files

George Reid, 1985–1989

Documented here are the commissioning, subsequent interactions and approval of Associate Professor W G McMinn's 6,000-word biography of Reid published in the *Australian Dictionary of Biography*, volume 11, Melbourne University Press, 1988, pp. 347–54. Fortuitously, McMinn had been preparing a full-scale biography of Reid, which appeared also under the MUP imprint the following year, and was able to draw on the file's research groundwork compiled by the ADB staff: copies of index cards from various sources, newspaper clippings, references to NSW government and Mitchell Library sources, and copies of birth, death and marriage certificates. Inevitably too there is correspondence with editors, and evidence of considerable editing. One ADB query related to the date the Labor Party adopted a 'fighting platform' (1904 or 1905), and another concerned a common ADB issue, how to succinctly summarise cause of death as detailed in the death certificate. In Reid's case, 'Cellulitis of Face 14 days Cerebral Thrombosis Coma Heart Failure 18 Hours' (which the ADB's medical expert had annotated: 'Could be an interesting sequence but insufficient detail. I'd omit') was reduced to: 'He died ... of cerebral thrombosis'. A final point of debate was the origin of the answer: 'It's all piss and wind, I'll call it after you', attributed to Reid when a heckler alluded to his large belly and asked what he would name his child. The general editor Geoff Serle asked McMinn in a letter of 14 December 1987: 'A vital point of scholarship! Your Reid story of piss and wind. Can you document it?', explaining that others believed it a Churchillian saying. McMinn replied citing two anecdotes from people claiming to be there though he first heard of it in 1953, including from A Y Jennings 'who claimed to be the heckler' and named the location (Newcastle) and date (1898) of the speech. The quoted response survived to be published. (ANUA 312)

KEVIN RUDD, 2007–2010

Australian National University student files

Thérèse Rein, 1975–1987

The file allows one to track Rein's time at the ANU where she gained an Arts degree in 1979 and qualified to undertake a Master of Arts in Psychology in 1981. It begins with an application to enrol as an Arts/Law student in mid-1975, which was deferred as she was technically too young, with subsequent changes in degree and subject preferences, and the deferment of an honours year. Also recorded are details of her employment with the ANU's Faculty of Economics and the Department of Trade and Resources, and brief enrolments in 1979 as a Master of Education (Counselling) student at the Canberra College of Advanced Education and in 1986 as a Bachelor of Letters student back at the ANU. (ANUA 78/764868)

Kevin Rudd, 1975–1990

The file relates to Rudd's years as an ANU undergraduate. It opens with a purposeful handwritten letter of declaration and request, and ends with an impressive list of results (ranging from Credit to Distinction) for subjects dominated by Linguistics, Asian Civilizations and Modern Chinese. In between there is the predictable evidence of his enrolments, payment of student union and other fees and brief changes of subject interest before the award of a first class honours Bachelor of Arts (Asian Studies) degree. There are also letters from Rudd, copies of those sent to him from the Registrar and others, and internal memos about him by his teachers concerning for example his 1979 'gap year' during which he undertook intensive language study at the National Taiwan Normal University's Mandarin Centre. The file shows he seriously contemplated studying law several times (in early 1978 as a combined degree, then in 1979 as a second degree), and there is reference to him having enrolled part-time in a Master of Arts in Strategic and Defence Studies. (ANUA 78/76A548)

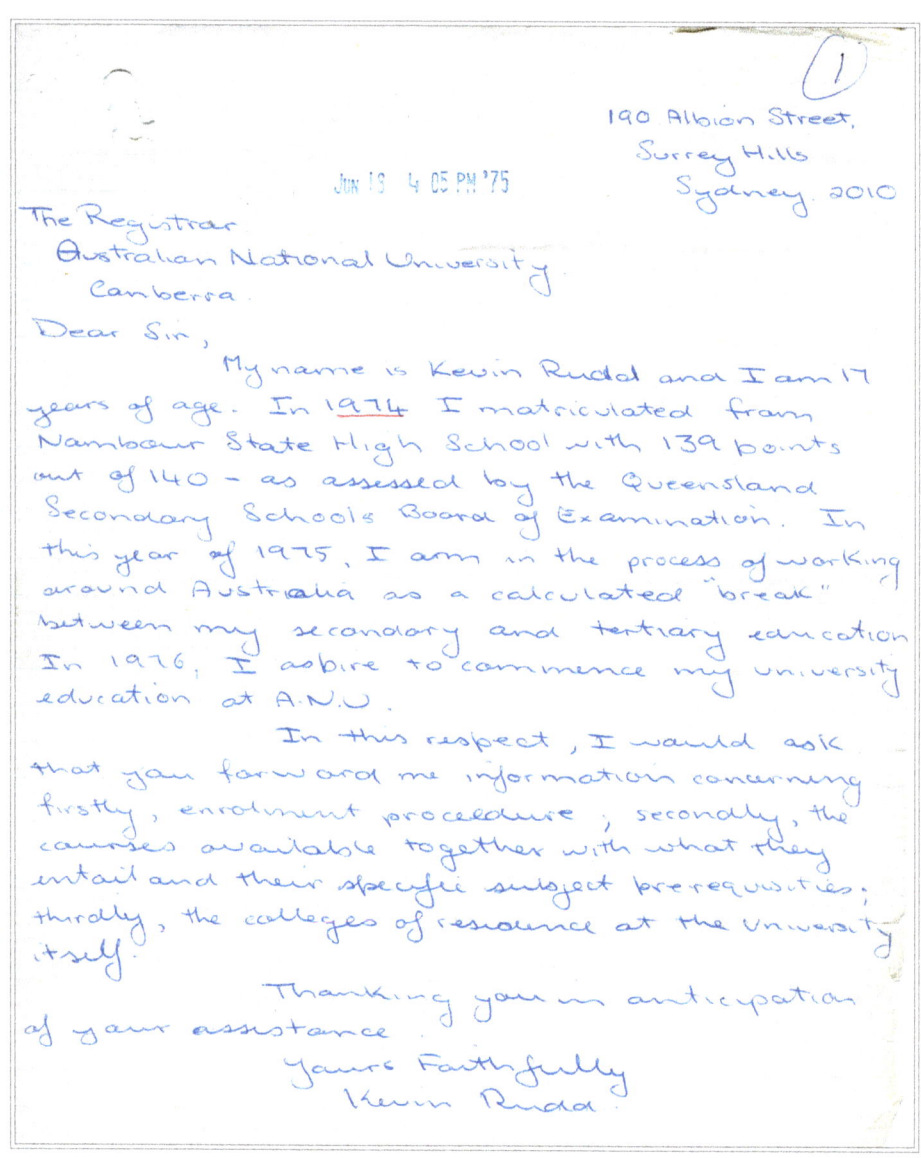

Kevin Rudd begins his association with the ANU in 1975, requesting information on enrolment procedures (ANUA 78/76A548)

JAMES SCULLIN, 1929–1932

Amalgamated Postal Workers' Union of Australia records

Government and Parliamentary members' correspondence files, 1920–1952

The APWUA and its predecessor before it was formed in 1926 represented postmen, sorters and linesmen employed by the Postmaster-General's Department. The files record the union's lobbying, advocacy and pursuit of redress, participation in inquiries, submissions on legislative amendments and negotiations for increased pay and improved entitlements and working conditions. The union also campaigned as part of the Combined Federal Service Unions, and courtesy copies of its letters will also be found here. The union was in contact with Scullin as leader of the opposition and the Parliamentary Labor Party (1928, 1929, 1932, 1935), as prime minister (1930, 1931) and as a backbencher deputising for Curtin (1942) during some of the worst years of economic hardship and industrial unrest. The matters canvassed included a five-day working week, a minimum living wage, the 1929 joint conference, preference for union members, government policy regarding retirement, deduction of tax from Commonwealth employees, and the discharge of temporary employees. (NBAC T35/22/1, 5–6, 13–14, 21, 27–8, 34, 39, 42)

Australasian Coal and Shale Employees' Federation records

Central Council minutes, 1928–1930

Scullin became prime minister following a 'landslide' federal election in October 1929. He inherited a volatile industrial situation on the northern coalfields of New South Wales and within weeks faced the collapse of the New York stock exchange. These minutes present the thinking of one of the key unions involved, and thus constitute important context for a fuller understanding of what Scullin was required to manage. They mention, inter alia, correspondence and meetings with Scullin as well as with other unions including the Australian Council of Trade Unions. (NBAC E204/1/4, E204/2/1)

Australian Dictionary of Biography files

James Scullin, 1987–1988

This file records the commissioning, subsequent interactions and approval of John Robertson's 3,500-word biography of Scullin published in the *Australian Dictionary of Biography*, volume 11, Melbourne University Press, 1988, pp. 553–7. It includes the usual papers such as clippings (some originals from 1959), reviews of Robertson's biography of Scullin published in 1974, photocopies of index cards, copies of various wills, birth, marriage and death certificates, drafts and corrigenda. The most surprising of these is the correction needed to the original entry which had Scullin abolishing rather than suspending compulsory military training. It had been repeated as 'abolished' three times in Robertson's published biography and the *Australian Encyclopaedia*, and had been missed by all ADB quality controls. (ANUA 312)

Australian Workers' Union records

Photographs, 1888–1986

Scullin is photographed standing on the balcony of the Australian Workers' Union Building in Ballarat. (NBAC N117/1370)

Christian Jollie Smith and Company records

Legal papers and correspondence, 1930–1931

Christian Jollie Smith and Company were solicitors who represented men appealing against charges of unlawful assembly made under the *Crimes (Intimidation and Molestation) Act 1929*. They had participated in riots triggered by a long festering lockout on the NSW northern coalfields during 1929–1930 which resulted in forty wounded and one fatally shot by the police, the cases becoming known as the 'Rothbury appeals'. The affidavits, judgements, correspondence, telegrams and clippings thus provide important context to Scullin's tortured and ill-fated prime ministership. (NBAC P15/8–10)

THE ARCHIVES

James Scullin, in a bowler hat, on the balcony of the Australian Workers' Union Building in Ballarat (NBAC N117/1370)

Federated Furnishing Trades Society of Australia records

Photographs, 1898–1940

A photograph of over 100 delegates to the Australian Labor Party conference in April 1919 in Melbourne includes Scullin. (NBAC T58/36/24, K2005)

Lake George Mines Pty Ltd records

Typescript document: 'Economic position of the Metalliferous Mining Industry', c. 1930

The thirteen-page document is annotated to indicate it was intended for Scullin and prepared by T Maughan 'about the beginning of 1930'. It is clearly written from an employer's viewpoint, and Maughan we know from other sources was the general secretary of the Australian Mines and Metals Association. The typescript refers to Scullin: 'As a native of Ballarat, the Prime Minister will not be insensible of the great part that gold mining has played', arguing that the industry has reached a crisis; it sees unions and high wages as a problem in the face of overseas competitors and it calls for 'this great primary industry' to be saved. (NBAC 67/142)

JOHN CHRISTIAN WATSON, 1904

Australian Dictionary of Biography files

John Christian Watson, 1988–1993

This file, both mundane and exceptional, documents the commissioning, subsequent interactions and approval of Bede Nairn's 4,500-word biography of Watson published in the *Australian Dictionary of Biography*, volume 12, Melbourne University Press, 1990, pp. 400–5. There are photocopies of *Sydney Morning Herald* index cards, *Who's Who* entries, newspaper articles, manuscript research notes by ADB staff, correspondence and annotated drafts. The file also includes a fascinating and highly entertaining exchange between the author and general editor John Ritchie over historical points, choice of words and phrases, word length and proposed changes; the key area of contention concerning Watson's early background, his British citizenship and the meaning of his visits back to New Zealand. (ANUA 312)

Australian Workers' Union records

Annual Conference minutes, 1896–1897

Among his many roles within the labour movement in the 1890s, Watson was a member of the Australian Workers' Union. His standing is evident from minutes of AWU annual conferences held in Ballarat in 1896 and in Sydney in February 1897. Watson was the returning officer at the former, which ran for eleven days from 1 to 11 February 1896. When a challenge to the president required a neutral chair to manage discussion to consider it, Watson took the chair for the first four days. He was formally thanked for 'the manner he had carried out his duties as chairman' and the following day voted a fee of £5/5s and a delegate's payment of 15/-. At the 1897 conference held in Sydney over seventeen days in February, he was asked to stand in for the delayed Creswick branch delegates until they arrived. (NBAC N117/2)

> 6
>
> Mr Gilbert moved } That Mr J C
> " Temple sec } Watson M L A
> be appointed chairman
> during the discussion of
> the protest.   Carried
>
> Mr Watson then took the chair.
>
> Mr McCook moved } That correspondence
> Gilbert seconded } be received
>   Carried
>
> Mr A Poynton M L A of
> Port Augusta who was present
> asked Conference to fix a day
> when his case could be taken
>
> Mr Gilbert moved } That the case
> " Toomey sec } of Mr Poynton
> and Port Augusta Branch
> be taken on Monday week
>   Carried
>
> Mr Gilbert moved } That Workers business
> " McCook sec } be dealt with on
> Saturday week 8th inst
>   Carried
>
> Mr McCook   } That Conference
> Macdonell   } adjourn till Monday
> morning at 10 oclock
>   Carried
>
> Conference at 12.30 adjourned
>
>   Confirmed
>   J Chris Watson
>   3/2/96.   acting chairman

John Christian Watson signed the minutes for the 1896 Australian Workers' Union convention as acting chairman (NBAC N117/2/6)

Ballarat Trades and Labour Council records

General correspondence, 1884–1923

Includes a folder of correspondence for 1905 with a two-page typescript letter signed on behalf of the Federal Labor Party by J C Watson and Frank G Tudor. They urge the Council to adopt a label under the new *Trade Marks Act* to signal the formation of a 'Union of Trades Councils' and propose a meeting at Trades Hall, Melbourne. (NBAC E97/7/1905)

Labor Papers Ltd records

Minutes of meetings of the Directors, 1910–1939

The minutes document Watson's six-year relationship, starting as 'organizer for the paper at a salary of £6 per week and 1st class fares & expenses for the year, as offered him by the shareholders at the second ordinary general meeting' (1st meeting of directors 13 January 1911, p. 39), shortly after being elected chairman of directors (1 March 1911, p. 40), and at the 1914 annual general meeting its managing director. The minutes, which Watson signed as meeting chair, record mostly mundane matters such as shares and debentures, his authority to act, staff appointments and fixing dates for shareholders' annual general meetings. Occasionally larger matters are discussed such as the purchase of land and the erection of a building in Pitt Street and Watson's remuneration (£500 p.a.) for coordinating this and practically single-handedly running the company. The last meeting he chaired, on 14 November 1916, records his forced resignation for supporting conscription (see also Chapter 3, 'Three Labor dismissals'). The minutes (pp. 144–6) present a sharp contrast to the tone of public meetings and newspaper cartoons of the day, his words suggesting a parallel with a more recent prime ministerial departure:

> The attitude of Mr J C Watson in connection with the conscription issue and his position of Managing Director & Chairman of Directors was next considered. Mr Watson explained his view & stated he did not feel justified in voluntarily resigning but if the Directors considered it would be in the best interests of the Company to resign he would do so. Mr Lundie then moved & Mr T Hyett seconded That in the best interest of the Company it was desirable for Mr Watson to resign his position as Managing Director & chairman of Directors. Carried.
>
> In resigning Mr Watson suggested that a special audit of the books be made to the 15th November 1916 & that a report be obtained as to the suitability of the machinery & plant installed for publishing a morning paper up to 24 pages. The suggestions were agreed to.

Mr Watson asked that his appreciation of the services rendered by Mr C Bamford the Business Manager, Mr H S Wynne the Engineer & Mr O E Foster, the Secretary, be placed on record.

Mr Rae moved & Mr Hyett seconded That the thanks of the Directors be tendered to the retiring managing director, Mr J C Watson, for his services while occupying that position. Carried. (NBAC N117/1531)

Minutes of the annual meetings of shareholders, 1910–1943

These minutes complement those for the directors' meetings noted above, and importantly cover the 1910–1911 period before the company was formally established. In particular, they record: 'A meeting of Promoters for the purpose of establishing a daily news paper' on 28 January 1910 when Watson was elected a provisional director. The minutes have him signing minutes and attending the first annual meeting 10 February 1910 and the first general meeting on 2 July 1910. They reveal Watson was initially elected one of the directors (p. 8) and appointed 'to organize for the Company' at a salary of £6 per week. At the following annual general meeting (p. 10) on 5 February 1912 he was chairman of directors. (NBAC N117/1534)

NSW Typographical Association records

Australasian Typographical Journal, 1890–1897

The Journal provides the broader context of the NSW Association's work and Watson's involvement detailed elsewhere in the minutes. Most monthly issues included a section headed 'Our Sydney Letter' which carried the occasional explicit mention. Thus issue no. 273 of March 1893 refers to Watson helping resolve a dispute when linotype machines were introduced at the *Daily Telegraph* and, with other Association officials, negotiate conditions and rates for machine operators (no. 287, May 1894). His final appearance (January 1895, p. 2547) was a report of his election as the first president of the NSW Provincial Council of the Australian Labor Federation. It concluded: 'From past experience he will doubtless prove a capable and efficient officer, and he carries the good wishes of all comps for his successful administration of the important position.' (NBAC T39/67/1)

Minutes, 1886–1894

The minutes cover monthly and special meetings of the board of management and of half-yearly and annual meetings of the Association. Watson was working at the *Globe* when he was accepted as a member at the monthly meeting of 26 June 1886 (T39/1/2, p. 1), but when he joined the Association's board of management it was to represent 'composing staff' at the *Australian Star*. From then until mid-1894 he was active in practically every meeting, though at one point he sought leave to return to New Zealand (T39/1/3, 19 December 1888, p. 1). He proposed and seconded motions, argued about rules, joined special committees and delegations, and was drawn into the debates and issues of the moment such as support for strikes and the Anti-Chinese League (T39/1/2, 7 July 1888, p. 451) and for industry-wide coordination through a Printing Trades Kindred Committee (T39/1/5, 25 March 1893, p. 102). It was during this time, the minutes show, that Watson came to know the industrial landscape and the labour movement. Through the minutes one can track his rise, serving first as the Association's delegate to the Trades and Labour Council, then one of its two vice-presidents, the only setback being his rejection for president in 1892 (T39/1/4, p. 223). When his links with the Association ended in mid-1894 because the Council folded, Watson had been its president three times. (NBAC T39/1/2–5)

Photographs, 1891–1927

Included in an album of photographs of the Association is a group photograph of delegates to the Interstate Labor Conference held in January 1900. In the front row, Billy Hughes in a straw boater is seated on the ground and beside him Watson in a bowler hat. (NBAC T39/74/26, K3808b)

Subscription books, 1884–1895

The books provide the financial detail of Watson's membership of the Association, the most intriguing aspect being to record him having paid 4/– as a casual member (as opposed to being linked to a specific workplace) in May–June 1894, two years earlier than biographers say he migrated from New Zealand. Given the industrial conflicts of the time, the emerging national union movement was called on to provide support to those on strike and in need. Watson is recorded contributing to the 1888 Unemployed Relief Fund, the 1888 Brisbane Strike and Unemployed Relief Levy, the 1888 Newcastle Miners Strike Levy, the 1889 Adelaide Compositors Strike Levy and the 1890 Defence Levy. (NBAC T39/13/1–2)

Sydney Wharf Labourers' Union records

Minutes, 1896–1897, 1899–1902, 1912–1913

Though rightly linked with Hughes (given his position as foundation secretary), Watson also participated in early meetings of the Wharf Labourers and its predecessor. In the mid to late 1890s, Watson was Labor's leading parliamentarian, prominent in the NSW parliament and when the new Commonwealth parliament began sitting, elected leader of the new Parliamentary Labor Party. As these minutes show, he joined Hughes in urging better organisation of unions across industries and across the country, explicitly noted as addressing three meetings in 1896. He reappears in the minutes in 1912. By then he was a labour movement elder working for the Australian Workers' Union, and one project in particular, what the minute taker called 'Daily Labor Newspaper'. At the union meeting of 26 June:

> Mr Watson who was heartily received gave a very forcible & able address in which he pointed out the advantages to be gained by the Unions taking shares in the paper and concluded with a strong appeal to the members present to show their sympathy by taking action in that direction at the earliest opportunity. Mr Watson at the conclusion of his speech was asked and answered several questions. (NBAC Z248/95, 97)

GOUGH WHITLAM, 1972–1975

Australian Council of Trade Unions records

Photographs, 1977

Whitlam is photographed with Bob Hawke, Sir John Moore, Sir Richard Kirby and trade union officials at the dinner celebrating the 50th anniversary of the ACTU on 3 May 1977. Margaret Whitlam and Hazel Hawke are also present. (NBAC N68/956–1010)

Australian Dictionary of Biography files

Sir George Knowles, 1981–1985

The file covers the commissioning, preparation and editing of a 500-word article by Whitlam which appeared on page 623 of volume 9 of the Dictionary published in 1983. Conveniently at the ANU at the time, he was suggested as author by the deputy general editor Chris Cunneen for reasons not recorded – though a factor may have been that Knowles (Commonwealth Solicitor-General, 1932–1946) and Gough's father Fred Whitlam (Crown-Solicitor, 1936–1949) knew each other well, and shared involvements with the University Association of Canberra and the Canberra University College Council. The author's characteristic and at times irritating love of accuracy and detail are evident in his correspondence with editors Geoff Serle and Bede Nairn. In one letter, he acknowledges his sister Freda's help in fixing the start date of Knowles' secretaryship of the University Association to 1928. This proved to be out by a year, prompting the file marginalia: 'Hooray Freda got it wrong'. (ANUA 312)

Hubert Lazzarini, 1995–1998

This file also fails to explain why Whitlam was asked by the ADB to write a 750-word piece on the federal politician and minister in the Curtin and Chifley governments, Hubert Lazzarini. However, the biography, which appeared in 2000 at pp. 68–9 of volume 15, is suggestive, noting that: 'Following the April 1951 polls, [Lazzarini] announced that he would not contest the next. Chifley thought that a local candidate should replace him. In a protracted contest E G Whitlam emerged from a final scrum of nine.' What is clear from the file is the author's enthusiasm for the research the writing involved, Whitlam staying in regular touch with general editor John Ritchie and sending as much to the ADB from his inquiries of, for example, the Land Titles Office and the Electoral Commission as it traditionally sent to authors. Not surprising then was his admission (letter of 4 June 1996) that he 'was carried away by the subject's exceptional ethnic background, electoral mobility and factional experience'. The Dictionary kept their internal assessments of the drafts largely from him ('Very flat & one dimensional. It's Pol Sci r/t [rather than] biography'), but it did negotiate a shorter final draft. By 1997, all concerns resolved, Whitlam was praising Ritchie's new book *The Wentworths* and the general editor was asking 'Dear Gough' if there would ever be a republic. (ANUA 312)

Harry Frederick Ernest Whitlam, 1999–2002

The file documents the production of a 750-word entry by Cameron Hazlehurst on Fred Whitlam which appeared in 2002 at pp. 540–1 of volume 16 of the Dictionary. Its contents conform to the standard: correspondence and emails with the editors, drafts, photocopies of clippings, index cards and birth, death and marriage certificates. As is often the case with these files, the most interesting feature is the exchanges about deletions and rephrasing. Hazlehurst, providing 915 words when asked for a maximum of 750, was nevertheless disappointed by the ADB's passing if succinct reference to Fred's son to the effect that he 'was to become prime minister'. He told them he thought 'my formulation was better – Gough liked it too'. The editors cut an entire section on Fred's siblings too, and reading the file, it is hard not to disagree that, as Hazlehurst emailed the deputy general editor on 1 March 2001, it was a shame that information about the brothers was deleted: 'it took a great deal of digging, and would be very useful to students of Gough's life as well'. (ANUA 312)

Australian National University Advisers on Legislation minutes

Minutes of meetings, 1951–1970

The minutes document H F E Whitlam's membership of the committee established in 1951 by Council to provide advice on statutes, rules, orders, aspects of the *Australian National University Act 1946* and ACT ordinances. He was a member from the beginning, attended most meetings, and when Professor Bailey was absent, took the chair. The minutes for 5 December 1969 noted Whitlam's resignation to be submitted to next meeting, just over two years before his death on 8 December 1971. (ANUA 200/1–5)

Australian National University correspondence files

Canberra University College – establishment of a National University, 1933–1938

This ANU file incorporates a top-numbered Canberra University College file from the 1930s, including clippings, correspondence and other papers. Among them are papers on a conference held on 26 April 1934 re proposals for a university for Canberra, specifically a typescript 'Summary of proceedings of a conference between the Council of the Canberra University College and the Council of the University Association of Canberra' which records H F E Whitlam's interventions. It also includes signed letters from Whitlam as secretary of the University Association of Canberra. (ANUA 53/14.1.0.77 part 1)

John Curtin Memorial Lectures, 1970–1984

The file documents the establishment and administration of the lecture program including a copy of the sixth lecture, delivered by Gough Whitlam and entitled 'Government of the people, for the people – by the people'. There is also correspondence from June–September 1975 between Vice-Chancellor Low, Whitlam and his office. (ANUA 53/10.02.2.47 parts 1–2)

National Fellowships, 1980–1997

The file includes a small number of papers on Whitlam's appointment by the ANU as a National Fellow. He was appointed on 14 November 1980 on the recommendation of the Honorary Degrees Committee. (ANUA 53/4.2.0.213)

Registration for National Service, 1965–1972

Australia's involvement in the Vietnam War, conscription, anti-war protests and the ANU's relationship with the Holt, Gorton and McMahon governments form the backdrop to this multi-part file. Students were refusing to register for national service, those pursued by the authorities were finding sanctuary on campus, and funds were being collected for the National Liberation Front. The Vice-Chancellor at the time, Sir John Crawford, tried to maintain the university's independence, and the privacy of student information, but for a time faced proposed amendments to the *National Service Act* aimed at requiring the addresses of draft resisters to be supplied to the government. The file includes correspondence, press releases, newspaper clippings, telegrams and legal opinions. Inevitably, it includes references to McMahon who was minister for labour and national service and Fraser who was minister for education and science under Gorton, and to Holt and Gorton as well. Finally there are references to draft resisters criticising Whitlam for arguing that they should give themselves up. (ANUA 53/4.0.0.22 parts 1–3 & C)

Australian National University Council minutes

Minutes of meetings, 1951–1954

The Council records at its 20th meeting on 12 November 1954 the creation of an advisory committee called the Advisors on Legislation and its membership which included Gough Whitlam's father, H F E Whitlam. (ANUA 198/7)

Australian National University Instructional Resources Unit recordings

Audio and video tapes, 1972–1995

The John Curtin Memorial Lecture delivered by Gough Whitlam in late 1975 was recorded by the Instructional Resources Unit. (ANUA 51/75002)

Australian National University photographs

Envelopes of photographs of people and events, 1948–2005

Gough Whitlam was a regular visitor to the University and appears in many photographs taken at events on campus. He was photographed with Vice-Chancellor Sir Leonard Huxley and Professor Dale Trendall, Master of University House in October 1962, with Professor Sir Ernest Titterton at the Research School of

Physical Sciences in 1973, delivering the John Curtin lecture in October 1975, and at a Convocation luncheon in 1978 speaking on Australia's regional opportunities and responsibilities. There are also photographs of Whitlam with Indira Gandhi, Prime Minister of India in 1973 and with Dr Stephen FitzGerald and Hua Kuo-feng, Chinese premier, in July 1976 (ANUA 225/1315). Whitlam launched Stewart Harris' book *This is Our Land* and was photographed with Paul Coe, the Indigenous spokesman in October 1972 (ANUA 226/478). He launched H C Coombs' autobiography *Trial Balance* in 1981 (ANUA 225/248). He was photographed with Rafe de Crespigny and two delegates from a Libyan Trade Mission in November 1979 (ANUA 226/552). As Australian Ambassador to UNESCO, he donated the *Journal of Pacific History*, published by the Research School of Pacific Studies, to the organisation in Paris in 1985 (ANUA 226/522). In December 1994 he attended a conference on campus on the Labor tradition in foreign policy. A drawing by Rik Bigwood of Whitlam, Gareth Evans and Arthur Calwell illustrated the event (ANUA 226/565). Margaret Whitlam was photographed at the Australian Playwrights' Conference at Burton Hall in May 1977 (ANUA 226/458) and at University House in 1990 (ANUA 225/1314). Gough's father H F E Whitlam was photographed at the dinner for the retiring Interim Council in July 1951 (ANUA 12/9).

Gough Whitlam with Indian Prime Minister Indira Gandhi, accompanied by ANU Vice-Chancellor (later Chancellor) Sir John Crawford in 1973 (ANUA 225/1315/1)

Australian National University staff files

Gough Whitlam, Visiting Fellow/National Fellow, 1978–1983

The two-part file documents the selection and administration of Whitlam as an ANU Visiting Fellow (1978–1980) then ANU's first National Fellow (1980–1981). It covers his conditions (research assistance and subsidised University House flat), remuneration, scholarly standing, and election as an Honorary Fellow of University House in 1982. The papers include internal memos and letters by the Vice-Chancellor Anthony Low, letters to him from Whitlam, students and members of the public, press items about protests when it was thought that Whitlam's tenure was to be extended, reports of overseas trips while a Visiting Fellow and copies of addresses he made during this period. (ANUA 19/4.2.4.50 & C)

Australian Workers' Union records

Photographs, 1888–1986

Whitlam is photographed with union officials Tom Dougherty and Charlie Oliver in the 1960s. (NBAC N117/1353–4)

Canberra University College minutes

Council minutes, 1930–1943

The minutes include reference to three Whitlams: Gough, Freda and their father Fred. They enable one to track Gough Whitlam's award and use of a scholarship under a CUC scheme established in 1930 to support Canberra-based Leaving Certificate students planning to attend university outside Canberra. They cover the initial award to study Arts at the University of Sydney and deferment while Whitlam studied Greek (meeting of 13 February 1934), the details of payments (£40 per term), annual results, granting of renewals (1935–1938), letters of support from H J Filshie, member of Council and headmaster of Telopea Park Intermediate High School, and the scholarship extension when Whitlam, having obtained an Arts degree, moved on to Law in 1938. The minutes also record the application by Gough Whitlam's sister Freda to sit for Honours, the meeting of 2 May 1939 noting this was deferred on technical grounds. She is mentioned again in the meeting of 17 February 1941 as one of a number of students who failed a subject the previous year, in her case Philosophy I. This subject was not planned to be offered the next year; in her case, the minutes note she might change to Economic History. The minutes also document H F E Whitlam's work as a member of the Council and a lecturer with the College, 1931–1942. They cover, inter alia, his appointment as a lecturer in Commercial Law (meeting of 23 February 1931), details of his students, his 'in kind' stipend and travel authorisation (26 March 1931), his and his wife's cash contribution of £10.10.0 towards the establishment of 'a University Trust Fund for the purpose of promoting the cause of University education and the establishment of a University in the Territory' (2 November 1934), involvement on Council committees (29 March 1940) and Council's appreciation of his service (3 February 1942). (ANUA 133/1–4)

George Crawford papers

Files and loose papers, 1951–1988

In the 1960s, when Whitlam waged a bitter campaign to change the internal structures and processes of the Australian Labor Party, the fiercest resistance came from the Victorian branch. One of the branch's key officials was George Crawford and his papers document an important part of the setting for that campaign. A strong supporter of peace and left-wing causes, he had also held state and federal positions with the Plumbers and Gasfitters Employees' Union of Australia. Crawford's papers also include material on the Victorian branch and federal executive of the ALP, the ALP Socialist Left and the Plumbers' Union. (NBAC Z494)

Jack Dwyer collection

Transcripts of speeches, 1968–1977

Jack Dwyer was a union delegate and official for the Federated Miscellaneous Workers' Union from the early 1940s until the mid-1970s. His collection of papers includes transcripts of speeches by Whitlam from 1968 to 1977. (NBAC Z296/15)

Michael Easson subject files

ALP Victorian Branch, 1970–1985

The file covers the power plays of factions (the Participants, Labor Unity, Socialist Left, Centre Unity and Centre Majority) within the Victorian ALP and union movement, and thus helps document the context to Whitlam's battles inside the labour movement leading up to and beyond gaining power in 1972. Subjects covered include the Combe/Ivanov Royal Commission, anti-uranium campaigns, re-affiliation of unions with the ALP, the Landeryou affair and ALP committee reports. In part accumulated from material sent to Easson by David Cragg (from Senator Ray's office), it comprises letters, newspaper clippings, photocopies of journal articles, leaflets, circular letters, policy discussion papers and how-to-vote cards. (NBAC Z514/34a)

Subject file on Gough Whitlam, 1970s–1990s

Among the hundreds of files compiled by trade union official Easson during 1973–1994 is a file on Gough Whitlam comprising mostly clippings, talks and similar material but also including a 1993 letter from Whitlam to Easson mentioning the Italian Socialist Party and ITAL Uil. (NBAC Z514/357)

D A Low papers

Folder relating to Whitlam's appointment as a Visiting Fellow, 1978–1980

The papers document the negotiations between the ANU Vice-Chancellor Anthony Low and Gough Whitlam which began five months before his retirement from parliament in July 1978 to his appointment shortly after as a Visiting Fellow in the Research School of Pacific Studies. They provide a genuine insider perspective of a controversial decision, from which one can piece together how the decision was internally negotiated, made and defended, and the media managed. The folder includes correspondence between Low and Whitlam, anonymous letters of protest from the public at the announcement of Whitlam as Visiting Fellow, press cartoons drawing on the speculation (especially a series of hilarious comic strip cartoons by Larry Pickering called 'The Ishbondogla Gang' published in the *Weekend Australian* in mid-1978), notes from academics re leaking of the news, extracts from the ANU Council and other official documents about the appointment, Low's chronology of the negotiation steps in the six months prior to the announcement on 14 July 1978, letters from supporters (especially Dr Stephen FitzGerald and Dr W S Ramson), doubters (Trevor Swan) and external advisers (J D B Miller), and memos some labelled 'Very Confidential'. (ANUA 55/35)

National Farmers' Federation records

Speeches and press statements by the Prime Minister, 1972–1977

As a national body whose aims include influencing government policies relating to farmers' interests, the Federation monitored statements issued by ministers on a broad range of economic, industrial trade and other subjects. The file on Whitlam has a range of transcripts of interviews, printed ministerial statements, national addresses and press releases, the concentration of documents dated December 1972 – March 1973 testifying to the Federation's close monitoring of the high activity and energy of the new government. There are also manuscripts notes on an NFF meeting with Whitlam on 20 March 1975, and copies of several letters to him. (NBAC Z135/59)

North Australia Research Unit records

Photographs, 1974–1997

Whitlam visited the ANU's Northern Territory campus in Darwin in August 1994 with Dr H C Coombs. There are several photographs of Whitlam with Coombs, Dr Deborah Rose and other staff. (ANUA 240/3)

Jill Waterhouse papers

Research material for University House history, 2002–2005

The file on 'University House History' includes a copy of the *ANU Reporter* for Winter 2004 with a photo of Whitlam (p. 15) and references to a 1981 ceremony at University House when he launched H C Coombs' autobiography *Trial Balance*. A second file contains letters by Whitlam sent to the University House Master, Professor John Richards, in October 2003 summarising his relationship and his father's with the University. As for University House, Whitlam stressed his being made an Honorary Fellow in 1982, his use of the House when staying overnight in Canberra and his work with a former House Master Ralph Elliott on Italian influences in Chaucer. There is also a photograph of Whitlam at the 3rd Wine Symposium in 1979. (ANUA 235/2, 4, 6)

Index

Note: references to photographs, illustrations and maps are in italics

Aboriginal land rights, 62, 65–6
    Fraser government and, 62
    see also under Gurindji people; Wave Hill Station
Aboriginal rights organisations, 64
Aboriginal workers
    struggle for equal wages and working conditions, 63, 64
        trade union support for, 64–5
    see also under Gurindji people; Wave Hill Station
Abschol
    visits to Wattie Creek sponsored by re land rights (1969–70), 65
Adelaide Steamship Company Ltd records
    Billy Hughes, 141–2
    Robert Menzies, 164
Alfred Deakin Prime Ministerial Library (Deakin University), 24, 25
Amalgamated Engineering Union records
    Ben Chifley, 92
Amalgamated Metal Workers' Union, National Office records
    Malcolm Fraser, 115
Amalgamated Postal Workers' Union of Australia records
    Stanley Melbourne Bruce, 84
    Ben Chifley, 92
    John Curtin, 103
    Arthur Fadden, 110–11
    Frank Forde, 113–14
    Billy Hughes, 142
    Joe Lyons, 157
    Robert Menzies, 164
    Earle Page, 176–7
    James Scullin, 181
Amalgamated Timber Workers' Union of Australia
    John Curtin and, 14, 72, 103–4
Amalgamated Timber Workers' Union records
    John Curtin, 103–4
    photographs
        John Curtin, *104*

Angliss Group
    and Wattie Creek land rights claim, 66
Anson, Stan (*Hawke: An Emotional Life*)
    and Bob Hawke and University House incident, 58
Anti-Conscription Campaign Committee
    and Billy Hughes and conscription, 40
ANU Archives
    papers about prime ministers in, 27–8
    see also Noel Butlin Archives Centre (NBAC)
ANU Liberal Club
    John Howard and, 139–40, *140*
archives
    about prime ministers, 22–3
    digitisation of, 24
    government policies on, 25
    official papers of prime ministers, 22
    papers, etc. *about* a prime minister, 18, 20, 27
    papers, etc. *by* a prime minister, 17–18, 27
    papers, etc. *of* a prime minister, 17, 18
    personal papers of prime ministers, 21–2
    prime ministers without papers, 19–20
    relevance, 20–1
    see also ANU Archives; National Archives; National Library; Noel Butlin Archives Centre (NBAC)
Archives Act 1983
    and Cabinet papers, 25
    and papers of prime ministers, 22, 23
Arndt, Professor Heinz
    and David Barnett, 71
    at CUC and ANU, 68
        Billy McMahon and appointment to CUC, 68–70, 162–3
    and Owen Harries, 71
    and Peter Henderson, 71
    and overseas trip with Malcolm Fraser (1980), 68, 70–1
        diary, 70–1, 115, 117
    and *Quadrant*, 71
    with Ross Garnaut and Peter Wilenski at relaunch of *Asian Pacific Economic Literature*, 69
    and *The World Economic Crisis: A Commonwealth Perspective* (1980), 70
    see also Heinz Arndt papers

audio tapes
    Stanley Melbourne Bruce, 75, 87
    John Curtin Memorial Lectures, 106, 192
    Bob Hawke, 127
    Paul Keating, 155
    Robert Menzies, 75, 167
    Gough Whitlam, 75, 192
audiovisual material on prime ministers *see* audio tapes; films; visual representations of prime ministers
Audrey Johnson papers
    Robert Menzies, 173
    photographs
        Bob Hawke, 133
        Billy McMahon, 163
        Robert Menzies, 173
Australasian Coal and Shale Employees' Federation
    and coal strike (1949), 92–3, 101
Australasian Coal and Shale Employees' Federation records
    Ben Chifley, 92–4
    Robert Menzies, 165
    James Scullin, 181
Australasian Typographical Journal
    John Christian Watson and, 187
Australian Agricultural Company
    William Barton and, 81
    Noel Butlin and records of, 13
    and wage inequality (Aboriginal workers), 63
    see also Australian Agricultural Company records; Pemberton, Pennie, *In the Service of the Company*
Australian Agricultural Company records
    Edmund Barton, 81
'Australian Conscription for Service Abroad Unnecessary and Unjust: A Reply to the Prime Minister' (booklet by 'W J Miles')
    and Billy Hughes and conscription, 40
Australian Council of Trade Unions (ACTU)
    archives of, 22
    Bob Hawke and, 14
        papers of, 22
    and struggle for equal wages and working conditions for Aboriginal workers, 63, 65

Australian Council of Trade Unions records
    Stanley Melbourne Bruce, 84
    Malcolm Fraser, 115–16
    and Gurindji strike and walk-off for equal wages and working conditions (1966), 63
    Bob Hawke, 123–7
    John Howard, 139
    Paul Keating, 155
    Robert Menzies, 165–6
    photographs
        Bob Hawke, 126–7
        Paul Keating, 155
        Gough Whitlam, 189
    struggle for equal wages and working conditions for Aboriginal workers in, 64
Australian Dictionary of Biography
    records of, 12, 27
        see also Australian Dictionary of Biography files
Australian Dictionary of Biography files
    Edmund Barton, 82
    John Munro Bruce, 84–5
    Stanley Melbourne Bruce, 85
    Ben Chifley, 95
    Joseph Cook, 102
    John Curtin, 105
    Alfred Deakin, 107–8
    Arthur Fadden, 111
    Andrew Fisher, 111–12
    Frank Forde, 114
    Harold Holt, 135
    Zara Holt, 135
    Billy Hughes, 142–3
    Sir George Knowles, 189–90
    Hubert Lazzarini, 190
    Joe Lyons, 157–8
    John McEwen, 160–1
    Robert Menzies, 166
    Earle Page, 177
    George Reid, 178–9
    James Scullin, 182
    John Christian Watson, 184
    Gough Whitlam, 189–90
    Harry Frederick Ernest Whitlam, 190
Australian Federated Union of Locomotive Enginemen
    Ben Chifley and, 14, 32, 36–7, 95–9

Australian Federated Union of Locomotive
    Enginemen records
  Ben Chifley
    Bathurst Branch, 95–6
    Federal Office, 96–7
    NSW Division, 97–9
  photographs
    Joe Lyons, 158, *159*
Australian Labor Party, Victorian Branch
  Bob Hawke and, 132
Australian National University (ANU)
  amalgamation with CUC, 4, 168, 171
  and Heinz Arndt and overseas trip with
    Malcolm Fraser (1980), 70
  Stanley Melbourne Bruce as
    Chancellor, 6, *7*, 11, 27, 44, 75, 87,
    88, 89, 177
  in Canberra (map), *3*
  establishment of, 158, 178, 191
    Ben Chifley and, 4, 99
  Malcolm Fraser and, 11, 27, 75
  Bettina Gorton and, 8–9
  John Gorton and, 9, 27, 75
  Bob Hawke and, 8, 9–10, 127–8
    doctoral student, 57
    see also University House incident
      (1957) involving Bob Hawke
  Billy McMahon and, 5
  Robert Menzies and, 5–6, 75, 167–8,
    171, 172
  prime ministers and, 1–2, 27–8
    buildings, plaques and foundation
      stones, 15
    earliest links, 2–4
    in NBAC, 14, 27–8
    in official documents (ANU and
      CUC), 12, 27
    photographs, 27
    students, staff, and other
      connections, 8–11
    the war and its aftermath, 4–6
  Therese Rein and, 8, 179
  Kevin Rudd and, 1–2, 8, 75–6
  as venue for visual representations of
    prime ministers, 72, 74–6
  Gough Whitlam and, 10, 75
  see also Canberra University College
    (CUC); a national university

Australian National University Advisers on
    Legislation minutes
  Billy Hughes, 143
  Harry Frederick Ernest Whitlam, 191
Australian National University audiovisual
    material
  Stanley Melbourne Bruce, 87
  Robert Menzies, 167
Australian National University Chancelry
    records
  Stanley Melbourne Bruce, 87
Australian National University
    correspondence files
  Stanley Melbourne Bruce, 87
  John Curtin, 105–6
  Malcolm Fraser, 116
  John Gorton, 121
  Bob Hawke, 127
  Harold Holt, 136
  Billy Hughes, 144
  Joe Lyons, 158
  Billy McMahon, 162
  Robert Menzies, 167
  Gough Whitlam, 191–2
  Harry Frederick Ernest Whitlam, 191
Australian National University Council
    minutes
  Stanley Melbourne Bruce, 88
  Ben Chifley, 99
  Malcolm Fraser, 116
  John Gorton, 121
  Bob Hawke, 127–8
  Billy Hughes, 144
  Robert Menzies, 167
  Harry Frederick Ernest Whitlam, 192
Australian National University History
    Project records
  Stanley Melbourne Bruce, 88
  Bob Hawke, 128
  Billy Hughes, 144
  Billy McMahon, 162–3
  Robert Menzies, 167–8
Australian National University Instructional
    Resources Unit recordings
  John Curtin, 106
  Gough Whitlam, 192
Australian National University Library
    records
  Robert Menzies, 168

Australian National University photographs
   Stanley Melbourne Bruce, 88–9
   Ben Chifley, 100
   John Curtin, 107
   Malcolm Fraser, 116–17
   John Gorton, 121–2
   Bob Hawke, 129
   John Howard, 139–40
   Paul Keating, 155–6
   Robert Menzies, 169
   Earle Page, 177–8
   Gough Whitlam, 192–3
Australian National University Public Relations records
   John Curtin, 107
Australian National University staff files
   Stanley Melbourne Bruce
      Chancellor, 89
   Ben Chifley, 100
   Laurie Fitzhardinge, 145
   Malcolm Fraser, 117
      see also Arndt, Professor Heinz
   Sir Leslie Melville
      Vice-Chancellor, 89, 169
   Robert Menzies, 169–70
   Gough Whitlam, 194
Australian National University Standing Committee minutes
   Stanley Melbourne Bruce, 89
Australian National University student files
   Bettina Gorton, 8–9, 122
   Bob Hawke, 129–30
   Therese Rein, 179
   Kevin Rudd, 179–80
Australian National University Students Association records
   Julia Gillard, 119–20
Australian Prime Ministers Centre, 26
   see also Round Table of Prime Ministerial Research and Collecting Agencies
Australian Society for the Study of Labour History, Melbourne Branch collection
   John Howard, 140–1
Australian Trade Union Congress (1916)
   and Billy Hughes and conscription, 38
Australian Union of Students
   Julia Gillard and, 119–20
Australian Women's Peace Army *see* Goldstein, Vida
Australian Woolgrowers' and Graziers' Council
   and Gurindji land rights claim, 66
Australian Worker
   and conscription, 37–8
   and Billy Hughes, 38, *39*
Australian Workers' Union
   and case for equal wages for Aboriginal workers (1917), 65
   and support for Aboriginal workers in Pilbara Strike (1946), 65
   John Christian Watson and, 184–5
      signature on minutes for 1896 convention as acting chairman, *185*
Australian Workers' Union records
   John Christian Watson, 184–5
   Gough Whitlam, 194
   photographs
      Ben Chifley, 100
      James Scullin, 182, *183*
Australian Workers' Union, Sydney Branch records
   Billy Hughes, 145
Australia's Prime Ministers website *see* prime ministers' portal

Ballarat Trades and Labour Council
   letter from Alfred Deakin to secretary of, *109*
Ballarat Trades and Labour Council records
   Alfred Deakin, 109–10
   John Christian Watson, 186
Barnett, David
   and Heinz Arndt, 71
Barton, Edmund
   depicted on program for banquet before leaving for England (1902), 72, *83*
   papers of, 21
   and seat of government, 2
   archives:
   Australian Agricultural Company records, 81
   South Australian Typographical Society records, 82–3
   Australian Dictionary of Biography files, 82
Barton, William
   and Australian Agricultural Company, 81

INDEX

Basic Wage cases
    Bob Hawke and, 123–5, 126
Beasley, Dr Margo
    on Billy Hughes, 151
    Wharfies: The History of the Waterside Workers' Federation of Australia
        on Billy Hughes' expulsion from union, 34
Belmonte, Jon, 141
    see also Jon Belmonte papers
Binns, Kenneth
    and Laurie Fitzhardinge on Joseph Cook, 102
Bourke's Melbourne Pty Ltd
    Bob Hawke and, 126
Brazil, Wendy *see* Wendy Brazil collection
Bridge, Dr Carl
    and ADB entry on Earle Page, 177
Brookes, Herbert
    papers of, 23
Bruce, Ernest
    and Stanley Melbourne Bruce, 91
    and Paterson, Laing and Bruce, 41, 90–1
    letterbooks, 90–1
Bruce family, 41, 91
Bruce Hall, 15
Bruce, John Munro
    in business, 41, 85
    archives:
    Australian Dictionary of Biography files, 84–5
Bruce, R L, 91
Bruce, Stanley Melbourne (Viscount Bruce of Melbourne)
    and ANU
        Chancellor, 6, *7*, 11, 27, 44, 75, 87, 88, 89, 177
        Stanley Melbourne Bruce Fund, 87, 89
    audio tape of, 75, 87
    and Ernest Bruce, 91
    the Businessman, 41–4, *86*, 91
    and Canberra, 1, 6
    civilised capitalist, 43–4
    and establishment of a national university, 4
    film of, 75, 87
    and J Grainger (returned soldier employee), 43
    papers of, 21
    and Paterson, Laing and Bruce, 14, 41–4, 90–1
    photographs of as Chancellor, 75
    public image of, 56–7
    and trade unions and arbitration, 84, 98
    archives:
    Australian Council of Trade Unions records, 84
    Australian Dictionary of Biography files, 85
    Australian National University audiovisual material, 87
    Australian National University Chancelry records, 87
    Australian National University correspondence files, 87
    Australian National University Council minutes, 88
    Australian National University History Project records, 88
    Australian National University staff files, 89
    Australian National University Standing Committee minutes, 89
    Keith Hancock papers, 90
    Paterson, Laing and Bruce records, 90–1
    Amalgamated Postal Workers' Union of Australia records, 84
    see also Bruce Hall
Burgmann College lecture
    Kevin Rudd and, 76
Burns, Philp and Company Ltd records
    Billy Hughes, 145–6
business
    prime minister with experience in, 41
Butlin, Noel, *13*
    and records of Australian Agricultural Company, 13
    see also Noel Butlin Archives Centre (NBAC)

Campbell, Mrs M D
    and ADB entry on Edmund Barton, 82
Campbell, Professor Colin, and John Halligan (*Political Leadership in an Age of Constraint: Bureaucratic Politics under Hawke and Keating*), 117, 130–1, 156–7
    see also Colin Campbell collection

203

Canberra
   Stanley Melbourne Bruce and, 1, 6
   Robert Menzies and, 1
   seat of government, 2–3
      and a national university, 2, 3
   site of national university in (map), *3*
Canberra University College (CUC)
   amalgamation with ANU, 4, 168, 171
      Robert Menzies and, 5
   appointment of Heinz Arndt to, 162–3
   L F (Fin) Crisp and, 8
   establishment of, 4
   Laurie Fitzhardinge and, 8
   Bob Hawke and, 9, 57
   Joe Lyons and establishment of a national university, 158
   James S Menzies and, 8
   Robert Menzies and, 168
   Earle Page and establishment of university in Canberra, 178
   prime ministers and, 8
   Freda Whitlam and, 8
   Gough Whitlam and, 8
   Harry Frederick Ernest Whitlam and, 8
Canberra University College records
   Robert Menzies, 170–1
   Earle Page, 178
   Freda Whitlam, 194
   Gough Whitlam, 194
   Harry Frederick Ernest Whitlam, 194–5
Carroll, Brian (*Australia's Prime Ministers: From Barton to Howard*)
   on Andrew Fisher, 112
   stereotypical labels for prime ministers, 41
Carroll, John
   on Robert Menzies and *Looking Forward* (Institute of Public Affairs), 54
cartoons and caricatures of prime ministers, 73
   Malcolm Fraser, *73*, 76
   Bob Hawke, 76
   Billy Hughes, *39*
   Robert Menzies, 73, *165*
Charlie Fitzgibbon papers
   Bob Hawke, 132–3
Chifley, Ben
   and Australian Federated Union of Locomotive Enginemen, 14, 95–9
      expulsion from, 32, 36–7, 96, 99
   biography of (by L F (Fin) Crisp), 8, 48
   and coal strike (1949), 92–4, 101
   and Cockcroft Building, Research School of Physical Sciences, 74, 100
   confronted by striking Katoomba miners in 1949, 72, 93, *94*
   dismissals, party-room coups and expulsions, 32, 36–7, 96, 99
   and Federal Labor Conference (1951), 72
   and Great Strike (1917), 93, 97, 98, 99
   and John Curtin School of Medical Research, 4, 74, 100, 107
      laying foundation stone of, 5
   photographs of at ANU, 5, 74
   and Premiers' Plan, 36, 37, 96, 99
   and Research School of Physical Sciences, 10
archives:
Amalgamated Engineering Union records, 92
Amalgamated Postal Workers' Union of Australia records, 92
Australasian Coal and Shale Employees' Federation records, 92–4
Australian Dictionary of Biography files, 95
Australian Federated Union of Locomotive Enginemen
   Bathurst Branch records, 95–6
   Federal Office records, 96–7
   NSW Division records, 97–9
Australian National University Council minutes, 99
Australian National University photographs, 100
Australian Workers' Union records, 100
Coal Mining Unions Council records, 101
see also J B Chifley Building
Christian Jollie Smith and Company records
   James Scullin, 182
Coal Miners' Mutual Protective Association
   Joseph Cook and, 102–3
Coal Mining Unions Council, 101
Coal Mining Unions Council records
   Ben Chifley, 101
coal strike (1949)
   Ben Chifley and, 92–4, 101

Cockcroft Building, Research School of
    Physical Sciences
    Ben Chifley and, 100
    Robert Menzies and, 167, 169
Cockcroft, Sir John, 11
    see also Cockcroft Building, Research
    School of Physical Sciences
Colin Campbell collection
    Malcolm Fraser, 117–18
    Bob Hawke, 130–1
    Paul Keating, 156–7
Colonial Sugar Refining Company Ltd/CSR
    Limited records
    Billy Hughes, 146
    photographs
        Bob Hawke, 131
Common Cause
    cartoon of Robert Menzies, 165
Commonwealth Arbitration Court
    Ben Chifley and AFULE award
        application to, 96–7
Commonwealth National Library
    and personal papers of prime ministers,
        21
Commonwealth Shipping Line
    Billy Hughes and, 146
conscription
    John Curtin and, 38
    Billy Hughes and, 31, 32, 35, 37–41,
        152
    and Labor split, 32
    John Christian Watson and, 31, 32, 186
convocation
    Ben Chifley and, 99
    Robert Menzies and, 167
Cook, Joseph
    Labor 'rat', 32
    archives:
        Australian Dictionary of Biography files,
            102
        Hartley District Miners' Mutual
            Protective Association, Lithgow Lodge
            records, 102–3
        Laurie Fitzhardinge papers, 102
Coombs Building *see* H C Coombs Building
Coombs, Dr H C
    and ANU, 100, 171
    on Ben Chifley, 100
    with Robert Menzies at laying of
        foundation stone of R G Menzies
        Building, 6

Vice-Chancellor, 122
    see also H C Coombs Building; H C
    Coombs papers
Copland, Sir Douglas, 11
    and Laurie Fitzhardinge and the writing
        of the biography of Billy Hughes, 49
Corbin, Alain (*The Life of an Unknown:
    The Rediscovered World of a Clog Maker in
    Nineteenth-Century France*)
    and lack of documentation, 20
Counihan, Noel
    caricature of Robert Menzies, 165
Crawford, George
    and Victorian ALP, 195
    see also George Crawford papers
Crawford, Sir John
    with Gough Whitlam and Indian Prime
        Minister Indira Gandhi (1973), 193
    Vice-Chancellor
        and privacy of student information
            during Vietnam War, 121, 136,
            162, 192
    see also J G Crawford Building
Cribb, Associate Professor Margaret
    and ADB entry on Arthur Fadden, 111
Crisp, Christopher
    and Alfred Deakin, 110
Crisp, L F (Fin)
    biography of Ben Chifley, 8, 48
    and CUC, 8
Crowley, Professor F K
    and ADB entry on Joseph Cook, 102
CSR Limited records *see* Colonial Sugar
    Refining Company Ltd/CSR Limited
    records
Curtin, Elsie
    and John Curtin School of Medical
        Research, 74, 107
Curtin, John
    and Amalgamated Timber Workers'
        Union of Australia, 14, 72, 103–4
    among 'Trade Unions' Officials' (1914),
        104
    biography of (by Lloyd Ross), 48
    and conscription, 38
    and establishment of a national
        university, 4
    and establishment of national medical
        research institute, 4
    prime ministers' portal and, 27
    and John Christian Watson, 33

and World War II, 105
archives:
  Amalgamated Postal Workers' Union of Australia records, 103
  Amalgamated Timber Workers' Union records, 103–4
  Australian Dictionary of Biography files, 105
  Australian National University correspondence files, 105–6
  Australian National University Instructional Resources Unit recordings, 106
  Australian National University photographs, 107
  Australian National University Public Relations records, 107
  D A Low papers, 107
  see also John Curtin Memorial lectures; John Curtin Prime Ministerial Library (Curtin University of Technology); John Curtin School of Medical Research
Curtin, John (son)
  and John Curtin School of Medical Research, 74, 107

D A Low papers
  John Curtin, 107
  Bob Hawke, 133
  Gough Whitlam, 196
d'Alpuget, Blanche
  papers of, 23
  Robert J Hawke: A Biography, 132–3
    and University House incident, 59
Danby, Michael
  on Bob Hawke, 132
Day, David
  as biographer, 48
  biography of Ben Chifley, 95, 96
Deakin, Alfred
  and Billy Hughes and Sir William Lyne, 108
  biography of (by John La Nauze), 48
  and Christopher Crisp, 110
  and Sir Frederic Eggleston, 110
  letter to secretary of Ballarat Trades and Labour Council, 14, *109*
  papers of, 21, 23
    digitisation of, 24
  and religion, in particular the Catholic Church, 110
  and seat of government, 2
  archives:
    Australian Dictionary of Biography files, 107–8
    Frederic Eggleston papers, 110
    see also Alfred Deakin Prime Ministerial Library (Deakin University); Deakin papers
Deakin papers, 17
SS Delfram
  and 'pig iron' dispute, 47
Democratic Labor Party
  and Labor split, 32
Devitt, Owen
  as LBJ, *138*
digitisation of archival material, 24
dismissals, party-room coups and expulsions, 31–7
  Ben Chifley, 32, 36–7, 96, 99
  John Gorton, 31
  Bob Hawke, 31
  Billy Hughes, 31, 32, 34–5, 152, 154
  Sir William Lyne, 31
  Robert Menzies, 31
  Kevin Rudd, 31
  John Christian Watson, 31, 32–3
  Gough Whitlam, 31–2
documentation policy, 25
Donnelly, Phyllis
  and Ben Chifley, 95
'Don't Scab: J C Watson, First Labour Prime Minister of Australia, talks to Australian Unionists on the Referendum' (National Referendum Council leaflet)
  re conscription, 40
Drakeford, A S
  and Ben Chifley, 96
Dwyer, Jack *see* Jack Dwyer collection
Dwyer, John V
  and inquiry into temporary employment in Commonwealth public, 114

Easson, Michael *see* Michael Easson papers
Eggleston, Sir Frederic
  and Alfred Deakin, 110
  see also Frederic Eggleston papers
Elder Smith and Company Ltd records
  Billy Hughes, 146–7

Elliott, Ralph
    on Bob Hawke and University House
        incident, 57–8
Engineers' Case
    Robert Menzies and, 98, 164, 174
Ennor, Professor Hugh (Sir Hugh), 172
    see also Hugh Ennor papers
ephemera, 14
    anti-conscriptionist, 40

Fadden, Arthur
    archives:
        Amalgamated Postal Workers' Union of
            Australia records, 110–11
        Australian Dictionary of Biography files,
            111
Federal Chamber of Automotive Industries
    records
        John McEwen, 161
        Robert Menzies, 172
Federated Engine Drivers' and Firemen's
    Association of Australasia
        Ben Chifley and, 97–8
        Malcolm Fraser and, 72
Federated Engine Drivers' and Firemen's
    Association of Australasia records
        Malcolm Fraser, 118
    see also Serge Zorino collection
Federated Furnishing Trades Society of
    Australia records
        photographs
            James Scullin, 183
        films
            Stanley Melbourne Bruce, 75, 87
            Robert Menzies, 75, 167
Fisher, Andrew
    death of, 111–12
    and establishment of a national
        university, 3
    papers of, 21
    and seat of government, 2–3
    and Waterside Workers' Federation, 14,
        111
        delegates to convention in 1912
            (with Billy Hughes), 72, *113*
    archives:
        Australian Dictionary of Biography files,
            111–12
        Waterside Workers' Federation of
            Australia records, 111–12

FitzGerald, Stephen
    and ANU, 11
Fitzgibbon, Charlie
    Bob Hawke in unpublished
        autobiography of, 132–3
    see also Charlie Fitzgibbon papers
Fitzhardinge, Laurie, 48
    and ADB entry on Billy Hughes,
        142–3
    on Billy Hughes and papers, 19–20
    biography of Billy Hughes, 8, 48–52,
        141–2, 143, 144, 145
        the commission, 49
        issue of rate of progress, 49–51,
            52
        vetting problems, 51
    and CUC, 8
    with Keith Hancock, Ross Hohnen,
        Mark Oliphant and Leslie Melville
        (1957), *50*
    and Kenneth Binns on Joseph Cook,
        102
    archives:
        Australian National University staff
            files, 145
    see also Laurie Fitzhardinge papers
Florey, Sir Howard (Lord Florey), 74
    Chancellor, 75, *122*
Forde, Frank
    papers of, 23
    will of, 114
    archives:
        Amalgamated Postal Workers' Union
            of Australia records, 113–14
        Australian Dictionary of Biography
            files, 114
        Institute of Public Affairs (Victoria)
            records, 114–15
Forde, Vera
    papers of, 23
former German New Guinea
    Billy Hughes and, 145–6
Foster, Stephen, and Margaret Varghese
    (*The Making of the Australian National
    University 1946–1996*), 88, 128, 144,
    162, 167
    see also Australian National University
        History Project records

Fraser, Malcolm
    and Aboriginal land rights, 62
    and ANU, 11, 27, 75
    and Heinz Arndt and overseas trip
        (1980), 68, 70–1, 115, 117
    caricature of in *Seamen's Journal,* 73
    cartoon of in *Woroni,* 76, 120
    Nyang Station (NSW), 118
        map, *119*
    and his papers, 19
    photograph of at Parliament House site, 72
    and Research School of Chemistry, 75, 116
    archives:
        Amalgamated Metal Workers' Union, National Office records, 115
        Australian Council of Trade Unions records, 115–16
        Australian National University correspondence files, 116
        Australian National University Council minutes, 116
        Australian National University photographs, 116–17
        Colin Campbell collection, 117–18
        Federated Engine Drivers' and Firemen's Association of Australasia records, 118
        Goldsbrough Mort and Company Ltd records, 118
        Heinz Arndt papers, 115
        Seamen's Union of Australia records, 118
        Serge Zorino collection, 119
        Wendy Brazil collection, 117
        see also Malcolm Fraser Collection (University of Melbourne)
Frederic Eggleston papers
    Alfred Deakin, 110

Gallery of Australian Democracy *see* Museum of Australian Democracy
Gandhi, Indira
    with Gough Whitlam and Sir John Crawford (1973), *193*
Garnaut, Professor Ross
    and ANU, 11
    with Peter Wilenski and Heinz Arndt at relaunch of *Asian Pacific Economic Literature,* 69
Geoff McDonald collection
    photographs
        Ben Chifley, 101
Geoffrey Sawer papers
    Robert Menzies, 174
George Crawford papers
    Gough Whitlam, 195
Gillard, Julia
    and Australian Union of Students, 119–20
    in *Woroni,* 76, 119–20, *120*
    archives:
        Australian National University Students Association records, 119–20
Goldsbrough Mort and Company Ltd records
    Malcolm Fraser, 118
    maps of Wave Hill/Wattie Creek area, 64
    photographs
        John McEwen, 161
Goldstein, Vida
    and Billy Hughes and conscription, 40
Gorton, Bettina
    and ANU, 8–9
    archives:
        Australian National University student files, 122
Gorton, John
    in academic procession with H C Coombs and Howard Florey, *122*
    and ANU, 9, 27, 75
    and conscription for Vietnam War
        privacy of student information, 121
    dismissals, party-room coups and expulsions, 31
    and Vietnam War, 14
    archives:
        Australian National University correspondence files, 121
        Australian National University Council minutes, 121
        Australian National University photographs, 121–2
        National Farmers' Federation records, 123
government archivist, 21
Grainger, J (returned soldier employee of Paterson, Laing and Bruce)
    Stanley Melbourne Bruce and, 43
Great Strike (1917)
    Ben Chifley and, 93, 97, 98, 99

Griffin, Walter Burley
    and site for a national university, 3
Grimwade, Geoffrey
    and Harold Holt, 56
Gunson, Niel
    on Bob Hawke and University House incident, 58
Gurindji people
    land rights claim, 62, 65–6
        trade union support for, 65–6
    strike and walk-off for equal wages and working conditions, 63–4
    see also Lingiari, Vincent
Gurindji Trust Fund, 66, *67*

H C Coombs Building
    Robert Menzies and, 75, 169
    reminiscences about, 58
H C Coombs papers
    Robert Menzies, 171–2
Halligan, John, and Colin Campbell (*Political Leadership in an Age of Constraint: Bureaucratic Politics under Hawke and Keating*), 117, 130–1, 156–7
    see also Colin Campbell collection
Hancock, Dr Ian
    and ADB entry on Harold Holt, 135
Hancock, Keith (Sir Keith)
    and Laurie Fitzhardinge and the writing of the biography of Billy Hughes, 49
    with Laurie Fitzhardinge, Ross Hohnen, Mark Oliphant and Leslie Melville (1957), *50*
    see also Keith Hancock papers
Harries, Owen
    and Heinz Arndt, 71
Hart, Phillip
    and ADB entry on Joe Lyons, 157–8
Hartley District Miners' Mutual Protective Association, Lithgow Lodge records
    Joseph Cook, 102–3
Hawke, Bob
    ACTU Research Officer and Advocate, *124*
    and ANU, 8, 9–10, 27, 75, 127–8
        doctoral student, 57
    and Australian Labor Party, Victorian Branch, 132
    and Basic Wage cases, 123–5, 126
        notes relating to 1964 case, *125*
    cartoon of in *Woroni*, 76, 120
    and CUC, 9, 57
    dismissals, party-room coups and expulsions, 31
    examining Ben Chifley's pipe and stand, *74*
    and J G Crawford Building, 9
    and maritime/waterfront dispute (1998), 126
    papers of
        ACTU, 22
    photographs of at various events, 72
    with Dr John Ritchie launching vol. 12 of ADB, *10*
    and Siding Spring Observatory, 9
    and University House incident (1957), 9, 56–61, 128, 133–4, 134
        archival sources, 59–61
        Disciplinary Committee, 60–1
        The Hawke Memoirs and, 58
        Hawke on, 61
        notes of Hawke's evidence to Disciplinary Committee, *60*
archives:
Audrey Johnson papers, 133
Australian Council of Trade Unions records, 123–7
Australian National University correspondence files, 127
Australian National University Council minutes, 127–8
Australian National University History Project records, 128
Australian National University photographs, 129
Australian National University student files, 129–30
Charlie Fitzgibbon papers, 132–3
Colin Campbell collection, 130–1
CSR Limited records, 131
D A Low papers, 133
Jack Dwyer collection, 131
Jill Waterhouse papers, 134–5
Mark Oliphant papers, 133–4
Michael Easson papers, 131–2
National Farmers' Federation records, 133
Sheet Metal Working Agricultural Implement and Stove Making Industrial Union records, 134

University House records, 134
Wendy Brazil collection, 130
Hawke, Hazel (*My Own Life: An Autobiography*)
  and Bob Hawke and University House incident, 59
Hawke Prime Ministerial Library (University of South Australia), 24
  and Bob Hawke's ACTU papers, 22
Haydon–Allen Building
  Robert Menzies and, 75, 169
Hazlehurst, Cameron
  and ADB entry on Harry Frederick Ernest Whitlam, 190
Heinz Arndt papers
  Fraser, Malcolm, 115
Henderson, Gerard (*Menzies' Child*)
  on influence of C D ('Ref') Kemp on Liberal Party of Australia, 54–5
  on Robert Menzies and Liberal Party of Australia, 54
Henderson, Peter
  and Heinz Arndt, 71
Hocking, Jenny
  as biographer, 48
  biography of Gough Whitlam, 19
Hohnen, Ross
  with Keith Hancock, Laurie Fitzhardinge, Mark Oliphant and Leslie Melville (1957), *50*
Holt, Harold
  and conscription for Vietnam War privacy of student information, 136
  Harold Holt impersonator in the 1966 May Day parade in Sydney, *137*
  and Institute of Public Affairs, 56, 136
  and Vietnam War, 14
  archives:
  Australian Dictionary of Biography files, 135
  Australian National University correspondence files, 136
  Institute of Public Affairs (Victoria) records, 136
  Waterside Workers' Federation of Australia records, 137–8
Holt, Zara (Dame Zara)
  papers of, 23
  archives:
  Australian Dictionary of Biography files, 135

Hone, J Ann
  and ADB entry on John Munro Bruce, 84, 85
Howard, John
  and ANU, 11
  with ANU Liberal Club students after presenting the Joe and Enid Lyons lecture in 1986, *140*
  and maritime/waterfront dispute (1998), 14, 28, 139, 140–1
  and Sir Roland Wilson Building, 11, 75
  archives:
  Australian Council of Trade Unions records, 139
  Australian National University photographs, 139–40
  Australian Society for the Study of Labour History, Melbourne Branch collection, 140–1
  Jon Belmonte papers, 141
  Wendy Brazil collection, 141
Hugh Ennor papers
  Robert Menzies, 172
Hughes, Billy
  biography of (by Laurie Fitzhardinge), 8, 48–52, 141–2, 143, 144, 145
    treatment of first marriage in, 51
  and Commonwealth Shipping Line, 146
  and conscription, 31, 32, 35, 37–41, 152
    caricature of in *Australian Worker*, *39*
  and Alfred Deakin, 108
  dismissals, party-room coups and expulsions, 31, 32, 34–5
  and former German New Guinea, 145–6
  Labor 'rat', 31
  and NSW Council for Relief of Spanish Distress, 152–3
  and his papers, 18, 19
  and Sydney Wharf Labourers' Union, 34, 148–52
    elected secretary 'unopposed' (1899), *149*
    expulsion from, 35, 152
  Testimonial, 14, 141, 146
  and Trolley, Draymen and Carters Union of Sydney and Suburbs, 34, 153
    expulsion from, 35
    with other members of the committee in 1905, *36*
  and Waterside Workers' Federation, 14, 34–5, 150–4

delegates to convention in 1912
  (with Andrew Fisher), 72, *113*
expulsion from, 32, 154
with John Christian Watson and other delegates to the 1900 Interstate Labor Conference, *34*
archives:
  Adelaide Steamship Company Ltd records, 141–2
  Amalgamated Postal Workers' Union of Australia records, 142
  Australian Dictionary of Biography files, 142–3
  Australian National University Advisers on Legislation minutes, 143
  Australian National University correspondence files, 144
  Australian National University Council minutes, 144
  Australian National University History Project records, 144
  Australian Workers' Union, Sydney Branch records, 145
  Burns, Philp and Company Ltd records, 145–6
  Colonial Sugar Refining Company Ltd records, 146
  Elder Smith and Company Ltd records, 146–7
  Laurie Fitzhardinge papers, 147–8
  NSW Combined Colliery Proprietors' Association records, 148
  NSW Typographical Association records, 148
  Phil Thorne papers, 152–3
  Sydney Wharf Labourers' Union records, 148–52
  Trolley, Draymen and Carters Union of Sydney and Suburbs records, 153
  Waterside Workers' Federation of Australia records, 153–4
Hurst, John (*Hawke: The Definitive Biography*)
  and Bob Hawke and University House incident, 58

Ian Turner collection
  Ben Chifley, 101

Institute of Public Affairs, 52
  Harold Holt and, 56, 136
  and Liberal Party of Australia, 54, 136, 173
  Billy McMahon and, 56
  Robert Menzies and, 54–5
Institute of Public Affairs (Victoria) records, 55
  Frank Forde, 114–15
  Harold Holt, 136
  Enid Lyons, 159
  Billy McMahon, 163
  Robert Menzies, 173
IPA Review, 52
  on Robert Menzies' retirement, *53*

J B Chifley Building, 15
J G Crawford Building
  Bob Hawke and, 9
  new
    Kevin Rudd opening, *9*, 75
Jack Dwyer collection
  Bob Hawke, 131
  Gough Whitlam, 195
Jill Waterhouse papers
  Bob Hawke, 134–5
  Gough Whitlam, 197
Joe and Enid Lyons lecture, 139
John Curtin Memorial lectures
  L F (Fin) Crisp, 8, 107
  Bob Hawke, 127
  list of, 105–6
  Gough Whitlam, 10, 75, 191, 192
John Curtin Prime Ministerial Library (Curtin University of Technology), 24
John Curtin School of Medical Research, 2, 15
  Ben Chifley and, 4, 74, 107
  John Curtin (son) and, 74, 107
  Elsie Curtin and, 107
  Robert Menzies and, 74, 75, 167, 169
  Kevin Rudd and, 2, 75
Johnson, Audrey *see* Audrey Johnson papers
Johnson, President Lyndon Baines
  wharfie Owen Devitt as, *138*
Jon Belmonte papers
  John Howard, 141

Keating, Paul
  at his ANU lecture on Commonwealth–State relations in 1994, *156*
  biography of (by Don Watson), 48
  archives:
    Australian Council of Trade Unions records, 155
    Australian National University photographs, 155
    Colin Campbell collection, 156–7
    Wendy Brazil collection, 156
Keith Hancock papers
  Stanley Melbourne Bruce, 90
Kelly, Paul (*The March of Patriots*)
  on John Howard and maritime/waterfront dispute (1998), 140
Kemp, C D ('Ref')
  influence of on Liberal Party of Australia, 54–5
  and Institute of Public Affairs, 54
  study tour to Canada, 114–15
  see also Institute of Public Affairs (Victoria) records
Knowles, Sir George
  archives:
    Australian Dictionary of Biography files, 189–90
Koutsoukis, Jason
  on Robert Menzies and *Looking Forward* (Institute of Public Affairs), 54

La Nauze, John
  and ADB entry on Alfred Deakin, 107, 108
  biography of Alfred Deakin, 48
  and Deakin papers, 17
  papers of, 23
Labor Papers Ltd
  John Christian Watson and, 14, 32–3, 186–7
Labor Papers Ltd records
  John Christian Watson, 186–7
Labor 'rats'
  Joseph Cook, 32
  Billy Hughes, 31
  Joe Lyons, 31
Labor splits, 32
Lake George Mines Pty Ltd records
  James Scullin, 183–4

Lampe, Eric
  and Billy McMahon, 56
Lang, Jack
  and split in NSW Labor, 32
Langmore, Di
  and ADB entry on Ben Chifley, 95
Laurie Fitzhardinge papers
  Joseph Cook, 102
  Alfred Deakin, 110
  Billy Hughes, 147–8
  Robert Menzies, 172
Lazzarini, Hubert
  archives:
    Australian Dictionary of Biography files, 190
Learmonth, F Livingstone, 148
  see also NSW Combined Colliery Proprietors' Association records
Lee, Dr David
  and ADB entry on John Munro Bruce, 85
  Stanley Melbourne Bruce: Australian Internationalist, 85, 90
Liberal Party of Australia
  influence of C D ('Ref') Kemp on, 54–5
  and Institute of Public Affairs, 54, 136, 173
  Robert Menzies and founding of, 54, 173
  see also Henderson, Gerard (*Menzies' Child*)
Lingiari, Vincent, 63
  and Gurindji strike and walk-off for equal wages and working conditions (1966), 63
  and Gurindji Trust Fund, 66, *67*
  and Wattie Creek land rights claim, 65–6
  correspondence with Vestey Company, 66
  Gough Whitlam pouring sand into the hand of, *62*
Lithgow Valley colliery (NSW)
  Joseph Cook and, 103
Lloyd, Clem
  and ADB entries on
    Joe Lyons, 157–8
    John McEwen, 160–1
Lloyd, Neil
  and ADB entry on Frank Forde (with Malcolm Saunders), 114

Lockwood, Rupert
  on Robert Menzies and 'pig iron' dispute, 45
Locomotive Enginemen *see* Australian Federated Union of Locomotive Enginemen
Looking Forward (Institute of Public Affairs)
  Robert Menzies and, 54, 55
Low, Professor D A
  and Heinz Arndt and overseas trip with Malcolm Fraser (1980), 70
  see also D A Low papers
Lyne, Sir William
  and Alfred Deakin, 108
  dismissals, party-room coups and expulsions, 31
Lyons, Enid (Dame Enid)
  archives:
    Institute of Public Affairs (Victoria) records, 159
  see also Joe and Enid Lyons lecture
Lyons, Joe
  and break with Scullin Cabinet, 158
  death of, 158
  and establishment of a national university, 158
  Labor 'rat', 31
  papers of, 21
  and 'pig iron' dispute (1938), 160
  Tasmanian minister for railways, with officials of the Australian Federated Union of Locomotive Enginemen, 72, *159*
  archives:
    Amalgamated Postal Workers' Union of Australia records, 157
    Australian Dictionary of Biography files, 157–8
    Australian Federated Union of Locomotive Enginemen records, 158, *159*
    Australian National University correspondence files, 158
    Institute of Public Affairs (Victoria) records, 159
    Phil Thorne papers, 160
    Waterside Workers' Federation of Australia records, 160
  see also Joe and Enid Lyons lecture

McDonald, Geoff *see* Geoff McDonald collection
McEwen, John (Sir John)
  photograph, 72, 161, 162
  archives:
    Australian Dictionary of Biography files, 160–1
    Federal Chamber of Automotive Industries records, 161
    Goldsbrough Mort and Company Ltd records, 161
    National Farmers' Federation records, 161
    New Zealand and Australian Land Company records, 162
Mackintosh, A K
  on Billy Hughes and former German New Guinea, 145–6
McMahon, Billy
  and ANU, 5
  and appointment of Heinz Arndt to CUC, 68–70, 162–3
  and conscription for Vietnam War privacy of student information, 162
  and Institute of Public Affairs, 56
  papers of, 22
  public image of, 57
  and Vietnam War, 14
  archives:
    Audrey Johnson papers, 163
    Australian National University correspondence files, 162
    Australian National University History Project records, 162–3
    Institute of Public Affairs (Victoria) records, 163
    National Farmers' Federation records, 163–4
McMinn, Associate Professor W G
  and ADB entry on George Reid, 178–9
Malcolm Fraser Collection (University of Melbourne), 24, 25
Mallory, Dr Greg (*Unchartered Waters*)
  on Robert Menzies and 'pig iron' dispute, 45
Maritime Worker
  on 'pig iron' dispute (1938), *46*
maritime/waterfront dispute (1998)
  Bob Hawke and, 126
  John Howard and, 14, 28, 139, 140–1

213

Mark Oliphant papers
  Bob Hawke, 133–4
Martin, Allan
  and ADB entry on Robert Menzies, 166
  on Robert Menzies and 'pig iron' dispute, 45
  papers of, 23
Mathews, Race
  on 'Victoria's War Against Whitlam', 14
Maughan, T
  and James Scullin, 183–4
Melville, Sir Leslie
  with Keith Hancock, Laurie Fitzhardinge, Ross Hohnen and Mark Oliphant (1957), 50
  to Keith Hancock on Laurie Fitzhardinge and the biography of Billy Hughes, 50
  Vice-Chancellor
    Robert Menzies and, 5, 11
    Australian National University staff files, 89, 169
Menzies, James S
  and CUC, 8
Menzies, Robert (Sir Robert)
  and ANU, 5–6, 11, 75, 167–8, 171, 172
    and Sir Roland Wilson, 11
  and Canberra, 1
  caricature of by Noel Counihan, *165*
  and Cockcroft Building, Research School of Physical Sciences, 167, 169
  and convocation, 167
  and Engineers' Case, 98, 164, 174
  and founding of Liberal Party of Australia, 54, 173
  government response to proposed Robert Menzies Library at University of Melbourne, 25
  and H C Coombs Building, 75, 169
  and Haydon–Allen Building, 75, 169
  and house for Professor Mark Oliphant, 170
  and Institute of Public Affairs, 54–5
  IPA Review on retirement of, *53*
  and John Curtin School of Medical Research, 74, 75, 167, 169
  and *Looking Forward* (Institute of Public Affairs), 54, 55
  and Billy McMahon's complaint about appointment of Heinz Arndt to CUC, 69, 163
  and James ('Jim') R Murray, 172
  'Out/Oust Menzies Campaign' (1953), 14, 174, 175
  on his papers, 19
  papers of, 21
  and 'pig iron' dispute, 14, 45–8, 165–6, 175, 176
  and R G Menzies Building, 6, 75, 167, 168, 169
    with H C Coombs at laying of foundation stone, *6*
    see also R G Menzies Building
  and Research School of Physical Sciences, 75
  and B A Santamaria, 173
  and Geoffrey Sawer, 174
  sobriquets, 45
archives:
  Adelaide Steamship Company Ltd records, 164
  Amalgamated Postal Workers' Union of Australia records, 164
  Audrey Johnson papers, 173
  Australasian Coal and Shale Employees' Federation records, 165
  Australian Council of Trade Unions records, 165–6
  Australian Dictionary of Biography files, 166
  Australian National University audiovisual material, 167
  Australian National University correspondence files, 167
  Australian National University Council minutes, 167
  Australian National University History Project records, 167–8
  Australian National University Library records, 168
  Australian National University photographs, 169
  Australian National University staff files, 169–70
  Canberra University College records, 170–1
  Federal Chamber of Automotive Industries records, 172
  Geoffrey Sawer papers, 174
  H C Coombs papers, 171–2
  Hugh Ennor papers, 172
  Institute of Public Affairs (Victoria) records, 173

Laurie Fitzhardinge papers, 172
Phil Thorne papers, 175
Seamen's Union of Australia records, 174
Waterside Workers' Federation of Australia records, 175–6
see also Menzies Virtual Museum (Sir Robert Menzies Memorial Foundation Ltd)
Menzies Virtual Museum (Sir Robert Menzies Memorial Foundation Ltd), 24
Michael Easson papers
　Bob Hawke, 131–2
　Gough Whitlam, 195–6
Miners' Federation *see* Australasian Coal and Shale Employees' Federation
Murphy, Dr Denis
　and ADB entry on Andrew Fisher, 111–12
Murray, James ('Jim') R
　and Federal Chamber of Automotive Industries, 161
　Robert Menzies and, 172
Museum of Australian Democracy, 26
　and Australian Prime Ministers Centre, 26

Nairn, Bede
　and ADB entries on
　　Joseph Cook, 102
　　John Christian Watson, 184
National Archives
　and archives about prime ministers, 22, 23
　and papers of Malcolm Fraser, 25
　and personal papers of prime ministers, 21
　and prime ministers' portal, 26
　see also prime ministers' portal
National Council for the Centenary of Federation
　and archives of prime ministers, 23
National Farmers' Federation records
　John Gorton, 123
　John McEwen, 161
　Billy McMahon, 163–4
　Gough Whitlam, 196–7
　photographs
　　Bob Hawke, 133
National Fellowship
　Gough Whitlam, 10, 116, 191, 194

National Library
　and archives about prime ministers, 22–3
　and personal papers of prime ministers, 21, 22
National Referendum Council
　'Don't Scab: J C Watson, First Labour Prime Minister of Australia, talks to Australian Unionists on the Referendum' (leaflet)
　　conscription, 40
a national university
　establishment of
　　Stanley Melbourne Bruce and, 4
　　John Curtin and, 4
　　Andrew Fisher and, 3
　　Joe Lyons and, 158
　　Harry Frederick Ernest Whitlam and, 191
　see also Australian National University (ANU); Canberra University College (CUC)
New Guinea *see* former German New Guinea
New Zealand and Australian Land Company records
　photographs
　　John McEwen, 162
Noel Butlin Archives Centre (NBAC), 13
　ACTU archives, 22
　　see also Australian Council of Trade Unions records
　collections of and prime ministers
　　documents, 14
　　publications and ephemera, 14
　papers about prime ministers in, 27–8
Norris, Dr Ron
　and ADB entry on Alfred Deakin, 107–8
North Australia Research Unit records
　photographs
　　Gough Whitlam, 75, 197
North Australian Workers' Union
　and struggle for equal wages and working conditions for Aboriginal workers, 63, 65
NSW Combined Colliery Proprietors' Association records
　Billy Hughes, 148
NSW Council for Relief of Spanish Distress
　Billy Hughes and, 152–3
NSW Typographical Association
　John Christian Watson and, 187–8

215

NSW Typographical Association records
    John Christian Watson, 187–8
    photographs
        Billy Hughes, *34*, 148
        John Christian Watson, *34*, 188
Numiari, Pincher
    and Wattie Creek land rights claim, 65
Nyang Station (NSW – Malcolm Fraser's childhood home), 118, *119*
    see also Goldsbrough Mort and Company Ltd records

Old Parliament House
    and Museum of Australian Democracy, 26
Oliphant, Professor Sir Mark
    on Bob Hawke and University House incident, 58, 60
    house for, 170
    with Keith Hancock, Laurie Fitzhardinge, Ross Hohnen and Leslie Melville (1957), *50*
    see also Mark Oliphant papers
O'Malley, King
    and a national university, 3
'Out/Oust Menzies Campaign' (1953), 14, 174, 175

Page, Earle
    with Stanley Melbourne Bruce, Chancellor of ANU, *7*
    Truant Surgeon, 177
    archives:
        Amalgamated Postal Workers' Union of Australia records, 176–7
        Australian Dictionary of Biography files, 177
        Australian National University photographs, 177–8
        Canberra University College Council minutes, 178
Parry, William
    and William Barton, 81
    see also Australian Agricultural Company
Paterson, Laing and Bruce
    Ernest Bruce and, 90–1
    Stanley Melbourne Bruce and, 14, 41–4, 90–1
    occupational health and safety, 44
    office of in London, *42*
    staff pension scheme, 44
Paterson, Laing and Bruce records, 42
    Stanley Melbourne Bruce, 90–1
Pemberton, Dr Pennie
    and ADB entry on Zara Holt, 135
    In the Service of the Company on William Barton, 81
personal papers of prime ministers, 21–2
Phil Thorne papers
    Billy Hughes, 152–3
    Joe Lyons, 160
    Robert Menzies, 175
photographs of prime ministers, 27
    at ANU, 74–6
    Edmund Barton, 72, 82, *83*
    Stanley Melbourne Bruce, *7*, 75, *86*, 88–9
    Ben Chifley, *5*, 72, 74, 93, *94*, 100, 101
    John Curtin, 72, 104, *104*
    Andrew Fisher, 72, 112, *113*, 154
    Malcolm Fraser, 75, 116–17, 118
    Julia Gillard, 76, *120*
    John Gorton, 75, 121, *122*
    Bob Hawke, *10*, 72, *74*, 75, *124*, 126–7, 129, 131, 133, 134
    Harold Holt, 137–8
    John Howard, 139, *140*
    Billy Hughes, *34*, *36*, 72, 112, *113*, 148, 153, 154
    Paul Keating, 155, *156*
    Joe Lyons, 72, 158, *159*
    John McEwen, 72, 161, 162
    Billy McMahon, 163
    Robert Menzies, *6*, 75, 168, 169, 173, 175–6
    Earle Page, *7*, 177–8
    Kevin Rudd, *9*, 75–6
    James Scullin, 72, 182, 183, *183*
    John Christian Watson, *34*, 188
    Gough Whitlam, *6*, *11*, *62*, 75, 189, 192–3, *193*, 194, 197
'pig iron' dispute (1938)
    archival sources, 47
    Joe Lyons and, 160
    Maritime Worker report on, *46*
    Robert Menzies and, 14, 45–8, 165–6, 175, 176
Powell, Graeme

on Deakin papers, 17
on prime ministers and recordkeeping, 19
Premiers' Plan
    Ben Chifley and, 36, 37, 96, 99
prime ministerial libraries, 23–4
prime ministers
    and ANU, 1–2, 27–8
        ADB records, 12, 27
        buildings, plaques and foundation stones, 15
        earliest links, 2–4
        in NBAC collections, 14, 27–8
        in official documents (ANU and CUC), 12, 27
        photographs, 27
        students, staff, and other connections, 8–11
        the war and its aftermath, 4–6
    archives and
        in ANU Archives and NBAC, 27–8, 31–76
        archives about prime ministers, 22–3
        official papers of prime ministers, 22
        papers, etc. *about* a prime minister, 18, 20, 27
        papers, etc. *by* a prime minister, 17–18, 27
        papers, etc. *of* a prime minister, 17, 18
        personal papers of prime ministers, 21–2
        prime ministers without papers, 19–20
        relevance, 20–1
        see also prime ministerial libraries
    with business experience, 41
    and Canberra, 1
    overseas travel of, 68
    sobriquets of / stereotypical labels for, 41, 45
    visual representations of, 71–6
        see also cartoons and caricatures of prime ministers; photographs of prime ministers
Prime Ministers Papers Project, 25
prime ministers' portal, 24–5, 26, 26–7
    and John Curtin, 27

Pullan, Robert (*Bob Hawke: A Portrait*)
    and Bob Hawke and University House incident, 59

R G Menzies Building, 15
    Robert Menzies and, 6, 75, 167, 168, 169
        with H C Coombs at laying of foundation stone, 6
    Gough Whitlam and
        in background at laying of foundation stone, 6
Radi, Dr Heather
    and ADB entry on Stanley Melbourne Bruce, 85
Reid, George
    death of, 178
    papers of, 21
    'piss and wind' story, 178–9
    and seat of government, 2
    archives:
    Australian Dictionary of Biography files, 178–9
Rein, Therese
    and ANU, 8
    archives:
    Australian National University student files, 179
Reith, Peter
    on John Howard and maritime/waterfront dispute (1998), 140
Research School of Chemistry
    Malcolm Fraser and, 75, 116
Research School of Pacific Studies
    Gough Whitlam and, 10
Research School of Physical Sciences
    Ben Chifley and, 10, 74
    Robert Menzies and, 75
    Gough Whitlam and, 10
    see also Cockcroft Building, Research School of Physical Sciences
Ritchie, Dr John
    with Bob Hawke at launch of vol. 12 of ADB, *10*
Rivett, Sir David
    and establishment of a national university, 4
Robertson, John
    and ADB entry on James Scullin, 182
    and James Scullin's paucity of papers, 20

Roderick, J M
   and University House incident
      involving Bob Hawke, 61
Ross, Edgar
   and coal strike (1949), 92–3
Ross, Lloyd
   biography of John Curtin, 48
'Rothbury appeals', 182
Round Table of Prime Ministerial Research and Collecting Agencies, 26
Rudd, Kevin
   and ANU, 1–2, 8, 75–6
      opening new J G Crawford Building, *9*, 75
   Burgmann College lecture, 76
   dismissals, party-room coups and expulsions, 31
   and incident on overseas trip, 68
   and new building for John Curtin School of Medical Research, 2, 75
   request for information on enrolment procedures, *180*
   archives:
   Australian National University student files, 179–80
Rutledge, Martha
   and ADB entry on Edmund Barton, 82

Santamaria, B A
   Robert Menzies and, 173
Saunders, Malcolm
   and ADB entry on Frank Forde (with Neil Lloyd), 114
Sawer, Professor Geoffrey
   on Stanley Melbourne Bruce, 88
   on Bob Hawke, 128
   and Bob Hawke and University House incident, 61
   and Robert Menzies, 174
   and question of treatment of Billy Hughes' first marriage in Laurie Fitzhardinge's biography, 51
   see also Geoffrey Sawer papers
Schellenberg, T R, 13
Scullin, James
   on balcony of Australian Workers' Union Building in Ballarat, 72, *183*
   and T Maughan, 183–4
   archives:
   Amalgamated Postal Workers' Union of Australia records, 181
   Australasian Coal and Shale Employees' Federation records, 181
   Australian Dictionary of Biography files, 182
   Australian Workers' Union records, 182
   Christian Jollie Smith and Company records, 182
   Federated Furnishing Trades Society of Australia records, 183
   Lake George Mines Pty Ltd records, 183–4
Seamen's Journal
   caricature of Malcolm Fraser in, *73*
Seamen's Union of Australia
   and support for Aboriginal workers in Pilbara Strike (1946), 65
Seamen's Union of Australia records
   Malcolm Fraser, 118
   Robert Menzies, 174
Serge Zorino collection
   Malcolm Fraser, 119
Serle, Dr Geoffrey
   and ADB entry on John Munro Bruce, 85
   and ADB entry on John Curtin, 105
   on Victorian premiers and papers, 20
Sheet Metal Working Agricultural Implement and Stove Making Industrial Union records
   photographs
      Bob Hawke, 134
Siding Spring Observatory
   Bob Hawke and, 9, 75
Simons, Margaret
   on Malcolm Fraser and papers, 19
Sir Roland Wilson Building
   John Howard and, 11, 75
sobriquets of / stereotypical labels for prime ministers, 41, 45
South Australian Typographical Society records
   Edmund Barton, 82–3
Spanish Civil War *see* NSW Council for Relief of Spanish Distress; Spanish Relief Committee
Spanish Relief Committee, 152
   Joe Lyons and, 160
Stanley Melbourne Bruce Fund, 87, 89

Sydney Wharf Labourers' Union
  Billy Hughes and, 34, 35, 148–52
  Billy Hughes and
    elected secretary 'unopposed'
      (1899), *149*
  John Christian Watson and, 188–9
  see also Waterside Workers' Federation
    of Australia
Sydney Wharf Labourers' Union records
  Billy Hughes, 148–50
  John Christian Watson, 188–9

Thorne, Phil, 152, 160
  see also Phil Thorne papers
Timber Workers *see* Amalgamated Timber
  Workers' Union of Australia
Titterton, Professor Sir Ernest
  with Gough Whitlam at Research
    School of Physical Sciences, *11*
trade union newspapers and newsletters
  visual representations of prime
    ministers in, 72–3
Trendall, Professor Dale
  and Bob Hawke and University House
    incident, 60
Trolley, Draymen and Carters Union of
  Sydney and Suburbs
  Billy Hughes and, 34, 35, *36*, 153
Trolley, Draymen and Carters Union of
  Sydney and Suburbs records
  Billy Hughes, 153
  photograph
    Billy Hughes, *153*
Turner, Ian *see* Ian Turner collection

University House
  Gough Whitlam and, 10, 75, 197
  see also Jill Waterhouse papers
University House incident (1957)
  involving Bob Hawke, 9, 56–61, 128,
    133–4, *134*
    archival sources, 59–61
    Disciplinary Committee, 60–1
    Bob Hawke on, 61
    notes of Hawke's evidence to
      Disciplinary Committee, *60*
University House records
  Bob Hawke, 134

University of Melbourne
  and government response to proposed
    Robert Menzies Library, 25
  see also Malcolm Fraser Collection
    (University of Melbourne)

Vale of Clwydd colliery (NSW)
  Joseph Cook and, 102–3
Varghese, Margaret, and Stephen Foster (*The
  Making of the Australian National University
  1946–1996*), 88, 128, 144, 162, 167
  see also Australian National University
    History Project records
Vestey Company
  and inequality of wages and working
    conditions of Aboriginal workers, 63,
    64
  see also Wave Hill Station
  and Wattie Creek land rights claim, 66
Victorian ALP
  Gough Whitlam and, 14, 195–6
Vietnam War
  John Gorton and, 14
  Harold Holt and, 14
  Billy McMahon and, 14
  privacy of student information and
    conscription for
      John Gorton and, 121
      Harold Holt and, 136
      Billy McMahon and, 162
      Gough Whitlam and, 192
Visiting Fellowship
  Gough Whitlam, 75, 194, 196
visual representations of prime ministers,
  71–6
  ANU as venue for, 72, 74–6
  see also cartoons and caricatures of prime
    ministers; films; photographs of prime
    ministers

wage inequality (Aboriginal workers)
  archival sources, 64
  Australian Agricultural Company, 63
  Vestey Company, 63
  see also under Aboriginal workers;
    Gurindji people; Wave Hill Station
Walker, T B C (Australian Woolgrowers' and
  Graziers' Council)
  on Aboriginal land rights, 66

Waterhouse, Jill
  and Bob Hawke and University House incident, 58
  and University House, 134–5
  see also Jill Waterhouse papers
Waterside Workers' Federation of Australia
  Andrew Fisher and, 14
  and Gurindji Trust Fund, 65
  Billy Hughes and, 14, 32, 34–5, 150–4
  see also Sydney Wharf Labourers' Union
Waterside Workers' Federation of Australia records
  Abschol-sponsored visits to Wattie Creek re land rights (1969–70), 65
  Andrew Fisher, 112–13
  Billy Hughes, 153–4
  Joe Lyons, 160
  Robert Menzies, 175–6
  photographs
    Andrew Fisher, 112, *113*, 154
    Malcolm Fraser, 118
    Harold Holt, 137–8
    Billy Hughes, 112, *113*, 154
    Robert Menzies, 175–6
  and 'pig iron' dispute, 47–8
  struggle for equal wages and working conditions for Aboriginal workers in, 64
Waterson, Professor D B
  and ADB entry on Ben Chifley, 95
Watson, Don
  biography of Paul Keating, 48
  papers of, 23
Watson, John Christian
  and *Australasian Typographical Journal*, 187
  and Australian Workers' Union, 184–5
    signature on minutes for 1896 convention as acting chairman, *185*
  and conscription, 31, 32, 186
  John Curtin and, 33
  dismissals, party-room coups and expulsions, 31, 32–3
  with Billy Hughes and other delegates to the 1900 Interstate Labor Conference, *34*
  and Labor Papers Ltd, 14, 32–3, 186–7
  and NSW Typographical Association, 187–8
  and seat of government, 2
  and Sydney Wharf Labourers' Union, 188–9
  archives:
    Australian Dictionary of Biography files, 184
    Australian Workers' Union records, 184–5
    Ballarat Trades and Labour Council records, 186
    Labor Papers Ltd records, 186–7
    NSW Typographical Association records, 187–8
    Sydney Wharf Labourers' Union records, 188–9
Wattie Creek
  Abschol-sponsored visits to re land rights (1969–70), 65
  maps of area in Goldsbrough Mort and Company Ltd records, 64
  see also Wave Hill Station
Wave Hill Station
  Gurindji land rights claim, 62, 65–6
  Gurindji strike and walk-off for equal wages and working conditions (1966), 63–4
  see also Wattie Creek
Wendy Brazil collection
  Malcolm Fraser, 117
  Bob Hawke, 130
  John Howard, 141
  Paul Keating, 156
West, Francis (*University House: Portrait of an Institution*), 134
White, Patrick
  correspondence of, 18
Whitlam, Freda, 8, 189, 190
  and CUC, 8
  archives:
    Canberra University College minutes, 194
Whitlam, Gough
  and ADB entries on
    Sir George Knowles, 189–90
    Hubert Lazzarini, 190
  and ANU, 10, 75
  biography of (by Jenny Hocking), 19
  and conscription for Vietnam War
    privacy of student information, 192
  and CUC, 8

dismissals, party-room coups and expulsions, 31–2
with Indian Prime Minister Indira Gandhi and Sir John Crawford (1973), *193*
John Curtin Memorial lecture, 10, 75, 191, 192
National Fellowship, 10, 116, 191, 194
and North Australia Research Unit, 75, 197
on oral history, 19
on his papers, 19
pouring sand into the hand of Vincent Lingiari, *62*
and R G Menzies Building
    in background at laying of foundation stone, *6*
and Research School of Physical Sciences, 10
    with Professor Sir Ernest Titterton, *11*
and University House, 10, 75, 197
and Victorian ALP, 14, 195–6
Visiting Fellowship, 75, 194, 196
and Wave Hill, 62–7
archives:
Australian Council of Trade Unions records, 189
Australian Dictionary of Biography files, 189–90
Australian National University correspondence files, 191–2
Australian National University Instructional Resources Unit recordings, 192
Australian National University photographs, 192–3
Australian National University staff files, 194
Canberra University College minutes, 194
D A Low papers, 196
George Crawford papers, 195
Jack Dwyer collection, 195
Jill Waterhouse papers, 197
Michael Easson subject files, 195–6
National Farmers' Federation records, 196–7
North Australia Research Unit records, 197
see also Whitlam Institute (University of Western Sydney)

Whitlam, Harry Frederick Ernest (Fred)
and ANU, 75
and CUC, 8
and establishment of a national university, 191
archives:
Australian Dictionary of Biography files, 190
Australian National University Advisers on Legislation minutes, 191
Australian National University correspondence files, 191
Australian National University Council minutes, 192
Canberra University College minutes, 194–5
Whitlam Institute (University of Western Sydney), 24
Wilenski, Dr Peter
with Ross Garnaut and Heinz Arndt at relaunch of *Asian Pacific Economic Literature*, *69*
Wilson, Alan
on Ben Chifley, 92
Wilson, Sir Roland
and Robert Menzies and ANU, 11
see also Sir Roland Wilson Building
Women's Political Association *see* Goldstein, Vida
The World Economic Crisis: A Commonwealth Perspective (1980)
Heinz Arndt and, 70
Woroni (ANU students' newspaper)
cartoon of Bob Hawke and Malcolm Fraser in, 76, 120
Julia Gillard in, 119–20, *120*
Wright, Professor R D
on Robert Menzies and H C Coombs, 171
Wright, Tom, 133, 134, 163, 173
see also Audrey Johnson papers; Sheet Metal Working Agricultural Implement and Stove Making Industrial Union records

Young, Walter J (Sir Walter)
and Billy Hughes, 146–7

Zorino, Serge *see* Serge Zorino collection

www.ingramcontent.com/pod-product-compliance
Lightning Source LLC
Chambersburg PA
CBHW060945170426
43197CB00024B/2981